Praise for Calm Brain, P

*"Calm Brain, Powerful Mind is an exceptional book. As someone who is always dealing with the constant pressures and demands of a busy personal and work life, this book helped me to better understand how to deal with and work towards eliminating my anxiety and stress. It helped me to better understand why I often feel the way I do and provided me with the tools and methods to work towards leading a stress-free life. I recommend **Calm Brain, Powerful Mind** for anyone looking for help to eliminate stress from their lives and become a better person."*

Simon Parkin, Best Selling Author of *Hiring Right* & Founder of *The Talent Company*, a Career Partner International Firm

*"**Calm Brain, Powerful Mind** truly achieves what the author set out to do - help people break their cycle of stress to achieve happier and more fulfilling lives. He does this by bringing us into his world and showcases how stress affects our lives and provides us with tools that are enshrined in scientific research and age old practices of meditation to achieve a more balanced and peaceful life. Many people today are constantly stressed. They are constantly seeking ways to achieve inner peace. If you are one of these people, this book is for you! It is an absolute read for those who want to truly develop practices to decrease stress in their lives and achieve happiness."*

Mina Mawani, Healthcare Executive

"Bravo! A transformative read...the quantum science behind the human potential and a clear roadmap to accomplishing its requisite inner peace."

Shelley Richardson, M.Ed., Publisher/Author/Educator

*"Through a holistic and multi-disciplinary approach, Aziz Velji has cleverly deconstructed the art and science of stress for the average person. The insights in this book are truly unique and transformative given the deep emphasis on heightened self-awareness as a basis of achieving sustainable mental well-being. I would strongly recommend **Calm Brain, Powerful Mind** as a comprehensive roadmap for anyone ready to embark on the journey of self-discovery and wellness."*

Sam Erry, Seasoned Executive and Values-based Leader in the public sector

"I found the content thoroughly engrossing from start to finish, as I keenly perused every chapter and illustration, not wanting to miss any of the profound "out of the box" ideas and discoveries. These have been developed masterfully chapter by chapter, for an effortless read and access to stunning epiphanies that will delight readers, resonating with their shared experience of stress in mundane life. The book achieves its purpose by using practical, everyday examples to express the reality that we each create for ourselves. The examples and tools used are incisive and elegant, drawing insights from the widest spectrum of disciplines. Probably no field of study of the brain-mind is missed in this compelling synthesis of science and wisdom."

Shiraz Hameer, Partner, MNP LLP

"What a great read! **Calm Brain, Powerful Mind** is so inspiring. As a lifelong career songwriter and creative person, I am always torn between my creative impulses and the ceaseless chatter of my unfocused mind. Aziz Velji describes, very engagingly, the limitless potential of a calm brain, and he takes the time to describe the brain's physiology in a relatable, connect-the-dots way."

Blair Packham, Musician/Composer/Educator

"This book is a well written and creatively illustrated self-help manual to help you achieve a calm, alert & stress-free mind around distractions and anxiety!"

Azim Jamal, Best Selling Co-author of The Power of Giving

"VERY impressive book... your acquired knowledge of the brain, psychology, physics and "the psyche" was incredible, and must've taken MANY years for you to research these things... I must admit, this is not the type of book I would typically read... I am... a very concrete black and white medical physician/educator... but I actually enjoyed what I read."

Dr. Jeff Habert, Medical Physician/Educator

"WOW!!! By far the best book I have read on the topic. You have succeeded in taking the woowoo out of what usually comes across as woowoo! You communicate clearly and convincingly that we need to understand our inner self. Your tools are simple and simply awesome. Available to all. I will need to gift this book to all my friends as soon as it's out in print. Please sign me *up for 10 copies. So grateful to have met you and to have had the opportunity to read this life changing book"*

Dr. Areef Nurani, Optometrist

*"Wow! **Calm Brain, Powerful Mind** is a compelling and powerful book AND easy to read! I enjoyed reading and learning about how stress affects us. My initial post-secondary education is in the sciences and I have not taken the opportunity to learn about meditation or philosophy. Aziz's book has given me an understanding of the ways that philosophy, meditation and brain science interconnect. Aziz's work on the evidence-based benefits of meditation is amazing. I found the information on stress and the development and working of the brain very useful not only for myself but also in relation to my charity work".*

Tricia Cisakowski, BSc MBA CMC

*"With mental health and work load stress becoming an increasing phenomenon in academia, I was intrigued by this book because it attempts to explain the science behind the practice of meditation. **Calm Brain, Powerful Mind** by Aziz Velji is an unassuming, non-academic text which links the relationship between developments in neuroscience, quantum physics, neuroplasticity and the teachings on meditation from the East...*

From the perspective of a student, early career researcher, professional, or for that matter, anyone who is walking life's journey, this book introduces the background one needs to prove to us that learning to silence that critical or egotistic voice in our head is the first step in learning to minimise stress and conditions relating to stress, such as imposter syndrome and academic exhaustion which are increasingly prevalent in higher education institutions.

Velji promises these techniques [in the book] provide clarity and enable the creativity to flow – not something that can be readily dismissed in this competitive world ... In a world that prioritises speed over quality (which we know so well in the academic world), this is a book that provides some useful answers but not in the form of a quick fix. It is important to understand this."

Nazlin Bhimani, Librarian

"In this day and age, all of us are trying to keep up with our everyday fast-paced life and are bombarded with tremendous stress. I absolutely love Aziz's book because he explains everything so well breaks everything down

so we can understand how to manage stress. This book is perfect for everyone, young and old."

Dr. Michael Lee, Chiropractor and Active Release Provider

"**Calm Brain and Powerful Mind** is an outstanding contemporary work that seeks to situate the practice of meditation, common to many cultures and faiths, in the context of scientific research. The book unfolds by socializing the reader to the relationship between living in survival mode and creativity, and artfully leads the reader through the challenges of our daily lives where we are more connected today, yet are lonelier than ever before. In tackling a complex topic, the author leads us on a four step journey in climbing a mountain to help us comprehend our personal view of the world, the mental stress in our lives caused by uncertainty, how the brain functions and how stress can be permanently abolished to realize transcendence and transformation. A must read!"

Nizar Sultan, Business Economist and Strategic Planner

Calm Brain, Powerful Mind

Abolish Stress to Unleash your True Potential

Aziz Velji

Paper Lantern
Publishing House Inc.

Copyright © 2018 by Aziz Velji

All rights reserved. No part of this book may be reproduced by any mechanical, photographic, or electronic process, or in the form of a phonographic recording; nor may it be stored in a retrieval system, transmitted, or otherwise be copied for public or private use—other than for "fair use" as brief quotations embodied in articles and reviews—without the prior written permission of the publisher.

The author of this book does not dispense medical advice or prescribe the use of any technique as a form of treatment for physical, emotional, or medical problems without the advice of a physician, either directly or indirectly. The intent of the author is only to offer information of a general nature to help you in your quest for emotional and spiritual well-being. Although every precaution has been taken to verify the accuracy of the information contained herein, the author and publisher assume no responsibility for any errors or omissions.

Cover design; Interior design and formatting; illustrations and drawings: John Mclachlan
Drawings: Diane Finlayson
Photo Tai Chi/Harmony: Georgina Chung

Publisher: Paper Lantern Publishing House Inc. Markham, Ontario
www.paperlanternpublishinghouse.com or calmbrainpowerfulmind.com
Printed in the United States of America
First Printing, 2020
Tradepaper ISBN   978-1-9990144-0-7
Digital ISBN   978-1-9990144-1-4

For Meena, Faheema, Scott and Amaya

Contents

List of Illustrations ix

Foreword by Jim Pappas xi

Introduction
I The Art of Ascending the Inner Mountain xix
II Mountain—The Preparation xxxi
III The Beginner's Mind xxxvii

Part I Our Personal World
Chapter 1 How We Live Today 3
Chapter 2 Consciousness—The Universal Intelligence 13
Chapter 3 Our Individualized Thought System 19
Chapter 4 The Monkey Mind 33
Chapter 5 The Walking Dead 39
Chapter 6 How "Dead" are We? 49
Tool for the Journey 1 Learning to Sit in Silence 53

Part II Realities of Stress
Chapter 7 Living in Survival 57
Chapter 8 The Anxiety Gap 63
Chapter 9 The Routine Trap 73
Tool for the Journey 2 Conscious Breathing 79

Part III Working of the Brain
Chapter 10 The Four-in-One Brain 83
Chapter 11 The Survival Brain 87
Chapter 12 The Emotional Brain 91
Chapter 13 The Conscious Brain 97
Chapter 14 The Famous Left and Right Brains 109
Chapter 15 The Right Brain Missing in Action 121
Tool for the Journey 3 Understanding the Brain Waves 125

Part IV The Science and the Art of Transformation
Chapter 16 The Science of Wholeness 133
Chapter 17 We are Machine 135
Chapter 18 A Paradigm Shift 139
Chapter 19 Quantum Billiards 149
Chapter 20 Our Mechanistic World 155
Chapter 21 The Holographic World 161
Chapter 22 Science and Mysticism 171
Tool for the Journey 4 The Art of Observation 177

Part V Process of Transformation
Chapter 23 Touch Points of Sanity 185
Chapter 24 Mountain—The Climb 197
Chapter 25 The Science and the Power of Meditation 205
Chapter 26 Witnessing Meditation 219
Chapter 27 Self-Inquiry Meditation 233

Part VI Transformation
Chapter 28 Mountain—The Summit 243
Chapter 29 The "Unconscious" Person Awakens 247
Chapter 30 Mountain—The Return 259

Glossary 269

Endnotes 279

Index 303

Acknowledgements 315

About the Author 319

Illustrations

1. The art of ascending the inner mountain xxi
2. Living in survival and living in creativity xxv
3. The anxiety gap 17
4. Brain development and the process of relaxation 21
5. The mind "iceberg" 23
6. The pendulum of thought 35
7. The screens of distortion 41
8. The four-in-one brain 85
9. Hand model of the brain (figures. 1, 2, 3, 4) 100
10. Maslow's hierarchy of needs 103
11. The famous left and right brains 111
12. Yin and Yang 113
13. Gateway into the subconscious 126
14. A classical Newtonian and a quantum atom 141
15. Hall of mirrors 142
16. Particles and waves 143
17. My wife and my mother-in-law 145
18. Billiard table 150
19. The art of observation (figures. 1, 2, 3) 177
20. The masks we wear 238
21. Our dual states of consciousness 245
22. Intellect, feelings and intelligence 254
23. Forces that shape our lives 261
24. The evolution of "me" (the integrated brain) 264

Foreword

If you are reading these words, you are most likely interested in the topic of stress—namely, what it is, how and why it can affect us, or, more importantly, how we can eliminate it from our lives. Considering that stress can affect our lives both emotionally and physiologically, it can have a potentially negative effect on the outcomes of our lives if we allow it.

I feel that one of the biggest contributors to stress is the rapid pace of change in modern society. And to make matters worse, the pace of change is increasing with each passing year. The dynamics of our culture are also changing. Traditional family and community structures are disintegrating, along with the support structures. People are feeling more isolated, lonely, and insecure. Social media is drawing people away from traditional communities and moving them to online communities. Social media has also become addictive (whether designed that way or not). This has created a society of unfocused young people trying to survive in an economy that demands ever-increasing specialized skills, self-control, and concentration. In business, traditional companies are folding and being replaced by tech hybrids like Uber and Amazon that displace millions of workers in the process. These former employees need retraining, and yet struggle to learn and adapt to a new information-based economy. The incidence of diseases (another form of stress) is also increasing rapidly because of pesticide-laden food, toxic environments, and toxic business practices like fracking. It is no wonder that we are so stressed.

I was one of these people who got caught up in this stress-laden world, with a struggling business, a broken marriage, and high levels of debt, as well as physical illness, loneliness, and even depression.

CALM BRAIN, POWERFUL MIND

After a number of years of chronic stress, I started to turn around my life, but I was still struggling with stress—although now hiding it better than before. That's when I met Aziz at my gym. He told me he was writing a book about how we could eliminate stress from our lives. I read his manuscript and asked him questions and started having discussions about his findings. I began to do the things that he outlined in his book. Eventually, I reached a turning point. In an instant, everything that I had read in his book suddenly came together. I finally understood. My life was now forever changed.

I learned that stress was a by-product of our ego and past programming by influential people, things, and experiences. Stress and anxiety were characterized by negative and limiting voices in our heads that dictate our decisions and actions. When we live with decisions and actions that were developed from fears, anxiety, limitations, lack of faith, and negativity, we end up perpetuating this state of mind, and with it, all the emotional and physiological consequences that result from it.

Aziz's book, **Calm Brain, Powerful Mind**, is designed to **help you eliminate stress**, not just manage it. When you read this book, you will see that it is not really possible to "manage" stress. Managing stress is not a strategy that can be maintained over the long term. The idea of managing stress is like juggling. It takes a great deal of effort and concentration to keep all the balls in the air. Eventually, you get tired, lose concentration, and a ball drops, or even worse, you have everything come crashing down. "Managing" stress is based on tips and techniques, not on a fundamental shift in mindset. This book teaches you how to shift your mindset... to dive deep into the root causes of stress and to reach a point where everything becomes clear... where you finally understand what is going on, and where you realize that *you can overcome this*, once and for all. The analogy used to illustrate this concept is reaching the mountaintop and suddenly realizing that

Foreword

you are able to see everything around you. This 360° mountaintop view of the world is reality. It is truth. It can never be taken away—it is permanent. Suddenly when you see what is real, you can never go back to what was an illusion—a self-made state of stress.

So how do you get there? How do you reach the point where you are calm, happy, and at peace? And more importantly, how do you stay there? The [very] short answer is through the practice of *meditation*.

I know what you're thinking—meditation? Are you kidding me? I know... I know. I was also skeptical at first. My logical left brain said, "How can a new age, yoga-based practice used by monks and cave-dwelling hermits help me overcome anxiety, fears, worry, and personal suffering? Well, that's exactly what happens. Aziz goes into great detail about what stress is, the causes, the science behind it, and the step-by-step process and tools needed to overcome it... once and for all. I have to warn you that the book is relatively long. I thought to myself— "Do I really need to read a 250+ page book to overcome stress?" The answer is a profound YES! And the reason is simple. You need to have a complete understanding of everything that can create, maintain, and ultimately eliminate stress, in order to really change your belief about what it truly is... a byproduct of your ego and the mind chatter. If your mind does not believe in something at the deepest level, it will never really accept it. You can try to fool your brain into believing something by repeating things over and over until they are blazed into your memory, but there will always be a nominal level of doubt in the background that will eventually sabotage you at some point. That's why many weekend self-help seminars do not create a lasting change in most people. They attempt to manage stress and change limiting beliefs through tactics and techniques. These do not quell the voices in the head; they simply subdue them for a period of time. Once the memory of the seminar fades, and we are thrown back into the realities of life, the negative voices of the brain rise up again and revive our state of stress.

I found that the concepts contained in **Calm Brain, Powerful Mind** were relatively easy to understand. Aziz goes into great depth about brain science, psychology, and the science of quantum physics to explain what stress really is, why it exists, how it originates, and how we can overcome it. He does not make assumptions about the ability of the reader to understand his terms of reference. That's why he provides a [very useful] *glossary of terms*. It helps the reader better understand the underlying brain science and quantum physics used in this book.

When I finally understood that the ego and the voices in my head were not real but were created from fear-based, negative influences, I was ready to accept the necessary change in my thinking needed to overcome my stress. In reality, what I was really doing was removing the overburden of garbage (my past programming and conditioning) that was obscuring my true state-of-being (my reality). Many people call this our spirit, or original consciousness. When my original consciousness was revealed, I knew that there was no turning back. I knew that I had uncovered the authentic me... something that was always there, waiting for me to liberate it from the control of the ego, and the voices in my head. The progress towards this discovery was gradual, but the change, when it happened, was instantaneous. It was just like climbing a mountain and only being able to see the countryside to the right, to the left and behind you. However, when you reach the summit, every part of the countryside becomes visible without obstructions. That was my transformation point—when I became aware of my inherent power. That was when I knew that I could achieve anything that I set my mind to... and I did.

Foreword

Reaching this transition point literally changed my life for the better. I reached a constant state of peace, calm, and happiness... knowing that I could never go back to the way it was. I was stress-free, thinking clearly, fully alert, and aware of each moment in time. In essence, I was accessing my inherent creativity, wisdom, and knowledge—*I was accessing my power.*

While the physiological and emotional benefits are powerful in their own right, the thing that has changed my life the most was gaining the understanding and confidence to *use* my power... the power to be able to do, be or have anything that I desired. This has made the greatest impact on my life. My confidence level has soared, and I am no longer risk-averse. I have liberated my creativity. My income has more than quintupled from the previous year. I am on track to achieving things that I only dreamt about in the past. When you learn to access your power (your natural state of being), ANYTHING is possible. Thomas Merton, a Catalan Trappist Monk, theologian, and writer, once described the rediscovery of your true state-of-being, as equivalent to "winning a cosmic lottery." He was absolutely right about that!

I must commend Aziz about **Calm Brain, Powerful Mind**. His only goal was to write a book to help people identify and reach a state of joy and happiness that is not only natural but also our birthright. This book is needed now more than ever before. It certainly changed my life, as I'm sure it will change yours as well. If you read this book and do the exercises outlined at the end of each section, you will achieve this state of peace, calm, and happiness, and finally, access your inherent power to positively change your life forever.

Jim Pappas
Fellow Traveller on Spaceship Earth

> "**If you can see, look...**
> **If you can look, observe...**"[1]
>
> From The Book of Exhortations

Introduction I

The Art of Ascending the Inner Mountain

"There are outer mountains and inner mountains. Their very presence beckons to us, calls us to ascend... sometimes you search and search for the mountain without finding it until the time comes when you are sufficiently motivated and prepared to find a way through, first to the base, then to the summit... ultimately, it is the climb which is the adventure, not just standing at the top."[2]
　　　　　　　　　Jon Kabat-Zinn, author, and meditation teacher

I have read a lot about mountain climbing as a metaphor for the inner journey of transformation or for that matter anything one does in life. I didn't realize how true this was until, while writing this book, I had an opportunity to climb the majestic, snow-capped Mount Kilimanjaro in Tanzania, Africa, with my life partner, Meena, and our friends Bruce Pausey and Ciara Behan. At

19,341 feet (5,895 meters) above sea level, it is the tallest freestanding mountain in the world. It is considered to be in the *extreme altitude* range, so acute altitude sickness, which commonly occurs above 8,000 feet (2,400 meters), is a threat if the body does not acclimatize properly. The climb took us through five different climate zones, each with its own terrain—from the cultivated areas at the base of the mountain, through the rainforest and low alpine moorlands to arid desert, and finally to the glacial or the arctic zone. Here the oxygen level is almost half that found at the base of the mountain. As one of our guides told us before our start, "This climb is like trekking from the equator to the North Pole and back in seven days."

Just like the four-stage journey one has to go through in climbing an external mountain—the preparation, the climb, reaching the summit, and returning to the base (Figure 1), there are four stages one has to go through in ascending the inner mountain of transformation. Each phase has its challenges, and we learn different things as we climb higher. Fear, uncertainty, and doubt are constant companions on the journey. Progress becomes slower as we climb because of the altitude... but each step takes us forward—closer to the summit, to our *natural state of being*. The change, when it comes, is instantaneous... but the progress is more gradual toward the point where change can occur. The implementation of what we experience in our life/lives is also slow and takes time. Every traveler goes through the same stages, but their progress through each milestone may be different. It does not matter when and from where one starts the journey because just like the bottom of the mountain is wide and it narrows toward the peak, all paths begin to merge as you get closer to the summit.

This book is the culmination of all the work I have done on the nature of mind, the nature of reality, and the *power* of the subconscious mind. It is about how we can understand and

The Art of Ascending the Inner Mountain

Figure 1. *The four stages of self-transcendence. It does not matter where one starts the journey because there are many paths to the summit.*

eliminate stress and, in the process, trigger a transformation within us. It is a journey into the mind to rediscover our natural state of being. It is about knowing ourselves.

My journey into my mind began some years ago, when I became interested in understanding the nature of mind, and how our thoughts affect our reality. My background is in engineering, science, and business management, which all emphasize the intellectual knowledge of the rational part of the mind. To understand the inner workings of the mind, I needed personal knowledge of the *irrational* or the intuitive part of the mind. Up until I turned my attention on my own mind, like most people, I didn't think the irrational right side of the brain had any useful function in today's world of science and technology. And so, I missed the opportunity to take any arts and humanities courses while in university.

I decided to rectify that missed opportunity by studying philosophy, psychology, meditation practices, and dreaming, especially lucid dreaming, or what is called Dream Yoga in the East. Along the way, I developed an interest in the brain and in neuroscience to better understand the relationship between the brain and mind. As a bonus subject, I also studied the new science of Quantum Physics, as if I had not done enough science already. But what I discovered, is that this discipline was nothing like the hard science (which is concerned with the external or *exoteric* world) that I had mastered many years ago. This new science is more "mystical" (concerned with the inner or *esoteric* world) than scientific, and it bridges the rational and the irrational worlds perfectly.[3] Its findings have brought about a shift in the way we view the world—they focus on *consciousness* rather than *matter* as the source of all creation.[4]

Many people have difficulty with the word *mystical* because it conjures up magical and occult practices and images of old men sitting in caves, or that the mystical path is only available to the

Introduction | Ascending the Inner Mountain

chosen few. Unfortunately, these images of mysticism have discouraged people from exploring the mystical path of self-discovery. The word mystical, according to the Merriam-Webster Dictionary means, "Having a spiritual meaning or reality that is neither apparent to the senses nor obvious to the intelligence."[5] Both the quantum physicists and mystics are dealing with this reality beyond the senses. Albert Einstein, (who was both a mystic and a scientist!), said that "The most beautiful and profound emotion we can experience is the sensation of the mystical. It is the power of all true science."[6]

To me, a mystic is anyone who undertakes the journey within himself or herself to experience their natural state of being. As Amit Goswami, author of *The Visionary Window, A Quantum Physicist's Guide to Enlightenment*, says, "Mysticism is not a belief system: it is a transformative system based on "see for oneself."[7] And spirituality is this process of going inward and *reconnecting with our true self.*

And so, realizing our true nature is neither mystical, nor a mystery as many people might assume—it is *being spiritual*. How can the life we are supposed to be living be a mystery? There is nothing mystical about spirituality or enlightenment. "Spiritual truth... is in fact profound common sense."[8] The ancient wisdom traditions and the present-day masters all speak to the same thing—namely, how to quiet or eliminate the voice of the ego that is playing in our head, the one that is creating fear and stress. The ego likes to judge everything that it perceives. It splits the world into *either-or* or dualistic thinking— "I like," "I don't like," "This is good," "That is bad," and so on. When the voice is not there, our mind is calm, clear and alert and we are enlightened to a new way of perceiving, one that is non-dualistic or united in nature. And so, stress and spirituality are actually two sides of the same coin.

This way of perceiving is built on our everyday way of looking at the world by giving breadth and depth to our daily experiences. In other words, it adds the intuitive and holistic (or a non-dual) perspective to our rational, linear, and detailed way of seeing things. This opens up the whole *undivided* world to us. It observes the entire forest as opposed to just seeing an individual tree. When we try to solve a problem without this unified method of perception, we simply immerse ourselves into the problem so much so, that we *become* the problem. We can't see the forest for the trees. But, when we step back, we separate ourselves from the problem... and are able to see the solution!

Learning to observe the world from a holistic perspective is what Einstein was referring to when he said, "You cannot solve a problem from the same consciousness that created it. You must learn to see the world anew."[9] Stress has been created by our everyday consciousness—our ego or false self. The rational, dualistic mindset can come up with coping mechanisms and wonderful drugs to counter the effect of our stress, but it can neither prevent nor eliminate it as long as the ego has its hold. For that, we need the holistic, intuitive mindset to observe the problem from a different perspective.

When our rational and intuitive parts of the mind start to work in harmony, our consciousness shifts to a higher state. It is as if we see with new, non-dualistic eyes. According to the Sufis, "a new organ of perception" comes into being,[10] or as poet William Blake described it, we experience a "cleansing of the doors of perception."[11] This way of observing is not new—it has always been there. It is just that we have identified ourselves with our thoughts, and this has restricted our ability to perceive and, in the process, forgotten how to observe. This higher state is *our natural creative state*—a state that is stress-free, fully alert, and aware. With the shift in consciousness, the world feels lighter, and it is fun to be alive again. Our internal reference point has now moved from the ego to our true self (Figure 2). This way of perceiving brings an end to our suffering. Now we begin to live in creativity. This state of creativity is our essence, our true nature which is also called our Buddha nature. The findings of quantum physics are now confirming that this *state of being* actually exists. As Amit Goswami pointed out in the *The Visionary Window, A Quantum Physicist's Guide to Enlightenment*, "[This state is] *consciousness, the ground of all being.*"[12]

Relationship between Living in Survival and Living in Creativity

Figure 2. *Most of us experience the world through the left half of the continuum and live in survival mode. Once we understand how our minds work and realize that thoughts are not real but are just mental concepts, the voice in the head begins to subside. The mind then becomes alert, calm, and therefore clear, and another way of perceiving emerges... bringing an end to our suffering. We then start to access the wisdom of our true self and live in creativity. But until then, our personal world revolves around the ego, and the voice in the head is our constant companion.*

The question often arises, "But, how can we know ourselves?" I believe that more important than "how to" is "want to." If you really want to know and are sincere, earnest, and receptive to change, the "how to" will fall into place. I have covered a lot of ground in the following pages, and have included many analogies, illustrations, drawings, metaphors, personal anecdotes, and practices to simplify and highlight some key points and ideas. *The process we are following is gradual, to allow us to become familiar and comfortable with the realized state... until it stabilizes.* Then we can operate from our natural state of being on an everyday basis.

Unlike in technical training or learning cognitive skills, there is no step-by-step or "how to" path leading to the natural state of being. To break the grip of the rational mind, we must start doing things consciously. Throughout this book, I have included tools for the journey, for you to begin the process of awakening. Incorporate these skills into your daily lives. They are designed to shift your consciousness from the *unconscious ego state* that most of us are operating from to becoming *conscious*. These practices vary from simple things you can do to break the unconscious, habituated way of doing things, to learning new skills that cultivate your attention and to bring you into the "present moment awareness."

Most people don't appreciate the power of their *attention*. Attention is our life force that keeps us awake and alert. Unfortunately, social media and marketing companies value our attention more than we do. Under a cloud of a chemically induced hypnosis for a dopamine fix (the brain's feel-good chemical), the social media companies slowly siphon off our attention "with [our every]... touch, swipe or tap [of the smartphone] 2,617 times a day"[13] or 2 to 3 times per minute. We do these actions unconsciously and, in the process, the technology and marketing companies keep us perpetually distracted. Without the focus and power of our attention, shifting our consciousness to a higher state becomes difficult, if not impossible.

Carl Jung, the Swiss psychiatrist who founded analytical psychology, warned that "the advancement of technology and materialism, now accepted by many to be stressors, would further widen the gap between the conscious and unconscious mind. As technology and materialism increased, people would spend less and less time cultivating their inner selves."[14]

Jung warned us about the dangers of technology and materialism in 1933, before the creation of the first supercomputers (in the 1940s), and the earliest form of the internet (in the 1960s),[15] and even before the push to make consumerism and "consumption a way of life" for us began in earnest in the 1950s.[16] Today, almost ninety years after Jung's warning, there are over two billion (and growing, with markets opening up in China and India!) smartphone and Facebook users. James Williams, a former Google strategist, notes that the tech industry has become the "largest, most standardized and most centralized form of attentional control in human history."[17] *And so reclaiming and training our attention must become a priority for us.*

Practices like mindfulness and other types of meditations will increase our attention and focus, and take us deeper into ourselves and into awareness—our true self, where the whole brain is finally integrated.

All you need to do is work on these practices and remain completely receptive. This state of being is not something to be achieved—it is something *to be rediscovered*. And so to our rational mind, the process may seem difficult or even impossible, because we are not working toward any goal. Here, once we have started on our journey, we have to let go and trust ourselves and let our intuition or common sense guide us. We must make this inner journey part of our life. It has to become our priority. As Jung, said, "The attainment of wholeness requires one to stake one's whole being. Nothing less will do; there can be no easier conditions, no substitutes, no compromises."[18] Only then will we enjoy doing the practices regularly.

I have also included thoughts from people who have undertaken this journey and who have influenced countless numbers of lives. It is my sincere hope that something in these pages will catch your attention, something you can relate to, that will make you want to undertake this journey. In time, if you persist, you will begin to notice a shift in your awareness.

Using the mountain-climbing metaphor that we started the introduction with, we will lay the groundwork for our journey in the first four parts of the book. In Part V, we begin our climb to the summit, and in Part VI, having reached the peak, we will return to our everyday world with our newfound knowledge.

In Part I, we look at how we develop our personal view of the world, which no one else has access to. This view creates the self we are most familiar with, the "I" that relates to the world. It is the everyday ego consciousness, the voice in our head, and the cause of all our mental suffering. The "I" is a mind-created mental structure born of memories, and our *name* holds this network of thoughts together. This nest of thoughts, and the "me" stories, become our conditioned or false self, and is unique to each of us.

In Part II, we see that mental suffering or stress is caused by uncertainty. The mind loves to be in control of situations and hates the unknown, something it cannot predict or control. That is why when we come across something unfamiliar, our anxiety level increases because our mind equates unfamiliarity as a threat to its well-being. We will see how this increase in anxiety affects us.

In Part III, we explore the brain. Did you know that we have four sub-brains in our head—reptilian, mammalian, primate and human—all doing their own thing? It is like putting an alligator, a dog, a monkey, and a human being in one room and asking them to get along. Whichever of these brains ends up in control depends on how conscious we are and the type of situation we are facing. We don't need to understand the detailed workings of the brain to know how to get in touch with our natural state of being—I didn't. But knowing a little bit about the brain will help us understand why we experience conflict in feeling, thinking, and interactions with others. We will also learn how stress triggers the instinctive survival mechanism of our primitive brains, and how it hijacks our higher-functioning human brain.

In Part IV, we will use the language of Einstein, rather than that of the mystics to look at what quantum physics has to say about our natural state of being. I have tried to simplify the terminology as much as possible to make the concepts easier to understand. Persist with it, and you will discover a fascinating new realm. This new science has brought about a paradigm shift in the way we view the world. The findings show that we cannot just stand back and watch the world as it goes by. This is because, in the process of watching the world, we are actually affecting it. Instead of being mere observers, we are participants in our world. Our every thought, word or action has an impact on everything in our surroundings. And so, if we want to, *we can alter the course of our lives.*

In Part V we see that to abolish stress permanently, we need to learn to switch off the voice in the head. The key to silencing the mind is to learn how to become aware and alert. Living in survival is living in our ego consciousness, or the person that we *think* we are. Living in creativity, on the other hand, is living in our natural state of being—the person that we *actually* are. The difference in how we live depends on our mindset. And, to change our mindset, we need specific techniques. Techniques are there to start us off, to break through our conditioning and to bring us into the here and now. In the beginning, the practicing these techniques will require some effort on our part, but we eventually reach a point where no further effort is needed.

Part VI looks at transcendence and transformation. Suddenly, one day we wake up and realize that the voice in the head, which for years had driven our thoughts and actions and made us anxious, is finally gone. Instead, it has been replaced by an unbelievable *silence*. This is not a passive silence, like being in a daze, but it is a silence in which we are completely calm, alert and aware of everything going on around us. And, *we realize that this is not a new state at all*. We had felt like this before on many occasions—when we were happy, or watching a sunset, or playing with our dog. Finally, we realize, we have returned home.

Introduction II

Mountain—The Preparation

"Targeting your thoughts—or what scientists ponderously refer to as "intention" and "intentionality"—appeared to produce energy potent enough to change physical reality... evidence suggests that human thoughts and intention are an actual physical "something" with the astonishing power to change our world. Every thought we have is a tangible energy with the power to transform. A thought is not only a thing; a thought is a thing that influences other things."[19]
Lynne McTaggart, author of The Intention Experiment

In climbing any mountain, everything depends on what I call the two principles of life—attitude and altitude... and they, in turn, depend on learning about, and understanding, the mind. Let me explain.

Our well-being depends on how well we adjust to our ever-changing environment, or how well we meet the daily challenges of life and this, in turn, depends on a clear, calm, and alert mind—failure to adapt, results in the daily stresses and struggles of life.

But how many of us are willing to spend the time to understand how our minds work? We do everything possible to avoid looking at our own minds because we are afraid to look within, to examine our inner workings, in case we find something that we consider *not good*. We seek mastery over our environment using science and technology, mastery over our physical bodies by eating healthy foods and exercising, but we never look at *understanding* and *mastering* our minds. The quality of our lives depends on our minds, yet the mind is one area that does not get any attention from us. And when we do work with our minds, we focus only on the rational, logical, thinking mind, which is the home of the ego. We try to make this mind sharper, more cunning, and more complex, thereby empowering the ego and leaving vast regions of the mind unexplored and underutilized.

The mind is a *thought-making machine*. Just like breathing, one of the functions of this human form is to produce thoughts. And like "our voices are the product of our ability to speak," we have the ability to think, and thoughts are the products of this ability.[20] It's a tool with which to understand and communicate with others, but our thinking is just a point of view, one view amongst billions! Unfortunately, we forget that *we* are the thinker of our thoughts and we let worry thoughts take over our minds. This is the constant chatter in the mind, the voice of the ego. It is the voice in the head that makes us anxious, produces stress, and the resultant suffering. Most of us are not aware of the mind chatter and as long as we are not aware of it, the chatter doesn't seem to bother us. We accept this background chatter as normal.[21]

The Two Principles of Life

"We are departing for the skies. Who has a mind for sightseeing?"[22]

Rumi, (1207-1273), Sufi mystic and poet

Attitude—how well we prepare physically and mentally for the journey will depend on our attitude to life. This is something that is under our control, something we can do something about. Even more important than the preparation is how receptive and willing we are to make the journey.

Our attitude is set with an *intention*. Intention begins with a desire for something. There is a single-mindedness and energy in that desire, and knowing a way to fulfill that desire. As we saw in the quote at the beginning of this chapter, intention is the targeted or focused thought that sets the course and gives us the energy to embark on the journey we are planning to take. Intention defines our path and gives us the right attitude to accomplish what we set out to do. Intention becomes *powerful* when it is set with a clear and alert mind. Confused thinking, on the other hand, will hamper our intentions with contradictions and compulsions that will pull us in different directions because we keep changing our mind about what we want, and in the process, we lose the powerful energy of intention. If our intention is clear, and well thought out, it will pull us toward where we are going. When we are earnest and committed in our approach, the climb becomes manageable. In fact, it becomes enjoyable.

Then before we start, we need to gather information and learn as much as possible about what we need for the journey. We can leave this task to our rational, logical mind because it understands and enjoys this kind of work. However, at some point, we need to make our move and take that first step. Otherwise, we remain stuck in the preparation or the information-gathering stage and don't move forward. It is very easy to convince ourselves that we are not ready yet, that we need to know more because we are afraid of change or of losing control. However, at some point, we need to take that first step toward wanting to experience. It is easier to talk and think about something than wanting to experience it.

How many times have we heard the old saying, "The road to hell is paved with good intentions"? We have intentions to do many things, but we don't follow through on them. Many of us have a tendency to sit comfortably at the base of the mountain and think about what it would be like to be on the summit and how good it will feel when we have done what we have set out to do, or what we want to do. We love to analyze, rationalize, intellectualize, and internalize, but we don't want to experience (because it takes too much effort). To internalize means we go deeper into the subject to get a better understanding, but that only increases our knowledge—*it does not change us*—it is all intellectual. Intellectual discussions, arguments, and debates are useful in our external world, but they don't transform us. And so, we fail to act, and the energy of the intention dissipates.

To transform, we have to become receptive, to become open. Every time we have an experience, it changes us... for example, love. We can have knowledge of love, or what love means by reading about it, but we cannot *know* love until we experience it. *Experience* will transform us. We have to *do it*, not just think about it. Thinking about something will never change us, but once we experience it, we are changed.

For intention to work; we need *attention*—they work hand in hand. While intention is the journey of where we want to go or what we want to do, attention is the step(s) that we take on this journey. As we will see in chapter 13, our prefrontal cortex or the *human* part of the brain is home of our intention, will, and attention. These are skills that can be enhanced by training our prefrontal cortex through mindfulness and other practices that we will discuss.

Altitude is the unknown, or what I call the "trust factor," something we have no control over. On our climb, we cannot predict the obstacles that we will face, whether it is the effect of the elevation on us during the physical climb or the effect of the ego on our inner journey. Both of these are out of our control, but this uncertainty should not frighten us. Dealing with uncertainty is the right, intuitive mind's specialty. And the way the right brain deals with uncertainty is by paying attention to what is happening in the here and now. Intention requires thought to set the course. Attention is what keeps us on the course. Attention requires no thought, just moment-by-moment awareness. It is the power of our natural state of being and the force for transformation. Whatever we pay attention to, or focus on, will thrive and grow. Attention *changes* what we observe. In other words, when we are attending to something, we are *giving it energy*. On the journey, we may not know what is going to happen in the next moment, but we can observe and attend to what is happening in the here and now. And so we have to let go and be completely present. We have to be patient and trust ourselves that we have prepared well, as we make the journey and adjust to the unknowns.

As soon as we start to pay attention to what is going on in our mind, we are already on our journey of transformation.

In addition to the skills of observation and attention that we discussed, we need what the Zen spiritual teacher Shunryu Suzuki calls *shoshin*... or a "beginner's mind."[23] So what is a beginner's mind?

Introduction III

The Beginner's Mind

"In the beginner's mind there are many possibilities, but in the expert's there are few."[24]
   Shunryu Suzuki, (1904-1971), *Founding father of Zen in America*

A Beginner's Mind Is an "I Don't Know" Mind
"If you believe you can or if you believe you can't—you are right."[25]
                              Henry Ford, (1863-1947), *industrialist*

Many of us say we have an open mind, but an open mind is not a beginner's mind. A tagline in an email someone sent me, read, "The mind is like a parachute. It works best when it is open."[26] An open mind says, "I know, but I am open to whatever you are saying." In this state of mind, there is resistance to new information because our preconceived beliefs and ideas will hamper the process of understanding. A beginner's mind says, "I don't know" and starts from there. Then the mind creates a longing to know in us and understanding comes. And so, we need to start each day anew without the baggage of yesterday. Then, every day will be a new discovery. Our focus is not on how fast we can complete the journey, but rather, on the journey itself.

A Beginner's Mind Is Patient
"Try to pose for yourself this task: not to think of a polar bear, and you will see that the cursed thing will come to mind every minute."[27]
Fyodor Dostoevsky, (1821-1881), Russian novelist and philosopher

Many times, you will find that your mind is restless and no matter how hard you try, it just won't settle down. If you are trying too hard, then you are doing the practice in the wrong way. Understanding the mind is not hard work. So if the mind is restless, let it be restless. Stop whatever you are doing and watch the mind as if you are a witness, an outsider to the mind. In fact, tell your mind to continue to be restless. You will notice that, in a short time, the mind will quieten down.

Actually, you can try this the next time you are upset, or unhappy or sad. Say, you are upset. Tell yourself, "okay, fine, be upset." Don't try and get out of that mood. Stay with it, feel it, watch it and soon the upset will dissipate because there is no one to fight with in your mind—you accepted yourself as you are. These conditions stay because we don't accept them and want to get rid of them. We make them a problem because we want to get rid of them. This is the difficulty—we can't seem to accept ourselves the way we are. We always think that we are not what is going on within us. What we *resist* stays, and what we *accept* is overcome or transcended.

This journey of transformation we have embarked on is the most important thing we will ever do in our life. And so, we have to be patient and take our time with the learning of the skills and working with the techniques. Transformation can happen, but it does take time. Realizing our true nature itself can happen in an instant, but we have to prepare the groundwork for it to happen, and that takes time. Most people are only interested in a quick-fix technique or solution that they think will change them right away—if not change, then at least to help them in their present situation.

I overheard two people in the gym just after New Year's Day discussing New Year's resolutions and how to bring about changes to their stressful lives. One of them said, "I wish someone could come up with a Reader's Digest version of what needs to be done in life... how to live our lives... no one gave me a manual, and I really don't have time to find out. There is just too much to do."

There is no Reader's Digest version of quick fixes to suffering or for anything in life. Quick fixes (like Band-Aids) hold us together for a short time until their effect wears off. Then we return to the place we started, but are worse off because now we must deal with our feelings of guilt and failure. We have to be willing and earnest in our desire for transformation, and it will require commitment and effort on our part. *Only we can pull ourselves out of the survival mindset—no one can do it for us.*

It is better to practice for a shorter time more often than sitting for a long period of time once in a while. Consistency and regular practice are important. We need patience because our mental conditioning is very strong and it is entrenched. How can we dislodge or break through the conditioning of twenty, thirty, sixty, or seventy years of living? The older we get, the stronger the conditioning gets, and the more defensive and stubborn we become. The wall of *mental concepts* grows very strong, and it becomes harder to crack.

A Beginner's Mind Is Loving and Compassionate

"Expressing the meaning of love in a story requires outer creativity, but becoming loving in one's life is inner creativity."[28]

Amit Goswami, quantum physicist and author

When I ask people if they love themselves, they respond immediately with, "Of course I love myself, we all love ourselves. What kind of question is this?" We all think we love ourselves, but if we truly did, we would not give ourselves such a hard time. If we are hard on ourselves, we are hard on others. If we love ourselves, we become kind to ourselves when we think we have made what we call "mistakes," and in turn, we are more compassionate, generous and forgiving of others. We automatically stop judging them and instead become receptive to them.

Just remember; every trait, every "flaw" we find in others, already exists in us. We are only able to identify the trait as a problem because we are familiar with it, we have encountered it within ourselves. We may not be aware of the trait because we have always avoided looking at ourselves, but if we dig deep, we will find it there. And then we project our "flaw" onto others, and say, they have that flaw.

To truly love ourselves, we have to accept ourselves as we are, or as Byron Katie, author and teacher of "The Work" method of self-inquiry, would say, "I love what is."[29] It doesn't mean we have to stay the way we are, but change can only happen once we acknowledge what we are. *This acceptance of what we are is the beginning of transformation.* We then begin to discover ourselves. Our sense of self gets stronger. Then change can happen. As long as the voice in the head is active, we are just moving in our mind. This makes it difficult to bring about any change because we cannot observe what is going on in our mind through the mind chatter. When we love ourselves as we are, we bring the voice in the head to a sudden stop. We are in the *now*. Then we discover that there is some *space* to observe ourselves without the interference of thoughts.

As we become more receptive to change, our behavior and our actions will change. Our behavior is a consequence of our attitude. Change the attitude... and the behavior and actions will change. We will then *never get bored or lonely again*! It is when we don't like ourselves that we seek out the company of others, or try to find "interesting" things to get us away from boredom. It is not that we should not go out or be around people. What it means is that we will not go to them out of boredom or loneliness but because we want to. *If we are "alive" (aware and alert) inside, then nothing is boring and you will never be lonely. But if we are "dead" inside, if we are sleepwalking through life, then everything becomes boring, because nothing holds our attention for long.*

A Beginner's Mind Does Not Discriminate
"If you are too clever, you could miss the point entirely."[30]

Tibetan saying

If we are operating too much in our left rational and logical hemisphere, it may take a bit longer to learn to silence our minds. Give the rational mind a rest because it is a hindrance to understanding ourselves. It will tie us in knots with its doubts and arguments. Instead of breaking things down, as we normally do, here, we are observing the mind *holistically*. To transform, we have to be receptive by invoking our intuitive side. And for that, we need a different kind of approach or language—not the everyday language of logic that we use to convince and persuade, but the language of love, because it is concerned with us and our well-being.

Also, we don't need the knowledge that we have acquired with our left-brain to observe our minds. Unlike with the rational concept of knowledge, where we can build upon a foundation of previously acquired knowledge, when we do our inner work, we cannot build on what someone else has experienced. *We have to go through the process ourselves.* For example, say we are learning a language, a left-brain activity. Once we have learned and memorized the alphabet, we can then build upon what we have learned and create words. We do not have to start from scratch and develop a new alphabet—we used someone else's alphabet for our purposes.

With inner work, if I describe the meditation process and write about the different states of mind that I have encountered during the practice, you cannot build on this knowledge… it is intangible. What you can do is use my experience and what I have found as signposts on your journey and discover the states yourself. Also, even if you were able to quiet your mind when you were meditating today, it is not guaranteed that tomorrow your mind will be quiet. You have to start from scratch each day with *a beginner's mind*—no expectations! And then the experiences will build up, and it will get easier as you progress.

A Beginner's Mind Is Like a Child's Mind—Curious, Excited, Happy, and Having Fun as It Is Learning

"The face of the wise man is not somber or austere, contracted by anxiety and sorrow, but the opposite: radiant and serene, and filled with a vast delight, which makes him the most playful of men… If someone has experienced the wisdom that can only be heard from oneself, learned from oneself, and created from oneself, he does not merely participate in laughter: he becomes laughter itself."[31]
                    Philo of Alexandria, (ca. 20 BCE–50 CE), philosopher

And finally, we have to learn to have fun while we are working on ourselves (to change). There are two ways to live in this world—either in moments of misery and suffering created by the voice in the head, or in moments of lucidity, clarity, and contentment when the mind is quiet. Actually, we are living both these ways now, but we only notice the misery and not the times we are happy. Most of us focus on the misery that we feel most of the time, and ask, "How can we make ourselves less miserable, less stressed?" We assume there is no way out of this misery or suffering. And, *so we turn to self-help books, most of which are geared to the art of survival of the ego for a quick and temporary relief of stress.* What can we do to make the present situation better? In other words, we ask how we can try and survive the best way we can. This is the survival mentality. We do not ask how we can change ourselves so that we do not suffer anymore.

Very few people focus on the moments of clarity and happiness, and ask, "How can we extend this clarity throughout the day?" When we are happy, we are in a different state of mind, our natural creative state. But we don't notice it, because these moments are few and far between, and anyway, we are too busy with our mind-chatter to notice. Even when these moments come, we can't seem to handle them. We are so used to discontent and misery that we never pay attention to when we are happy or contented. We are thrown off balance and question why we are happy when there is so much work to be done… and in the process, we feel guilty, become serious, and lose these precious moments. Then these precious moments just become fleeting memories of peace and respite in our never-ending cycle of suffering.

We have to start becoming receptive to these moments of clarity if we are to end our suffering. To become familiar with this state, we need to remain in that feeling, and fully experience that moment of clarity. We have to learn to stay with whatever situation or experience brings on these feelings of joy, happiness, or clarity, for as long as we can. Only then, will we begin to see what these experiences feel like.

It is easier to change and transcend from a baseline of happiness than one from misery. When we are filled with love, fun, laughter, and enjoyment, we are open and receptive to new things, and new ways of doing things. Then every technique will bring about a change. When we are miserable, we are closed and defensive—we want to stay where we are because it is safe. If we are miserable, then no technique will work, because we will find problems with it, and we will lose interest very quickly... so lighten up and have some fun.

Part I
Our Personal World

Chapter 1

How We Live Today

"He [man] cannot stop the flow of his thoughts, he cannot control his imagination, his emotions, his attention. He lives in a subjective world of 'I love,' 'I do not love,' 'I like,' 'I do not like,' 'I want,' 'I do not want.' He does not see the real world [which] is hidden from him by the wall of imagination. He lives in sleep."[32]
   G I. Gurdjieff, (1866-1949), Russian mystic, writer, and teacher

The Lady in the Gym
   Some time back, one early morning at my previous gym, I saw a woman exercising on a treadmill in front of me. You could not help but notice her, because not only was she loud, but because of what she was doing while she was working out. For the next half-hour, while she was on the treadmill, her mind was on six different activities. She was watching a crime show on the small television screen mounted on her machine and listening to

the iPod strapped to her left arm. She was having a conversation with the person on the elliptical machine next to her, telling her how busy she was and all the things she had yet to do during the day. She was glancing at the big television screen on the wall in front of her which was on the news, weather, and traffic channel and walking.

She seemed anxious, impatient, and unhappy, or at least she didn't seem to be having much fun. It was as if she was on a mission to complete all the things she had planned for herself in that half-hour or so—something like checking off items on her mental to-do list, while probably at the same time thinking of all the items still pending on the list and trying to figure out when and how she would tackle them all before the end of the day.

This way of living is a microcosm of how many of us live and function in our society today. And of course, many of us would ask, "And what is wrong with us trying to catch up on the things we need to do when we just don't have enough time in the day to complete them all?" We would also say that this way of living was a fact of life in our fast-paced, technologically oriented, stress-filled society, and if we didn't do this, we would never be able to accomplish everything we have set up for ourselves. In fact, many self-help books in the market today tell us to prioritize our life and advocate doing multiple things at the same time to become even more efficient in the time we have, all so that we can manage to stay on life's treadmill.

The Treadmill of Life

We are caught up on life's treadmill, tethered to work 24/7 by technology, and pushed forward by priorities and to-do lists. Even though we know our stress level is too high (and that it is affecting our health, family, relationships and other areas of our lives), we tend to put up with it. Instead, we justify being stressed by saying it is the price we have to pay for our fast-paced life, and of course, we think living with stress is the norm because everyone is stressed. In fact, it becomes a bragging right, "How my life is more stressful than yours." Short-changing our sleep and personal activities and feeling overwhelmed, we nonetheless keep going, toward breakdowns, disillusionment, and unhappiness. Just when we think we have attained a balance in different areas of our lives or some semblance of normalcy, something slips through our fingers, and we start over again.

Multitasking, swinging between memories, guilt, and regrets of the past and the hopes, worries, and expectations of the future, makes *our lives superficial and mechanical* because we never delve into anything in depth. We never spend any time in the present, where life is, but we do everything to *avoid the here and now by keeping busy*. Intellectually, we are aware that we need to slow down because we are skipping chunks of our lives, but our mind keeps pushing toward all the things that we still need to do.

Fuelled by desire (to accomplish our goals and to accumulate more things) and fear (that we may not be able to do so), our life has become a struggle to survive—running faster to stay where we are. *Sometimes it feels like we are just spinning our wheels and sleepwalking through life*. No matter how much we struggle to achieve all the things we want, there is still more to achieve. It never stops—there is always a desire for more and more. We are never satisfied with what we already have. We want it all, and we want it now, and we don't mind what we have to go through to get it.

Running on the treadmill, we keep chanting mantras— "mind over matter" or "no pain, no gain"—to push us faster and harder even when we are hurting, or when our lives are falling apart. Moments of clarity throw us off balance because most of the time we are not clear and lucid. Rare is a person who knows when to step off this treadmill and find happiness. Stepping off does not mean an end to our aspirations. It means we have control over our lives again.

When we are young, stress just flows through us—it just moves in and out of us all the time. At least it used to be like that when I was young. Now it is different. Today's kids are getting into the "stress" game. Stress is becoming part of their everyday vocabulary. They watch how we react to things, and they start to mirror our behavior in the events and situations they encounter in their lives. It is not uncommon to hear kids as young as nine and ten complain about how much stress they are under and how much stress their parents put on them. Ann Zimmerman, a reporter for the *Wall Street Journal*, says that we put so much pressure on our kids that they are stressed all the time. We don't even let kids have time for free play anymore. She says that toy manufacturers are now coming up with what they call "snack toys"—games and toys to fill in the "time between the organized activities" for busy kids who only have "bite-size bits of time to play." The toy makers are even revamping many of the board games so that they can be played at a "more frenetic pace."[33] This trend of squeezing playtime between organized activities makes children lose their joy of life, playfulness, spontaneity, and creativity; they are becoming like us—tired, bored, and dull.

We keep ourselves busy with all the activities because we are afraid to be on our own, with our own minds. We are afraid to be alone. When we are busy, we forget ourselves. We don't even know what to do when we have some time to ourselves or when we go on vacation. A couple of days into the vacation, we are bored and turn on our laptops and smartphones to get in touch with the office (despite having promised ourselves that we wouldn't). Relaxation is an escape into social media, television, shopping, alcohol, and drugs.

Chapter 1 How We Live Today

Shopping or consumption of goods and services has not only become a way of life for many of us but, as Annie Leonard, an environmental activist and a critic of excessive consumerism, says, consumerism now defines us. Advertisers use every means possible to sell us this way of life—to make us feel miserable as we are and to try to convince us of what we need to be, do, and buy to make ourselves happy. So, we always want to be something other than what we are, to be somewhere else other than where we are right now, and to do something other than what we are doing; this way of living is a recipe for unhappiness, discontent, and anxiety... which are all triggers for stress. Ms. Leonard talks about consumerism in "The Story of Stuff" video:

"The purpose of advertising is to make us unhappy 3,000 times a day; it tells us that our hair is wrong, our skin is wrong, our furniture is wrong, we are wrong. But it can all be made right if we just go shopping... we are in this ridiculous situation—we go to work, maybe to two jobs, come home and we are exhausted and plunk ourselves on our new couch and watch television and the commercials tell us we suck... and so we go to the mall to buy something to feel better and then you have to go to work more to pay for the stuff you just bought and you come home, more exhausted, more tired, watch more television and go to the mall again—caught in this treadmill."[34]

Many of us are forced off the treadmill because we can't keep up with the stress. We move to slower pastures to tend whatever little gardens we have in our minds, spending the rest of our lives disillusioned and disappointed, blaming everyone and everything—except ourselves—for the way life has turned out.

The Wired Ego
"The attention economy incentivizes the design of technologies that grab our attention... it privileges our impulses over our intentions...

privileging what is sensational over what is nuanced, appealing to emotion, anger and outrage... the dynamics of the attention economy are structurally set up to undermine the human will."[35]

James Williams, former Google strategist

Technology, especially the wired world, instead of making our lives more efficient, has created a whole slew of other problems. Companies like Facebook, Apple, Google, and others not only narrow our worldview and reinforce our conditioning, as we will see in chapter 5, but, as we saw in introduction I, they are draining away the very power that we need to break through our programming—*our attention...* our creative, transformative force.

These companies harvest our attention little by little using "every possible neuroscience and psychological trick" to hook us to their smartphones and apps and in the process hijack and control our minds.[36] In fact, as Ramsay Brown, co-founder of Dopamine Labs, a very aptly named company, says, "[the technology companies] are now in the business of designing brains not just designing software."[37] Look at the implication of these words; the tech companies are telling us what to think, when to think, and what to do. In other words, *we have now lost control of our own minds.*

A 2013 Microsoft study found that thanks to "our always-on portable devices," we can multitask more, but our attention span, which was twelve seconds in 2000, had been reduced to eight seconds by 2013, less than that of a goldfish (nine seconds). Furthermore, it is becoming increasingly difficult for us to "focus in environments where prolonged attention is needed... and we are displaying more addiction-like behaviors."[38] And it is not only when we are using the smartphones. Another study has shown "that the mere presence of smartphones damages cognitive capacity—even when the device is turned off."[39]

Chapter 1 How We Live Today

We have become socially inept and easily distracted, with short attention spans. Laden with anxiety, we are lonely and easily bored, sharing our lives with others on social media moment-by-moment. Thus, we document our lives online and have a following on Twitter, Facebook, Instagram, and other social media sites, counting the number of "likes" to make us feel better and secure. These fleeting, momentary sense of pleasure are timed to be delivered to us by the companies when these companies know we are feeling down. Facebook, for example, has the ability to "identify when teens feel "insecure," "worthless," and "need a confidence boost,"[40] so they target the individual teen with a feel-good reward—a "release of dopamine in the brain."[41]

Instead of turning inward to understand ourselves, we turn more and more to the online world because we find it better and easier to deal with than our inner world. In our online world, we say and do things that we would not dream of doing in a one-on-one interaction. We go to sleep and wake up with texts and emails buzzing in our ears. Many of us wake up in the middle of the night to respond to these intrusions because we believe we will miss something important if we don't respond immediately. It is estimated that "Eighty-seven percent of people wake up and go to sleep with their smartphones."[42]

We look to this world of cyberspace and to the external world to provide us with happiness and fulfillment—we love taking pictures of what is going in our lives and moving on to the next thing more than actually staying with an encounter and experiencing it fully. Not only do we not find happiness and fulfillment, but this behavior also leads to moodiness, social withdrawal, and loneliness because we are moving further away from our center.[43] It affects our relationships, our work, and everything else we do. We have become so hooked on these devices that doctors and psychologists have started talking about internet addiction because these devices trigger the same neurological connections in the brain that are active when one is addicted to gambling or drugs.[44]

Many young technology company engineers and designers, who were involved in creating the many features of the social media apps that are so addictive, are beginning to realize some of the unintended consequences of these technologies. As Sean Parker, Napster founder and former president of Facebook says, "Facebook, like other social media, was designed to exploit people's psychological vulnerabilities... *God only knows what it's doing to our children's brains.*"[45] These tech workers are not waiting to find out. Not only are they slowing reducing their use of smartphones and social media apps, but they are sending their children to private schools which prohibit smartphones and laptops.[46] But most of us don't even realize the addictive nature of these smartphone apps and, even if we do, we can't seem to be able to break our dependency on them or... *we just don't care.*

Lurking Just Under the Surface—A Cocktail of Emotions
"The wise understand the ignorant, for they were themselves once ignorant. But the ignorant do not understand either themselves or the wise, never having been wise themselves."[47]

Sufi saying

Even though there is an undercurrent of anxiety, restlessness, unease, fear, and feelings of dissatisfaction and frustrations with everything that is going on in our lives, we seldom pay attention to these signs of mental disturbances or inner turmoil. We feel unfulfilled and unhappy, no matter what we do, how much we struggle, or how hard we work. Sometimes, it feels like life is just a game of survival, and it is slipping away, just like fine beach sand flowing through our fingers. Even if we do stop and try and understand what is causing this unhappiness, we don't stop long

Chapter 1 How We Live Today

enough because we don't have the time. We can't or don't even know where to begin to spend some time with ourselves in silence to find the answers to what is troubling us.

Why am I so stressed? Why am I doing this to myself? What is the purpose of life? Is life just a struggle to survive? Do I have to continue suffering? When does my suffering end? Or does it ever stop? Is this all there is to life? Why am I not happy even though I have everything to make my life comfortable? Why am I so lonely even though there are people around me all the time? These kinds of questions cross our mind regularly but soon forgotten as our "busyness" pushes them aside. We plow through life, with our heads hunkered down, saying that we have no time for these distractions because we have all these things that need doing—feed our family, worry about our finances, worry about what is going on at work and in the world, and on and on. We don't even have time to fall sick without feeling guilty.

Before we look at how we can eliminate stress, we need to look at how we create stress by the way we experience the world. Did you know that we create our own experience of the world? Not only do we shape our own unique worldview, but we create multiple versions of it during the day, depending on the state of mind we are in. Our thoughts, needs, hopes, expectations, and desires keep our personal world going. For example, if we are angry at someone, we tend to ignore everything else and keep thinking about the incident that provoked our anger, over and over again. So at that moment, our personal world revolves around our anger. Or, if we are hungry, we tend to ignore everything else and look for food; at that moment, our personal world revolves around food. Rumi put it this way: "What a piece of bread looks like depends on whether you are hungry or not."[48]

So how does our personal view of the world come about... and what does it look like? To get into that, we need to talk about how consciousness and mind are related.

Chapter 2

Consciousness—The Universal Intelligence

"A human being is a part of a whole, called by us 'universe,' a part limited in time and space. He experiences himself, his thoughts and feelings as something separated from the rest... a kind of optical delusion of his consciousness. This delusion is a kind of prison for us, restricting us to our personal desires and to affection for a few persons nearest to us. Our task must be to free ourselves from this prison by widening our circle of compassion to embrace all living creatures and the whole of nature in its beauty."[49]

Albert Einstein, (1879-1955), theoretical physicist

Consciousness

Consciousness is intangible and difficult to define, but most simply, it is what gives us life. It is life itself. The sages and seers call consciousness the ground of all being from which everything comes, and into which everything goes back. It is invisible, but we can see its manifestations everywhere. It is the universal intelligence that runs trillions of chemical and electrical processes in our physical bodies, keeping us alive without us either consciously doing anything or being aware of what is going on. It is the background on which everything happens, and there is no duality or subject-object split. It just is. In essence, consciousness is what we are... called by different names—universal intelligence, God, no mind, original mind, divine self, presence, quantum consciousness, awareness, natural creative state, cosmic consciousness...

Mind

This all-pervading consciousness can have different manifestations in the universe, but, in the physical form, it appears as, what we call, the mind. Even though the brain is powerful and has billions and billions of neurons or nerve cells, without consciousness, it cannot function. In other words, consciousness gives life to the brain in the form of mind. And so, the mind is simply "a working brain, a brain in action... there is no mind without the physical expression of life through a functioning brain."[50] There are, however, many levels of mind, but the two important ones we will be discussing here are:

1. Our Original Consciousness: Our original or the natural state of being which is our innermost essence, our center, and the deepest level of mind.

    This level of mind is our highest state of consciousness, pure awareness. It animates every cell of our body. This

Chapter 2 Consciousness—The Universal Intelligence

natural state of being is common to all and is the state of our mind before our ego (our conditioned, self-memorized framework of habits, beliefs, attitudes, behaviors, and conditioned responses) comes into being in early childhood around the age of three or four years. This state is also called "primary," or our *present moment awareness*. In Chan Buddhism, it is called the "original spirit... the host [or]... the master."[51] It is unconditioned and is always awake and alert. It is our creative realm, and we are in touch with our innate intelligence or wisdom. This *awareness* is what we are in essence.

In this state of consciousness, we are watching everything that is going on—there is no subject-object split or duality. It is just one state—*pure observation*, without any interference of what is being experienced. *We see things as they are in their pristine nature.* In other words, we are completely in the here and now—experiencing whatever we are experiencing at the moment. We are aware that we are aware. We have access to this state when we have insights or when we are happy, lucid, and contented. But mostly, our true nature has become the forgotten state of mind.

2. Ego Consciousness: Our ordinary, everyday mind or wakeful consciousness—our top-most or superficial mind.

    Memories are created once we experience the same object or situation multiple times, and are an essential part of the learning process. These memories start to affect what we actually see through our everyday consciousness. Memories or mental concepts are just *thought forms*—the labels that we attach to what we observe, and are what our brains use to understand the world around us. They are made on the periphery, around the innermost essence of who we really are, and form a "wall of thoughts" that then defines us. Thus, we observe the world through this filter of thought forms... eventually identifying with them—*limiting or constricting our awareness,* and altering what we are really observing. Ultimately, we lose touch with reality, and we are then, what is called, "unconscious." This state of mind is our "secondary" awareness (compared to our "primary" awareness of Original Consciousness). It is the beginning of our conditioning and the formation of the *ego or the superficial false self*. In the process, we begin to lose touch with our innermost essence, of who we really are.

From then on, we are not actively engaged with reality and are *lost in thought*, mostly never to recover unless something jars us awake in the later years. Even though we may think that we are conscious (just because we are awake and not sleeping), we may not be. In fact, this is the case with most of us, as we will see in how much we operate from our conditioned self and are not conscious of what is going on around us. We are then on automatic control; so for most of us, there is no difference between being asleep and being awake. And this way of perceiving the world is the reason for our incessant suffering.

We have moved away from our innermost essence and now reside on the periphery, becoming egocentric. We forget who we are and take on an identity of who we *think* we are. This false identity then becomes the world of our ego-self, our very own unique worldview, or "our individualized thought system,"[52] which no one else has access to. It is the self we are most familiar with, the "I" that relates to the world. It is our ordinary everyday consciousness, and the noisy, restless, anxious, chattering (voice in the head), mind. It is our personality, the role (or more correctly, the roles) we play in this life. The ego-self in Chan Buddhism is also known as "conditioned conscious spirit… the guest [or]… the servant."[53]

The wall of thoughts, which pushes us away from our innermost essence, makes us forget who we truly are. This forgetting creates what I call the "Anxiety Gap"—*the gap between who we think we are (our ego consciousness) and who we actually are (our original consciousness).* This gap is dependent on our conditioning (Figure 3).

The Anxiety Gap
(The gap between who think we are and who we actually are)

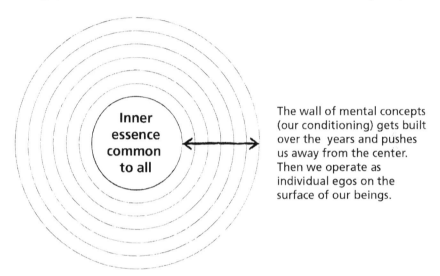

Figure 3. *The Anxiety Gap is directly proportional to how conditioned we are. As our conditioning increases and moves us further away from the center, the more anxious, stressed, and superficial we become. We have moved away from the center and are residing on the periphery of our essence operating as individual egos and observing the world through the wall of thoughts and the reality we have created through our perception of what is.*

The ego in itself is not bad, but once we get more conditioned and entrenched in who we think we are, and get further away from who we are, then the ego becomes a problem. The more conditioned we are, the louder the voice in our head becomes, and the more difficult it is to face our everyday living challenges… and so we become more anxious, fearful, and lonely.

This inadequate response to our problems leads to mental anguish, suffering, and stress of daily living.

I prefer the terms *host* (master—unconditioned) and *guest* (servant—conditioned) to our original consciousness and the ego consciousness, as they represent the perfect relationship between the different manifestations of the universal consciousness within us. These terms are a good reminder of the *temporary* nature of the ego and the *permanent* nature of the innermost center or the original self in the human form.

Chapter 3

Our Individualized Thought System

"Your beliefs become your thoughts
Your thoughts become your words
Your words become your actions
Your actions become your habits
Your habits become your values
Your values become your destiny"[54]
  Mahatma Gandhi, (1869-1948), Indian civil rights leader

The Ego and our Conditioning—the Beginning of Our Unique, Individual Worldview

Many of us believe that the world we perceive is real and that everyone perceives the world in the same way. What we don't know is that the world we see and experience is the mirror image, a reflection of our mind and our thinking. The world is neutral, neither good nor bad, but our thinking gives it meaning based on our conditioning (our habitual way of thinking or our mindset). And because our thinking is affected by our conditioning, our view of the world is unique and so we all see the world differently. In fact, our worldview changes constantly, at each moment, depending on our thinking, feelings, and emotions. We see and hear what we want to see and hear—what fits and supports our point of view or our outlook.

No two people, not even identical twins, will view the world in the same manner, and so we all act and react to things differently. And yet many people insist that their view of life is accurate and try to force their viewpoint on everyone else not realizing that theirs is just one of an infinite number of possible worldviews. Unfortunately, many of us never move beyond our personal worldview and spend the rest of our days reinforcing and defending this view.

So how does our personal view of the world or our individualized thought system come about, and what does it look like?

Brain Frequencies and Mental States
"Children are the vibrant, wandering butterflies who transform into caterpillars inching along the grown-up path."[55]

                Alison Gopnik, author of The Philosophical Baby

To understand how our personal viewpoint develops and why it is so hard to change the way we perceive the world, it is important to know something about our *brain-wave frequencies* and the various *mental states* they create[56] (Figure 4). Although most people think we have only two states of mind—the active or awake state during the day (or the beta state) and the one at night

The Inverse Relationship between Brain Development and the Process of Relaxation

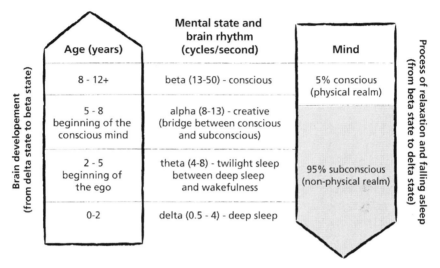

Figure 4. *Understanding how the different brain waves relate to different states of the mind will help us understand the process of transformation we are undertaking.*

when we are in deep sleep (or the delta state)—there are actually two more states between them. These are the alpha or the creative state and the theta or semi-awake state. Understanding the various mental states will help us to understand the process of inner creativity of change and transformation, which we will be discussing later. Once we become familiar with these different states, we can bring them on at will. For example, when we are stressed, we will know that we are in the high beta zone and will need to calm ourselves by slowing the wave frequency to the lower beta and the higher alpha level (*the calm and alert state*)—by say... conscious breathing (see tools for the journey 2 and 3).

The brain's activity produces various kinds of electrical waves that can be measured by an electroencephalogram (EEG). The quantity and strength of these waves will change, depending on the individual person and the activity they are involved in. All the brain waves are present in the brain at any one time, but the predominant wave will determine the mental state during a particular activity. The waves are divided into bandwidths—the higher the vibrations or frequency (measured in cycles per second), the faster the brain activity. Different waves represent different states of mind; and in general, we go from the subconscious state of very low-frequency delta waves that we encounter in deep sleep (with almost no brain activity) to the theta waves of the twilight zone (the semi-awake state between sleep and wakefulness but still subconscious). From there, the brain vibrations increase to the creative frequencies of the alpha state (becoming conscious—this alpha state connects the subconscious and the conscious minds), to the higher frequencies of our conscious state or the beta waves when we direct our attention to the outside world.

The terms *conscious*, *subconscious*, and *unconscious* can create a lot of confusion because we tend to use them in many different ways. Here is what I mean when I use these words to talk about the mind.[57]

Subconscious: Just like an iceberg, where the majority of the iceberg is hidden below the water, most of our mind (over 95%) is hidden or subconscious (Figure 5) and runs our subconscious automatic body processes like breathing, blood circulation, and the pumping of the heart. The subconscious mind also includes our conditioned framework of beliefs, habits, and attitudes that we have accumulated since when we were young. Within the subconscious mind, there are many levels and at the deepest level is our original mind or natural state of being.

Chapter 3 Our Individualized Thought System

The Mind "Iceberg"

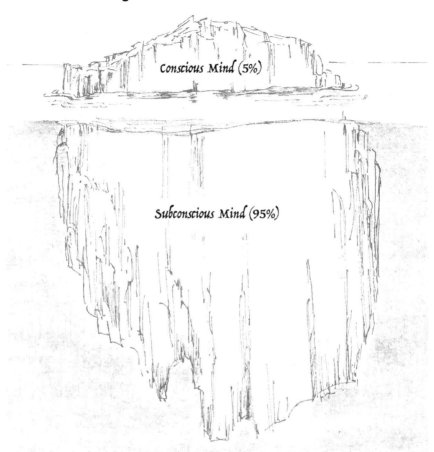

Figure 5. *Even though the conscious mind is about 5% of the total mind, many of us use much less than 5% of the mind. To be conscious is to be awake and alert to what is going on in our environment. Most of us operate from our habitual conditioned self and are not aware of what is going on around us, and as a result, our responses become "unconscious" and automatic. We have handed over the responsibility of the day-to-day living to our subconscious mind and then sleepwalk through life. Even when we are briefly aware, the pull of the subconscious mind, which is a million times more powerful than the conscious mind, is hard to resist and we go back to our automatic way of thinking and doing things.*

Conscious: The remaining 5% of the mind that is visible, is our conscious, analytical, rational, logical left-brain mind. Its primary focus is on the external world. It is our everyday mind, and home of the ego. To be conscious is to be awake, to be aware and alert to what is going on in our lives.

Unconscious: When we are "lost" in thought, we are awake, but lose awareness of our actions, behaviors, and surroundings. Our responses then become automatic and "unconscious." This robot-like lack of awareness is different from the medical use of the term "unconscious" that is applied to someone who is unresponsive to his or her surroundings because of brain injury, or under the effect of anesthesia. In this condition, the person doesn't have the ability to respond to the environment at all.

Just as we go from the subconscious to conscious mind when we awaken from deep sleep, children start their life journey in the subconscious delta region and progress to higher conscious brain wave activity as they grow and their brains develop. Each state plays an important role in their mental development. As they progress through the different mental states and start becoming conscious, their experiences begin to get stored as memories. This collection of memories is the beginning of their conditioning and the formation of the ego or the superficial self with which most people identify as their *real self.*

Let's look at this process of mental development in more detail by focusing on the brain waves in children as they develop.[58]

From Birth to Two Years Old

"Babies are explorers and adults are exploiters."[59]

Alison Gopnik

From birth to about two years of age, infants' brains emit very slow delta brain waves in the region of one-half to four

Chapter 3 Our Individualized Thought System

cycles per second, and so the infants function primarily from their subconscious level. During this period, the flow of information from its environment is all one way—inward—and is accepted into the subconscious without any resistance from the child. At this age, all brain development takes place in the right brain hemisphere.[60] The conscious, rational, logical, left-hemisphere brain is not active yet. *There are no thoughts in the child's mind, and the child is completely in the present moment.*

From Two to Five Years Old

As the child's brain develops, its brain activity increases to between four to eight cycles per second. These frequencies are associated with the theta waves, and the child still functions from its subconscious. In this subconscious theta state of mind, children are extremely suggestible. In fact, this is the state of mind that hypnotherapists bring their patients to when they are trying to change the patients' old behaviors, by programming in new ones.

Children at this age don't rationally or logically think in a linear, focused way (a left-brain activity). Instead, they learn (continuously) by observing, imagining, exploring, and using free association, which is a right-brain activity. Young children are much more aware and conscious of everything in their surroundings. They are always in *the present moment*. Gopnik describes this awareness as "the lantern consciousness of childhood as opposed to the spotlight consciousness of ordinary adult attention. You are vividly aware of everything without being focused on any one thing in particular."[61]

To experience the world in relation to itself, the child has to develop a separate identity—its ego. This developing identity is reflective of the child's upbringing based on parent-societal expectations. The ego is like a beacon, a surveillance system, and a tool to assist the child to navigate our world, and to discover itself as an independent entity—to put its unique stamp on its domain. It is the child's personal point of view. The ego gets its start in the left-brain hemisphere with the first conscious "I" thought.

With the ego consciousness just beginning, the child's internal state, according to Gopnik, is "more like wandering than voyaging—a journey of exploration rather than conquest," where everything is happening in the *here and now*.[62] In this state, there is *no concept of time*. Thoughts come and then for a while they cease.

For adults, the internal consciousness moves in a straight line. Our mind swings continuously from the memories of the past to the plans and anticipations of the future, never stopping to experience what is happening in the here and now. When we do stop, we tend to focus on a specific thing that interests us (or what our ego-self is interested in, at that particular moment) like a spotlight. We ignore everything else in our surroundings because our awareness is constricted by our conditioning. This is because we tend to live in our ego-world and have forgotten what it's like to live like children, in the present moment, and in our natural state of being.

Our consciousness is more like a child's "when we are traveling in an unfamiliar country or practicing a type of meditation that emphasizes clearing the mind and being present in the moment."[63] The sights, sounds, smells and the feel of an unfamiliar place or a country, can literally take our thoughts away and the mind becomes quiet, aware and present. *Meditation* has a similar effect on us. It has the *power to shift our consciousness* by *expanding our attention into awareness*. This is the expanded or heightened sense of awareness of our true self that we discussed earlier. While children operate from this state of mind subconsciously, we can learn ways to consciously access and use

Chapter 3 Our Individualized Thought System

this natural state, in order to perceive the world differently and eliminate stress.

Five to Eight Years Old

The child's brain waves start to speed up to alpha waves between eight to thirteen cycles per second. The child still functions mostly in the realm of the subconscious, but now the conscious mind has started to develop. The alpha state overlaps the subconscious and the conscious minds.

As the boundary between the subconscious and conscious minds has not yet solidified, children can go back and forth between these two minds with ease. *During these early years, the child is a master at using both hemispheres of the brain.* And, as we will see in chapter 14, she learns through creativity and intellect or what is called "dual-brain processing."[64] She doesn't see a difference between her inner world of imagination and the outer world of reality. Here the child is becoming creative—she looks at problems holistically, and so, is able to combine information in different ways to help her understand. Her mind is relaxed but alert, or in a state of passive or primary awareness. *This natural state of mind is conducive to accelerated learning.* She is still very much right-hemisphere dominant, but the left hemisphere is now coming into play much more with the ego development gaining dominance. The child has no self-image, as yet, because the ego-self is in the early stage of development, and conditioning hasn't started to take hold.[65]

The child learns something new and then uses this information to understand whatever she encounters. In other words, she meets the new experience with the memory of the previous experience. This process results in the constant creation of new memories. Then the memories start to get entrenched, as the child keeps repeating and recalling these memories.

In our early years, observation and creativity play a big part in our accelerated learning process. Then comes our education system, which is based on the society's emphasis on academics, with the aim of producing knowledge workers to keep up with advances in technology. So begins the skewed, lopsided development of the left brain, rational, intellectual, scientific mode of thinking. As a result, the creative right-brain wisdom is sidetracked because it is not deemed useful for acquiring technical knowledge.

In the absence of the quiet, intuitive presence of the right-hemisphere wisdom, the ego begins to leverage the rational mind functionality to take control of the mind, and so we begin to live more and more in our minds. Our locus of consciousness thus shifts from our natural state to the activities of the left-brain, or our everyday ego consciousness.

As a result, creative activities that the child is involved in start to fall off the radar, and the creative learning decreases over time. She begins to lose her connection to the intuitive mind as her conditioning increases, thereby losing access to her inner intelligence. And so, the child starts to fall back on her conditioned, learned behaviors and responses. Loss of creativity, and the increase in conditioned habitual responses go hand in hand, and in the process, she begins to lose the art of accelerated learning.

As she grows, every thought, belief and memory that arises, every emotion she experiences, every behavior and action she performs, everything she picks up from her parents, coalesce around the "I" thought. Her name acts as a repository of "the I-hood," which stores everything as memory. She creates a framework of mental concepts about everything, including her experiences, to help her understand what she is perceiving and to make it easier to communicate her understanding to others. So in other words, this framework of mental concepts is a make-believe

Chapter 3 Our Individualized Thought System

or virtual world, because these earliest concepts are imaginary and fused with reality. For example, the word "moon" is not the actual moon. It is a concept (a description) that the society has agreed to call that planetary object we see in the sky.

The collection of these memories as a framework of mental concepts is what is called our conditioning. As we saw in chapter 2, the wall of memories gets built up over the years, and pushes the child away from her innermost core (her essence) to the periphery. Here she operates as an individual ego on the surface of her being. Then she begins to observe the world through this wall of memories—through her past—and slowly starts *to get identified with them*. This conditioning becomes the center of her personality, the ego-self—just a collection of mental concepts, but it gives her an idea of who she thinks she is. Without this "I" thought, the other thoughts cannot exist; because, for the ego, everything exists in relation to itself.

The framework of habits, behaviors, attitudes, and beliefs that the child builds in her mind is not an entirely new framework. It gets its start from the child's parents, and with teachers, and other people in her life. In other words, the child is conditioned even before she starts to add her own experiences to the framework of mental concepts. The child's parents indoctrinate her in the social ground rules and expectations. These include but are not limited to, religious, political, cultural, and societal beliefs—on how they think the world operates, and the child's place in that world. The child then adds her own personal memories, experiences, knowledge, and desires to the information she has received from others.

By seven or eight years of age, when the child's conscious mind starts to become active, she has already gathered and learned most of the information that she is going to use for the rest of her life. All these acquired attributes, her beliefs, behaviors, and attitudes, get stored as programs in the subconscious mind, and become part of her ego... her personality.

Remember these are not her beliefs, behaviors, and values. She accepted what she received from others as facts, as she was not able to *consciously* evaluate this downloaded information. As Dr. Bruce Lipton, the author of the Biology of Belief, noted, "We are realizing that 70% or so of the programs are disempowering, limiting and undermining who we are."[66] The reason for such a high percentage of self-sabotaging programming is because most parents are not enlightened to conscious parenting and, as a result, they *are operating from their own programming*, and children at this age do not have a concept of cause and effect. So a simple remark that's directed to the child, like, "You are stupid," or "You don't deserve that toy because you misbehaved," is taken as a fact by the child and stored away, never to be forgotten.[67]

Once these beliefs, have been programmed into the subconscious mind, the child's life will unfold according to these stored programs—she will not deviate from them. And as Gandhi said in the quote at the beginning of this chapter, these beliefs will then become her destiny, unless she realizes the impact of this subconscious programming later on in her life, and consciously decides to change it.

Eight to Twelve Years Old and Onward

As children develop into their teens, their brain activity increases and they move progressively into the fully awake, higher beta wave frequency that is common to adults. Now they are conscious of their external environment, and in the process, are becoming more rational, logical, and alert. Their brain waves develop from low beta (thirteen to fifteen cycles per second) to mid beta (fifteen to twenty-two cycles per second) to even higher beta (twenty-two to fifty cycles per second), the range usually observed in adults when we are *anxious and stressed*. Having the

Chapter 3 Our Individualized Thought System

right brain waves (lower beta and higher alpha) however, allow us to be focused and alert when we are completing our tasks.

The boundary separating the conscious mind from the subconscious mind solidifies around the age of twelve. Now the child is mostly operating from the conscious mind—the left, rational, analytical brain. The right brain is working in the background. Both brain hemispheres function throughout our lives, but the access to the creative force starts to weaken as the focus turns outward, to the external environment, and the left-brain emphasis on logical and analytical thinking. Children who are able to maintain their creative activities continue to use both sides of their brains.

From this age on, the teen starts to become "lost in thought," unless an unsettling experience, great suffering, or another major change in life situation such as the death of a loved one, "wakes" her up. As we saw in chapter 2, the "wall of memories" (or thoughts) pushes her away from the innermost essence, and so she now resides on the periphery of her being... becoming *egocentric*. The child slowly forgets who she is and takes on the identity of *who she thinks she is.* And, again as we saw in chapter 2, this forgetting of her innermost essence is the beginning of her anxieties, boredom, and loneliness, as she begins to live a superficial life. She may not notice these feelings at this young age because she is just starting on her life journey, and will be busy with many things. However, these feelings will become more pronounced in the later stages of her life. This identity of who she thinks she is, or the ego, is the self that we are all familiar with.

The conditioned ego framework becomes rigid as she gets older and accepts her beliefs, attitudes, and perceptions (that she has accumulated) as truth. Everything that she then experiences will be affected by what she has experienced and learned to date. So if what she learned is not true, and, as we saw earlier, most of the beliefs and conclusions she took on when she was young were not true, then the new things that she learns will be based on these "untruths" and so will be conditioned and therefore skewed.

After adolescence and the beginning of adulthood, we are capable of questioning our beliefs and everything we have learned, rather than simply accepting the teachings and learning involuntarily. However, by the time we become adults, we are busy and focused on our education, careers, and family, and we do not notice the effect of our conditioning. For most people, this process of involuntary learning without challenging the status quo continues for a long time and never stops. And as a result, our beliefs become more and more rigid and entrenched, and it becomes harder for us to let them go even if we know they are not true. There is no one to tell us that the ego is just a *conditioned self* because most of us are not even aware that there is anything else besides the *ego identity*...

Chapter 4

The Monkey Mind

"The mind is like a monkey, inebriated, stung by a scorpion and seized by the demon, all at the same time. Like a monkey it displays habitual restlessness—it can travel in many different directions and give us myriad thoughts in no time at all. Under the influence of alcohol, it has endless designs, cravings and delusions of grandeur. The scorpion sting brings out the envy and jealousy within us. Not only do we want that grandeur for ourselves, we hate it when someone else gets it. Seized by the demon, it is obsessed with vanity and pride about its own delusions, conclusions and points of view."[68]
Sanskrit shloka

The ego mind by its very nature is restless and in a constant state of turmoil, as the above analogy from the Sanskrit *shloka* (verse) shows. It is always on the move. Every thought has a story attached to it (something that happened in the past, something that is happening currently, or something we expect to happen in the future). The thought is triggered when we give attention to it. The mind grabs the thought and doesn't let go, and the back and forth of the mind keeps the story alive. The same thoughts keep looping around in different configurations as if they are trying to draw our attention to them, to see which formulation will grab our attention and make us react.

The mind acts like the pendulum of a grandfather clock that goes back and forth—thoughts go from the past to the future, sweeping through the now but never stopping there long enough to appreciate what the now really feels like (Figure 6). The past is anything that happened a moment ago to years ago. It is the arc of the pendulum from the point of now (at this moment) to all the way back. The swing to the left (the past) creates space for thoughts because memories, regrets, guilt, and missed opportunities need space to work in. Thoughts work by association, with one thought after another traveling horizontally with offshoot branches like a tree. When our experience triggers a certain memory, a slew of other thoughts come into being, and hence thoughts need a lot of space to expand.

In contrast, the future is what will happen from the next moment on, to wherever our imagination takes us. It is represented as the arc of the pendulum from the point of now, i.e., at this moment, to all the way forward (the future). The swing to the right also creates space as anticipation, expectations, hopes, and worries all need space to work with. These thoughts also work by association in a linear manner.

Chapter 4 The Monkey Mind

The Pendulum of Thought (The voice in the head)

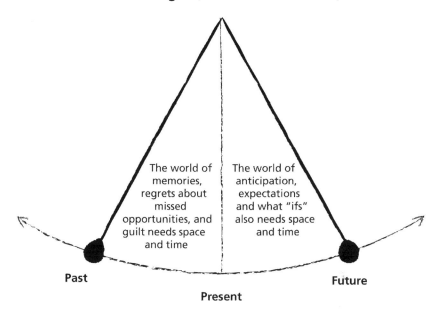

Present is just a point with no space and time associated with it. It is the *now*. Here the world stops. Since there is no space and time to move horizontally, we move vertically and go deeper into what we are experiencing.

Figure 6. *The swing of the pendulum is dependent on our conditioning. The more conditioned we are, the wider the arc of the swing and the louder and more insistent the voice in the head. The momentum of our thoughts swings the pendulum from left to right, from the past to the future, just skimming the present. Once in motion, the momentum does not allow the pendulum to come to rest. If once in a while the pendulum does stop, in the now, the thoughts kick in and force the pendulum back on its swing. The mind only exists in the past and the future. In the present, there is no such thing as mind. There is just awareness.*

The now is this point in time, just a dot between the past and the future but with the potential to expand vertically to infinity, or as Eckhart Tolle, author of *The Power of Now*, describes it, "walking along the razor's edge of Now."[69] At this point, no time or space exists. Now we are in touch with *what is, or what is happening right now*. This is reality, and there is no space for thoughts because reality does not need thoughts. As soon as a thought appears, we have moved away from what is going on in the here and now. Since there is no space in the now to move horizontally, we move in a vertical direction—we go deeper and deeper in the experience that is happening in this present moment. The deeper we go, the more we connect with life—our inner reality... our natural state of being.

Hence the majority of our thoughts have nothing to do with reality (with what is happening now). But it has everything to do with things and events that have already happened (what we did, what we should have done, what we could have done) and things and events that we think will happen in the future (what we will do if it happens again, our hopes, anticipations, expectations).

We are now trapped in what is called the *net of psychological time*. This time is different from the chronological or clock time that moves linearly—past, present, and future—and that we need to manage our day-to-day activities. Psychological or inward time is a mental concept, an idea, or a thought, an illusion, created by the ego and goes from the past to the future, avoiding the present moment. As we have seen, in the present, there is only awareness—we live in the here and now, where time does not exist. And so, *to live in awareness is to live in our natural state of being.*

To add to this, we continuously scan our environment for potential or perceived threats, and when we don't find any problems we make them up (what can go wrong—what if it doesn't work out), and then spin our wheels worrying about them—going nowhere.

The pendulum of thought, this back and forth movement, over and over again, creates the voice in the head, reinforces our habitual, conditioned way of thinking and keeps us in the prison of the illusionary psychological time. This continuous movement of thought is the voice in the head... that constant chatter that most of us are not even aware of. It weaves stories around the fact of what happened—giving it a positive spin to make us feel better, and then it believes what it has created. Through self-talk, we reinforce the ego-self. By talking to us continuously, the voice tells us that it is dealing with our concerns, and they are a priority. Notwithstanding the fact that at least 85–90% of our thoughts are the same thoughts we think every day, it makes us believe that our every thought is important and that we are doing something about it by thinking.

The voice is loud and insistent. It is the voice of our parents, our teachers, our friends, etc., one that has been with us all our lives. It is the voice that we use to motivate us. We think that without the voice, who would drive us? Who would guide us? Who would motivate us? But we don't realize that *the same voice is the source of all our anxiety*, which leads to *stress and mental/physical fatigue*. It is the voice of beta mental state which means, the higher the frequency of beta brain waves, the louder and more persistent the voice. It is neurotic, insecure, anxious, fearful, and at times, malicious. Once we are operating at this level of mind and keeping alive the psychological time in our mind, it is hard for the brain to slow down. And yet, most of us operate at this level on a daily basis.

Chapter 5

The Walking Dead

"You know, as we age, we just get 'more-so'... so if you were a whiner and a complainer at 30, you are apt to complain even more by the time you reach 70... and if your tendency was to boss everyone, to tell them how to live, chances are you will be insufferable by 60. More-so."[70]

Nancy Routley

Adulthood

As we get older, we close our minds to learning new things, and we start to age mentally. As we saw in chapter 3, our conditioning (cultural, education, assumptions and beliefs) acts as a frame of reference for everything we do and perceive in life. The content of our thoughts comes from this conditioning, and it colors everything we encounter and experience in the world. So in a way, our ego contaminates and corrupts our every thought and experience, and hence *there is no new thought or original experience.*

Our assumptions about the world around us, based on our conditioning, also prevent us from understanding the true nature of the world as it filters and screens out anything that does not fit what we already know. We focus only on the things that reinforce our long-held beliefs. To make matters worse, technology is creating a "filter bubble" to increase the distortion of what we already perceive.[71]

Technology companies like Facebook, Google, Amazon, and Netflix, and online news companies like HuffPost, use algorithms (powerful software), to mine the vast amounts of data we provide online. Basically, they analyze our habits and give us what we prefer. They not only offer suggestions of products to purchase but limit and edit the kind of information that we see on the sites based on what we have purchased or searched before. Some sites even tailor the news that we get and we don't even know what gets left out. No two people searching for the same thing will get the same search result. Now we are truly living in our own *virtual filter world bubble!*[72] This "filter bubble" not only narrows the worldview even further, and but it reinforces our conditioning (our subconscious programming).

But what most of us don't realize is that even the worldview that we perceive through our own eyes, without the filter of technology, is already distorted by our conditioning. And this misperception (of what we see) is a much bigger problem than the filtering screen of technology.

In the process of these distortions, we lose touch with reality, and begin to live in our mind... in the mental concepts that we have developed (Figure 7).

Here is a practical example of what I mean. Let us say we have a particular political view. We will then tend to read newspapers, watch newscasts or visit internet sites that reflect

Chapter 5 The Walking Dead

Screens of Distortion
(Filters we place between us and the world we perceive)

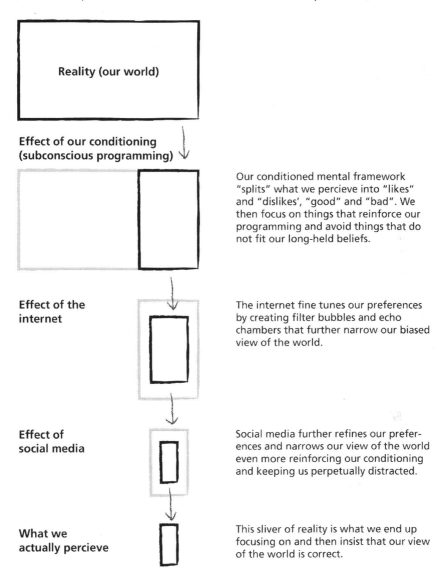

Figure 7. *We expect our life to unfold according to our view of the world and of course, it doesn't. This limited way of perceiving creates the stresses and struggles of our daily living.*

and promote our political opinions believing that what we are getting is accurate news. Anything that does not mirror our beliefs we will tend to ignore or disregard. And as we saw above, the internet and the social media are very "helpful" in this regard and will tailor the news we get based on our searches. We don't realize that the particular political view we hold is already biased and is as a result of our conditioning. We are comfortable thinking and doing the same things repeatedly because we feel secure in these thoughts and actions—there are no surprises. That's why it is so hard to give up our old beliefs and values, even when we have doubts about them because the ego-self does not want to admit that it is wrong. When our long-held beliefs are threatened, we fight back because we wonder how something we have been saying for all these years could be wrong. Then we spend the rest of our lives defending our beliefs and values.

According to psychologists, our personality or the person we think we are is fully formed when we reach our thirties.[73] What this means is that for all intents and purposes, we *are mentally dead* and *become prisoners of our conditioning (programming)*. We are now set in our ways and think we know everything there is to know about life. We become mentally stunted, and we stop growing. In other words, whatever we were yesterday, we are that today, and *unless we bring about a drastic change in ourselves today (and not the superficial, incremental kind of change that some self-help books advocate), we will be that in the future.*

We have learned and established a framework of habits, beliefs, and behaviors over the years and turned them over to our subconscious for implementation or response (within this framework) as required. As we saw in chapter 3, the majority of the content of this structure was subconsciously downloaded from others in the first six to seven years of our lives, without any conscious oversight from our conscious mind. Subsequent to that, we added our own experiences, memories, and knowledge to this existing content. This turning over of our conditioned framework

Chapter 5 The Walking Dead

to the subconscious happens because once an attitude, behavior, or habit is repeated often enough, it becomes automatic. As a result, our subconscious mind, which makes up of over 95% of our mind, and controls all our physical automatic actions (such as breathing and heart rate without our involvement) takes over. And so, we are no longer conscious of our conditioning. We lose control over it. The conditioning becomes dead to us. Now we react and respond to the life challenges automatically from this conditioned framework, in the same way, every time as required.

Look at the implication of this—over 95% of what we think, feel, say, and do is unconscious and automatic. And, again, as we saw in chapter 3, almost 70% of the subconscious programming is disempowering, and limiting and undermines who we are. In other words, after our identity completely forms in our thirties, most of us *go on autopilot and sleepwalk through the rest of our lives*, never "waking" up unless something serious shakes us from this slumber. Even when we are briefly aware and conscious (less than 5% of the time), the pull of the subconscious mind is hard to resist, and we go back to our automatic way of living and doing things. The reason why we slip back into the subconscious mind is that "the conscious mind's prefrontal cortex can process and manage relatively measly 40 nerve impulses per second. In contrast... the subconscious mind's platform can process 40 million nerve impulses per second. That makes the subconscious mind's processor 1 million times more powerful than the conscious mind's."[74]

If we take away the seven to eight hours that most of us spend sleeping, it leaves us with about 5% of the waking hours that we are conscious, or approximately fifty minutes (spread over the remaining day) that we are awake and aware of what is happening. This limited awareness is why *most of the self-help books don't work* when we are trying to bring about a change in ourselves because, *to change, one needs to be awake and alert*. The books may help in the short run, but we slip back to our reactive behavior over time. As we saw in chapter 3, this conditioned, automatic way of living gets more and more entrenched in the subconscious, as we get older. Then, fear and anxiety become our constant companions as our usual way of doing things is never adequate for the challenges of life, which are always in constant flux.

The challenge is always new, but our response is always the same (old and conditioned), the way we had solved a similar problem in the past. The old (our conditioned self) is rigid, not flexible to deal with the new, which is unpredictable, uncertain and always evolving. The encounter between the conditioned self and the challenge creates a disturbance in the mind as the response is insufficient. *This inadequate response creates anxiety and fear, which are the components of stress.*

We want life to fit into our framework of beliefs, our parameters. We want it to flow according to our plan, based on our experience. We try to use logic and rational thinking to understand life, but we don't succeed, because life is not logical; it is not rational. It does not flow in a sequence of events. Life is uncertain, unpredictable, multidimensional, and chaotic—everything is happening at the same time, so logic and rational thought can never understand the complexities of life.

Here is an everyday example to illustrate this point. Let's observe the scene unfolding at a busy downtown intersection. As we watch with complete attention, we experience the many things that are happening in front of us all at the same time. We are fully aware of all the sights, smells and sounds surrounding us—a couple of runners on the sidewalk to our left, cars waiting for the lights to change on the east and west sides of an intersection, cars travelling north and south rushing through the same intersection, people with smartphones in their hands crossing the road without even looking up, the sunlight reflected

Chapter 5 The Walking Dead

from the window of the bakery in the corner, the various buildings housing different kinds of businesses surrounding the intersection, the sound of the jackhammer tearing into a pothole in the side street on the right of us causing a minor traffic jam, the smell of the car fumes, and much, much more.

We can never understand or perceive this big picture of events using our logical, rational thought. As we shall see in chapter 14, the function of the intellect is to deconstruct the big picture perception of what we are experiencing (in the here and now) and break into smaller chunks of thought forms, in order to create coherent mental concepts, as it tries to understand and remember what is happening in front of our eyes. In the process of breaking down of the big picture into smaller bits, we lose the multidimensional, unpredictable, and chaotic nature of the reality around us.

And that is the beauty of life. You cannot sit back and say you understand life—you have to be involved with it moment-by-moment.

Our continuously chattering, noisy mind makes us anxious, vigilant, tense, and afraid, keeping the brain's beta wave levels high. We are always in the crisis mode, waiting for something to happen (usually something we have worried about). We have become paranoid and hypervigilant. We are fearful and anxious about everything.

And when some things happen, even the smallest incident or event, like a perceived slight or criticism, becomes a crisis, because we are unable to cope with it, which creates a cycle of anxiety. As we will see in chapter 9, our stress then engages our brain to go into survival mode, a state that is usually triggered when we face external threats such as being attacked by a wild animal. However, the brain reacts, not only to the external threat but also to the internal threat caused by anxiety linked to the voice in the head. With this internal threat, *we are now under siege from our thoughts*—a matter of survival. *This survival reaction, is so powerful and automatic, that it often overwhelms and even hijacks the thinking brain*[75] because we don't know how to calm these impulses. In fact, studies have "found that prolonged stress causes degeneration in the area of the brain responsible for self-control."[76]

As Joe Dispenza, author of *Evolve your Brain: The Science of Changing Your Mind*, says "Living in stress is living in a primitive state of survival common to most species. When we live in survival, we limit our evolution, because the chemicals of stress will always drive our big-thinking brain to act equal to its chemical substrates. In effect, we become more animal-like and less divine."[77]

We then depend on our automatic, conditioned response (ingrained in our psyche) to address the new threat. Most of us spend our waking hours in this anxious, high-beta brain wave state. This is the state of mind that defines us. We begin to live in our minds, and the voice in the head becomes our constant companion. Now we are truly in the *survivor mode*.

Stress attracts more stress, and as it keeps building, it starts to squeeze our "aliveness" out of us. We become, what I call, the "walking dead,"— sleepwalking through life, and just surviving. When we were young, we were full of joy and full of life, sensitive and curious about everything. Now, we are always tired and have become dull, bored and insensitive. We don't seem to have time for joy and happiness anymore. We don't even smile, and when we are happy on those precious few occasions—we feel guilty. We become serious and walk around as if we are carrying the weight of the whole world on our shoulders.

We start to age prematurely. We look at things cynically and negatively, and everything becomes a source of irritation. We stop enjoying life; we become less and less creative until we are just operating from our conditioned self. We feel that we are losing control of our life. Even the smallest decisions that we have made thousands of times before begin to overwhelm us, and all of a sudden, we don't know what to do. We are just trying to keep on top of things, trying to stay afloat.

Our enthusiasm for life wanes. We become emotionally detached. We become bored with our jobs and have difficulty getting ourselves going in the mornings. *"Same old, same old"* becomes our standard answer when someone asks us how we are or what is new.

To compensate for the way we are feeling inside, we try to build up our external environment by buying bigger homes and cars, and going on numerous vacations... but inside we are in a rut—we have already died. As an old saying goes, *"most of us die at thirty and wait to be buried at eighty."* Psychologist Charles Garfield put it this way: "The only difference between a rut and a grave is how deep it is."[78] This then is our predicament—living in survival mode and not even knowing that there is a way out of it!

Chapter 6

How "Dead" Are We?

"More than by fear of going astray, my hope is that we will be moved by the fear of remaining shut up within structures which give us a false sense of security, within rules which make us harsh judges, within habits which make us feel safe."[79]
   Pope Francis, *Evangelii Gaudium* (*The Joy of the Gospel*)

A Max Planck Institute study, using Functional Magnetic Resonance Imaging (fMRI), found that the subconscious brain arrives at a decision seven to ten seconds before we are consciously aware that a decision is even needed. "Your decisions are strongly prepared by brain activity. By the time consciousness kicks in, most of the work has already been done," said study co-author neuroscientist John-Dylan Haynes.[80] To the brain, which makes decisions instantaneously, a seven to ten-second time lag is an eternity. This time lag would suggest that everything in our life is predestined, or in other words, we lack a free will to make decisions. Actually, we do have a free will, but it is limited by the ego, which in itself is only able to select from the choices provided by the conditioned self.

When we are conditioned, it means that we operate from a certain set of parameters or framework within our profile (our ego self). The ego-self includes, but is not limited to, beliefs, likes, dislikes and so forth that we have picked up over time. In short, we are conditioned. As we saw in the last chapter, this framework of conditioned behaviors resides in the subconscious.

Hence, even before we become conscious of a decision that we want to make, our subconscious (or our innate intelligence) already knows what we are going to decide about seven to ten seconds before we make the decision. It is as if, once we are in the survival mode, and operating in a habitual manner, our innate intelligence puts us into an autopilot mode and runs our life for us very efficiently. And so, we do the same things over and over again—we greet people the same way, we say the same things, we get angry in the same way and about the same things, and we choose the same things, such as one flavor of soft drink. So, we do have a choice, but the choice is within this framework of responses or specific parameters, a limited-ego free will.

However, the decision we make subconsciously is reversible—in fact, we have almost ten seconds to change our mind, but our mind is busy with chatter (the voice in the head), so we don't know that we even have a choice. It doesn't matter how intelligent we are (one of the study participants was Marcus Du Sautoy, Professor of Mathematics at the University of Oxford—and he definitely did not like the result!)—if we are conditioned as most of us are, this seven to ten-second time lag will still apply. Our innate intelligence wants to guide us, but when we are conditioned, our survival mode kicks, in and our

Chapter 6 How "Dead" are We?

instincts take over. Then we only react to the situations based on our parameters and framework that was previously put into place.

I believe that this ten-second delay is caused by our ego-consciousness, our conditioning[81] When we move beyond our thoughts and into our natural state of being, *communication is instantaneous*, as quantum physics has proven (we will look at this later in chapter 21), and hence there is no lag time. And then we just act... instantly.

Before we move to the next section on the realities of stress, let us look at the next tool for our journey—learning to sit in silence.

Tool for the Journey 1

Learning to Sit in Silence

"All man's miseries derive from not being able to sit quietly in a room alone."[82]
  Blaise Pascal, (1623-1662), French mathematician and scientist

Learn to sit quietly with yourself without reading, watching television or playing with your smartphone. When you are quiet, you are alone with your thoughts. Initially, this will be very difficult to do, if you have never done it before. Up to now, your attention has been focused on the outside world. All of a sudden, your attention is turned inward to your internal world, and the ego cannot bear the spotlight on itself. It doesn't like what it sees. It is not that your thoughts are bad or ugly. It is just that you have never observed your own thoughts before and it makes you (your ego) uncomfortable for a while. You squirm and are filled with fear because you don't know what to expect. It is the unknown. We fear silence because we are impatient. We are so used to doing something all the time that suddenly when we sit quietly *"not doing" anything*, we don't know what to do. We start to get bored and fidgety.

Another reason we don't like silence is that we have become used to the noise around us. In fact, silence starts to become uncomfortable after just 4 seconds, and we become anxious.[83] Stay with the practice—don't move away and escape into doing "things." Face the fear you are encountering. It is the fear of the ego facing "death" because *when the mind is quiet, there is no ego.* Start with a few minutes and gradually extend sitting-in-silence to longer periods of time. With practice, your old conditioning begins to break down. The voice in your head slowly subsides, and for the first time, you experience inner peace. This experience of inner peace is the beginning of your love for silence.

Part II
Realities of Stress

Chapter 7

Living in Survival

"Pain is physical; suffering is mental. Beyond the mind, there is no suffering... Pain is essential for the survival of the body, but none compels you to suffer. Suffering is due entirely to clinging or resisting. It is a sign of our unwillingness to move on, to flow with life."[84]
  Sri Nisargadatta Maharaj, (1897-1981), Indian mystic and teacher

What is this suffering that affects so many of us in so many areas of our lives? *It is mental anguish or stress.* It is a disturbance of the mind caused by our restless and anxious, chattering mind, the voice in the head. To live with suffering, and to be free from suffering, are not two separate things. They are just two different ways of perceiving the world; one way of looking makes us suffer.

A slight shift of consciousness, however, frees us from suffering, and living becomes a delight... pure joy.

So it all comes down to what we believe about stress, or how we look at stress and suffering. Is stress a necessary part of life? Can we do anything about stress except to try to manage its consequences? Is stress our own nightmare and invention? If we are happy living in stress and the suffering it brings, there is no need to change. But, by understanding how our mind works and bringing about a change in the way we perceive the world, we can change our relationship with ourselves, and our environment, and thereby eliminating the cause of stress.

Our normal, natural state of mind is one of peace, free from conditioning—a silent and creative mind. However, most of us are oblivious to the experience of this state of being. This is because we've never experienced it, or at least that is what we think. In reality, we do experience a quiet mind regularly, but we tend to override it with our noisy thoughts. And even when we are consciously aware that we are in this state of mind, we want nothing to do with it. Why? We believe a calm, quiet mind is a boring, dull, dead mind, where nothing exciting happens, and where thinking stops, and hence the propensity to override this state of mind.

Stress starts with the way we view things and circumstances—it begins with our thoughts. *Stress doesn't exist... except in our minds.* The events, situations, actions, or conditions that we encounter are *neutral*. As Shakespeare wrote in *Hamlet*, "There is nothing either good or bad, but thinking makes it so."[85] So it is the "spin" that the voice in the head puts on what we perceive that troubles us and makes us feel anxious and upset.

The spin is our way of looking at the world, through our screen of conditioning (a collection of our past experiences). It is a framework of mental concepts that makes us respond in a certain way. It is our individualized thought system, our personal world. It affects everything we do. We have provided the brain with a framework of ideas, beliefs, opinions, attitudes, and conclusions with which we have created our "virtual" world of mental concepts. It is within this world that we live our lives, anxious and fearful of venturing out because we are afraid of uncertainty. This *virtual world* is the *ego*, or what we call *our personality*.

The neural networks in our brain have become entrenched in certain ways of doing things, so we don't deviate much from those pathways. As a result, the ego takes over our subconscious programming and tries to make our life easy and uncomplicated. The reality is that we don't like change. We are only comfortable with the things that we already know. There are no surprises, no spontaneity, no creativity—just automation and efficiency... or simply *sleepwalking through life.*

And so, stress is the result of the meeting of the old and the new—our old framework of conditioned thinking meeting everyday challenges. In other words, *the voice in the head, which is the voice of the ego, tries to pre-empt the unfolding of life.* The size of the gap between how we think the world should unfold, and how it actually unfolds, is proportional to how stressed we are. Life is unpredictable and chaotic, but we want it to unfold according to our plan, according to what we want, according to our likes and dislikes—and of course, life doesn't. The more rigid we are in our thinking and the further away we are from what is actually happening in the world, the more anxious and fearful we get. We then perceive everything as a threat to our well-being. The unwillingness to flow with life is resisting reality. As long as we resist what is happening, we will create "problems," which we then try to "solve" in our mind by *worrying* about them.

Hence, we are *always stressed* because all we do is worry—a running commentary of what could have been, should have been, didn't happen, and on and on. If we listen to this voice of the ego, we will notice that it is anxious, insecure, fearful, and frustrated—in other words, it is paranoid and neurotic. Unfortunately, for most of us, arguing or resisting reality is our way of life.

What does the voice in the head sound like? Do you know someone who is always commenting, complaining and judging everything going on around them— "This looks good," "I don't like how that person dresses," "The weather is terrible," "That person is so stupid... how could he do that?" "I wouldn't do that if I were her," and on and on? Now imagine that that person is in your head. That is what the voice in the head sounds like. That other person who is always commenting, complaining, and judging, is just externalizing the mind chatter, and when that person gets tired they will stop, but *the voice in our head never stops*—except when we go to sleep, but even, then, it starts talking in our dreams.

And yet most of us believe that our chattering mind is alive, active, alert and full of life and energy. We love the war and the anxiety that goes on in our minds. It is invigorating! It feels as if we are doing something and that we are in charge. Many of us think we would get bored and lonely with a calm and quiet mind because there would be no one to talk to in our heads. We have become addicted to certain kinds of behaviors, emotional responses, and the voice in the head, and we don't want to give them up. Joe Dispenza put it this way: "Each time we have a stress reaction... we tend to associate people, places, things, times, and events with the adrenal hit, the chemical rush, the high, that makes us feel alive."[86] We have now become addicted to stress.

And of course, we project this way of thinking on the world as US General George S. Patton did when he so succinctly said, "I love war and responsibility and excitement. Peace is going to be hell for me."[87] Is there any wonder why there are so many wars going on in the world? *If we are at war with ourselves, how can there ever be peace in the world?* And when there is peace, it is more a brief interlude while we get ready for the next war.

Many psychologists, medical experts, and self-help gurus tell us that stress is a way of life in this high-tech, fast-paced world. Technology today, especially the internet and social media, while making our lives easier in many ways, hasn't done anything for our basic human nature (fear, insecurity, and discontent). Instead, technology has accentuated our neurosis, and the triple heads of anxiety, fear, and loneliness, the key ingredients of stress, have become our default state of mind, gnawing at us throughout our lives.

Most of us think that living in stress is our normal way of living. Even though stress and suffering (mental distress) mean the same thing, it has become socially acceptable to say, "We are stressed" than to say, "We are suffering." The former conjures up an image of us working hard and struggling to make a living. It shows that we are not slacking off by taking time to rest and that we are indispensable at work. And, of course, we say stress is for self-motivation. It's a "badge of honor" that we proudly wear. In fact, we even identify with stress: "I am more stressed than you are." Suffering, we think points to something that is wrong with us. It denotes laziness, weakness or "mental issues." People look at us and think (and many will tell us) that we are not working hard enough, or taking life seriously enough. To them, as long as our suffering is not caused by physical discomfort, everything else is just our imagination, and that we should be able to "pull" ourselves out of it.

Many of us, who believe that stress and working long hours is good for us, are believers in the long-standing business concept of *survival of the fittest*. To us, people who want to get rid of stress and lead simpler lives, are wimps. We believe that we should fully participate in the rat race by working long hours and accepting stress as being part of this commitment. That is the recipe for success. The dream of a simpler life is just that—a dream. To us, there are no options—either we get stressed, or we leave the "fast track" and are labeled as "failures."

And yes, the medical community does acknowledge that stress is not good for us and that it causes physical and mental health issues. It is estimated that up to 90% of our visits to the doctor are related to stress.[88] Studies have also shown that an excess production and constant release of the stress hormone called cortisol detrimentally affects the development of our brain, and our "ability to fight infection and even cancer."[89] And yet, these same doctors say that we should learn to manage stress, because not only can we not eliminate it, but also, we actually need some stress in our lives in order to motivate us. Then we try to learn how to manage and cope with stress.

And so, to manage stress, we have developed gadgets that monitor our heart rates, and smartphone apps that remind us to breathe consciously to calm ourselves down when we are stressed by providing us feedback on our heart rates and sweaty hands. Many of us even try to manage stress by using relaxation and mindfulness techniques. These are powerful techniques to decrease stress, but we only use them as *stopgap fixes*, never trying to understand the root causes of stress. For a few moments or so, we quieten down, but as soon as the "busyness" returns, we are back where we started.

Some of us try to drown the voice in the head by drinking alcohol, taking drugs, or by being entertained, but this doesn't help us for long, as we are back where we started from, once the cloud of fogginess, forgetfulness, and distraction dissipates.

Chapter 8

The Anxiety Gap

"What can we gain by sailing to the moon if we are not able to cross the abyss that separates us from ourselves? This is the most important of all voyages of discovery, and without it, all the rest are not only useless, but disastrous."[90]
   Thomas Merton, (1915-1968), Trappist monk, writer and mystic

The Basic Anxiety of Loneliness
   Loneliness, that feeling of emptiness, is not the failure to connect with others, as many believe. It is the failure to connect with ourselves. How can we get in touch with our true nature, when we are not even able to *be* with ourselves, to see what is going on in our minds? In fact, most of us don't even want to admit that we are lonely. And when we do feel lonely, we look for the causes of loneliness (living alone, self-absorbed society, social

media, or poorly planned urban spaces) outside of us but that is the wrong place to start. We look for comfort from others because we cannot live with our minds. We keep busy and try to fill the void in us with material goods, or with the company of other people to avoid reconnecting with ourselves... *to make us forget about ourselves.* It can be easy to live with someone else, but it is very difficult to live with our minds. And, so when we are alone and not doing anything we are bored and become anxious.

As Elizabeth Renzetti, a *Globe and Mail* columnist points out, "Loneliness is our baggage, a huge and largely unacknowledged cultural failing... It is the great irony of our age that we have never been better connected, or more adrift."[91]

Many people also wrongly assume that loneliness comes with old age. In reality, *we have always been lonely* (irrespective of age or the type of work we do), but we have kept our loneliness hidden by our "busyness."

As we age, we slow down, and have difficulty being busy all the time—that is when most of us come face to face with our loneliness, and it is terrifying. Unfortunately, by that time, there is not much we can do about it because we are plagued by health issues and other challenges of old age.

We are anxious because, as we saw in chapter 3, everything we know about ourselves has been given to us by others, and to which we have added our experiences. This knowledge is our conditioned ego self, our personality, and it is time and place dependent. What is real is our essence, what we came with *before* our programming modified us. The programming has made us *forget who we really are,* and this forgetting is the cause of the underlying anxiety that we carry around with us. It is a feeling of uneasiness, of something missing in our lives. *This anxiety gap, the gap between who we think we are and who we really are, is the foundation on which stress or suffering is built.*

Chapter 8 The Anxiety Gap

This basic anxiety increases, as we get more and more entrenched, in our conditioned behavior. As a result, the voice in the head gets louder and more insistent. We don't notice this voice as much because it is covered up by our daily flurry of activities. When we are not busy, we tend to drown the noise in social media or entertainment, and as a result, we are hardly aware that our mind is chattering. And sometimes when we find that we have nothing to do, we will try to do anything possible, just to avoid being alone with our thoughts, even inflicting pain on ourselves.

In a series of experiments conducted at the University of Virginia to explore the state of being alone with your thoughts, Professor Timothy Wilson found that generally, people do not enjoy being on their own with their thoughts. The volunteers in the studies were both male and female and ranged in age between eighteen to seventy-seven years. Wilson noted that "Our study participants consistently demonstrated that they would rather have something to do than to have nothing other than their thoughts for even a fairly brief period of time."

In fact, in one interesting experiment, he found participants preferred pain rather than being left by themselves with their own thoughts. The professor asked university students to spend fifteen minutes in an empty room without windows, "entertaining themselves with their own thoughts." In the room, he also placed a small device that would administer "a severe static shock... not a huge jolt, but it was a little painful." He explained the nature of this device to the volunteers and told them that they could touch it if they wanted to. He found that almost half of the volunteers ended shocking themselves at least once during the time they were alone in the room because "they seem to want to shock themselves out of boredom, so to speak."[92] We are terrified to be alone with ourselves as this creates a great deal of anxiety within us.

The low-level anxiety and tension we experience and that we try to avoid responding to is the result of feeling out-of-sync with our real selves, a state of off-centeredness. Deep inside us, we know we are more than the life we are leading. It is the superficiality of the life that we lead, which is causing the discontentment. It is as if we are skimming over life to get to the end... and when we near the end, we are afraid of what we will find and try everything possible to delay it. However, if we are able to be with ourselves, we can begin the journey of healing and of reconnecting with our real selves now, while we are physically and mentally healthy.

How else does the voice in our head (our conditioning) add to this basic anxiety?

The Resistance to Reality—To What Is (Real)

Our chattering mind does everything possible to avoid facing reality, by not accepting what is happening right now, and this resistance creates turmoil in our minds. We always think that the present moment is not good enough, or that it is an obstacle that we need to overcome. And so we reach for the next moment, or something in the future that we think it will be better, but when we reach it, the next moment becomes the present moment. We continuously keep reaching for the future, forgetting that the future, when reached, also becomes the now moment—a reality. In the meantime, *we avoid living in this moment*. As Byron Katie, author and teacher of "The Work," a method of self-inquiry, often says, "Stress is an argument with reality."[93] So what do we mean by reality?

Let's take a simple example of a traffic jam, something most of us face every day. What happens when we are caught in a traffic jam on our way to work in the morning? We sit in the car fuming, thinking thoughts like, "Why doesn't the city do something about these roads," "If only I had left home a little

Chapter 8 The Anxiety Gap

early, I wouldn't have been caught in this traffic," "I am always late—my boss is going to get upset with me again," and on and on the mind goes. *This voice in the head is self-torture or misery by a thousand thoughts.* By the time we get to work, we are already stressed out, and ready to chew out the first person we encounter... and we haven't even started our day yet! When you think about it, there are three things playing out here: the traffic jam (the fact), our thinking (the process), and our thoughts (the mental concepts about the traffic jam).

The traffic jam is a reality (a fact). We can see the cars backing up, we can hear the drivers honking, and trying to change lanes and we can see some waving of fists—this is real. It is what's happening right now. It is something we feel, see and hear. This traffic jam is definitely not the place we want to be at this time. We would rather be somewhere else. But this is where we are, and no amount of frustration, and anxiety about the missed meeting, or being late to drop off our kids at school, is going to make the present situation (the traffic jam) go away. Trying to avoid the present moment is actually resisting the present moment—arguing with reality, as Byron Katie would say... and we will always lose (this argument) by becoming stressed.

Then there is our thinking and our thoughts. Thinking is real because it is our ability to think, to produce thoughts. However, the thoughts themselves are not real—they are worry-thoughts, mental concepts, the voice in the head. Thoughts take us away from where we are—the here and now. For example, we just can't seem to let go of the thoughts of the traffic jam, and we might even use the incident to vent about all the things we think are wrong in our lives. Unfortunately, as we saw in introduction II, we forget that we are the thinker of these thoughts, and thus can stop them anytime we want. Instead, we let them take over our mind because "at least we are doing something, instead of just sitting in the car."

This voice in the head is what causes the anxiety and frustration, and it is the beginning of stress—just words, continuous chatter, mental concepts of things one has no control over, of events that have already happened in the past, and the things that may occur in the future.

This resisting or non-acceptance of what is happening is how we respond to the traffic jam or other "stressful" situations in life every time—the same response, the same upset—expecting a different result, but getting the same outcome. The voice of the ego is *the voice of insanity*, which we take as "normal," because most of us suffer from it.

The Inadequate Response to Challenge

As we saw in chapter 3, our minds are conditioned, and we keep building within that same framework. When we are young, our thinking is very flexible, so we keep learning and coping with everything that comes our way. But as we get older, we start to become rigid in our thinking. Then most things make us anxious. We want things to be the same, or to behave in the same way, as we are used to, but nothing stays constant, except for our framework of conditioning. In fact, even our conditioning does not remain constant—it gets more and more entrenched, and therein lies the problem.

The function of the ego is to make every experience old because it itself is old and conditioned. It likes routine and wants to know what exactly to expect in the future. It needs the past memories to make sense of what it is encountering in the present. The ego is afraid to touch the present without these supportive memories. It uses the past as a crutch, and without the past, it cannot face the world. The ego does not like the unknown, something it cannot control. But life is uncertain and chaotic; it does not follow any rules. *Every moment is new*, ever-changing, and exciting, but we cannot keep up with the changes because our

Chapter 8 The Anxiety Gap

minds are conditioned and inflexible. And so, we don't have the capacity to adapt to all the new experiences that we face every day.

The more inadequate our responses to the challenges, the more anxious we get. Anxiety is caused by the gap between our conditioning and the new situations that life brings to us, each and every moment—as this gap widens, our anxiety increases. This is the "disconnect" in our lives, which causes so much of our suffering—the conditioned mind is living in the past, but we can only live in the present moment. Stress isn't caused only by our reaction to the events or situations happening at this moment, but it can also be caused by thinking about something that has happened in the past, or thinking about something in the future, like a meeting that we are going to have with our boss tomorrow.

It is not that we don't have the capacity, or the creativity to solve the problem effectively, it is that we tend to override our creativity with our rational, conditioned mind. We want to play it safe, and do things the way we have always done them. Once in a while, when we are facing a challenge and are completely present and attentive, we can deal with what is happening without our conditioning, without our memory and we can solve the problem creatively. We feel good, and know that that was the right solution. It makes us happy and satisfied, and this solution leaves no trace in our memory or is not added to our worry list. But this happens only rarely. *These are moments of lucidity, clarity, and happiness, which are the hallmarks of our natural state of being that we rarely recognize.* It is when our mind is occupied by the voice in the head, with the worries and agitations of the past, and the future, that we are not fully present that creates an inadequate response which then causes anxiety. And, since most of the time we are on automatic control, we are like an absentee landlord, unaware of what is going on. And, so anxiety builds on anxiety. It becomes a continuous process—we keep entrenching the inadequacy of the response in our memory by thinking of it over and over again, in a never-ending cycle.

Our Habit of Constant Worrying

"Over the years your bodies become walking autobiographies, telling friends and strangers alike of the minor and major stresses of your lives."[94]
Marilyn Ferguson, (1938-2008), author of The Aquarian Conspiracy

We create the world around us—if we think something disturbs us, then this thought will become alive for us—it will take on a life of its own. Every time we react to something with fear and anxiety, whether it be an external event, or thoughts in our minds, the reaction causes us mental turmoil. As we saw in chapter 4, the majority of our thoughts have nothing to do with reality, yet we are perpetually worried, and anxious about everything all the time. It is as if we carry a list of things to worry about, and as soon as something on the list doesn't happen (and as we know, most things we fear never materialize), we replace it with something else to take its place—to make sure that some worry always occupies us.

We even get stressed when we want to go on a vacation, as we worry about all the work that we are leaving behind, and all the work that will have piled up upon our return. We may worry about the kind of food we will be served or the kind of people that we will meet. We may come back from vacation so unhappy and stressed, that we start planning our next getaway, our next vacation. Sometimes we may decide that since going on vacation is too stressful, we will just take Fridays off from work, and take three-day weekend mini holidays instead.

But the fact is, that it doesn't matter where we go, we will always be anxious—even if we go to a resort, where everything is calm and slow-paced, we will not be happy because we will think it is too boring. We will always find a problem or something to worry about and be unhappy. *We are the problem because nothing satisfies us.* Whatever we want, our thoughts will provide it and make it real for us. And so, *we create our own stress.* Once we understand this simple concept, *our stress will start to disappear.*

Chapter 9

The Routine Trap

"If we lack emotional intelligence, whenever stress rises the human brain switches to autopilot and has an inherent tendency to do more of the same, only harder. Which, more often than not, is precisely the wrong approach, in today's world."[95]

Robert K. Cooper, neuroscientist and author

What Happens When We Are Stressed?
Stress shifts our brain into the survival, or protective mode, with its instinctive fight, flight, or freeze responses. Threatening, unfamiliar, or uncertain situations, raise the brain's level of anxiety and pushes it to work in the higher range of the beta wave frequencies. This shift in the brain wave activity triggers the brain's early warning system—the amygdala (located in the midbrain). As a result, our brain goes into our survival mode of

fear and anxiety. Now our mind's attention is completely focused on finding a way out of the immediate, and potentially dangerous situation.

The amygdala is designed to protect us from both external and internal threats. This almond-shaped structure located deep in the brain, that served our mammalian ancestors so well is now helping to protect us not only from real physical dangers (a wild animal attaching us), but also from the "imagined-in-the-head" (anxiety and fear created by the voice-in-the-head) threats that we inflict upon ourselves every moment. *In other words, we are literally being attacked by our thoughts.* The mystics have always said that a "chattering, voice-in-the-head mind is actually a disease (or "dis-ease"—a lack of ease or harmony within the body). The triggering of the amygdala by our anxious thoughts is a warning to us that the voice in our head is also a danger to us, and has become *a real threat to our well-being.* This is in contrast to the calm, focused, and alert state of being needed to be productive at our work and in our day-to-day tasks.

When the amygdala is triggered, the brain shuts down all unnecessary bodily functions, including thinking and digestion of food. All the blood and energy are redirected to the arms and legs to outrun or fight the "enemy." At the same time, it triggers a cascade of stress hormones and directs the adrenal glands to flood the body with chemicals like adrenaline and cortisol to prepare it to respond to the threat. And because the body is in this heightened state of responsive action, we are not able to "think" because thinking takes *too long* to respond to the threat (and we would be dead). Therefore, to keep us alive, our bodies naturally default to automatic or instinctive responses, such as fighting or running away from our threat.

Once the physical danger has subsided, the amygdala switches off the survival mode mechanisms, and we go back to our baseline normal body operations and growth mode. However,

Chapter 9 The Routine Trap

with a *psychological* threat (i.e., stress and anxiety which in reality is not real, but "imaginary" in nature), the amygdala cannot switch off, and that's because the threat is continuous and ongoing. The worries and anxieties continue and are never-ending. We can be in either one of two states—1) growing, energizing, and being creative, or 2) protecting ourselves and regressing—we cannot do both at the same time. As Bruce Lipton observed, "Mechanisms that support growth and protection cannot operate optimally at the same time... humans unavoidably restrict their growth behaviors when they shift into a protective mode... a sustained protection response inhibits the creation of life-sustaining energy."[96]

And that's why many times when we are under a great deal of stress, our brains can freeze momentarily, even though we are not in a real, physical, and threatening fight or flight situation. When our brains freeze, we don't know what to do next or, we become very defensive and just want to get away from what's happening as quickly as possible.

For many of us, this is our state of mind all the time. And as such, there is no new thinking or creativity—because we are in the protective/survival/regressive *"same old, same old"* way of living, with all its imagined stressors, and all the stress-related automatic, responses that it entails. *We are now caught in the routine trap.*

Even if the thinking function were available to us, in this stress-induced state-of-mind, it would still not help us calm the instinctive survival responses of our more primitive brains, because it uses *logical, rational thought* to try and overcome these responses. When someone is afraid of a perceived threat, and we try and explain that the fear they are feeling is all in the mind and is not real, they simply don't believe us—the explanation is not effective. *Intellectualizing* fear does not get rid of it. And so, our thinking or rational mind *cannot solve the problem of stress.* Only when we step back and observe/understand the thoughts that are creating the fear (and then let them go), do we overcome this state of fear. This way of looking at stress and anxiety is from a new and different vantage point—a function of the mind that eludes most humans.

And so, in our attempt to overcome this state of mind, we try to run inside ourselves to hide. We become defensive and build a wall around ourselves so that we don't get hurt. The problem with walls is that, apart from trying to keep people and perceived stressful situations out, they also keep us in. We become our own prisoners. And since we are almost always stressed, most of us are governed by these survival instincts, and their automatic, habitual, conditioned responses.

Hence, we are always in the automatic, habitual way of responding and doing things. We are stuck in this state of mind, and so, change is difficult. We just can't seem to break away from this cycle. We then run on anxiety and fear (created by our imagined threats) and on our insatiable desires and wants for more and more (created by the emptiness in us, as we saw in the last chapter). Mentally, we create a dog-eat-dog, survival-of-the-fittest world. Thus, we are always engaged in fighting and competing—against the clock, against traffic, against people. And worst of all, we are fighting with ourselves—inside our heads. Everything becomes a fight or flight situation to survive. It is a self-inducing problem, a problem of our own making in which we are trapped.

Our zest for life is slowly squeezed out, and we don't seem to have the energy or the enthusiasm to get involved in new things and new projects (or even getting out of bed in the mornings!). We are not as creative as we used to be. We keep forgetting things, and our brain seems to freeze right in the middle of doing something. We also tend to overeat in this state because, while in the fight or flight response mode, the body thinks it needs

Chapter 9 The Routine Trap

additional fuel to outrun or outfight the threat. In fact, we tend to crave carbohydrates because they can be converted to energy fast.[97]

We think this way of living is normal because everyone is living the same way. Happiness becomes elusive as we start to focus more and more on the external world to survive. Then we look for pleasure to try and fill the void within us. The only thing we are concerned with is our own welfare and our personal safety. We don't trust anybody and fear everything and everyone. We become hyper-alert or super-vigilant and paranoid, always waiting for something to go wrong—or for something to "attack" us. And so, we are in the fighting mode, and constantly looking over our shoulders and worrying about the potential threats that the future holds. Then everything becomes urgent, and a top priority. We are then completely engrossed in trying to survive, and so there is only one option left—struggle.

There is hardly any joy, laughter, humor or play in our lives—this is a dangerous world, and life is serious. We are obsessed with food, sex, greed, power, and exploitation, and manipulation of the environment, and people. We cannot take time to rest or catch a breath because we don't know when trouble will strike us. We feel old and tired well beyond our years. Actually, studies have shown that every stressful thought leaves behind a permanent scar and not only is the stressful thought detrimental to our health, but it also ages us in the process.[98] Stress builds upon stress. We begin to get used to a base level of stress, and then as additional stress starts to pile on, our tolerance for stress increases. And before we know it, we are operating from a very high beta frequency level, and we are constantly anxious.

So If We Know What Stress Does to Us, Why Haven't We Done Anything to Eliminate It?

Why? Because we just don't know what to do. Stress is a problem that our intellect cannot solve because it is tied up in knots by our voice in the head. We have learned to survive in this world using our analytical, rational left-brain very well, but the intellect on its own is not able to control our instinctual, survival-mode responses to things. It does not know how to break us out of this "stress loop." The rational mind can take us to the moon, but it doesn't know how to prevent or to end stress. And so, we come up with coping strategies to manage our stress, but they don't succeed. We end up dealing with the outcomes of stress—health issues for example: like hypertension or the constant use of stress-reducing prescription drugs. We end up getting overwhelmed by our primitive, animal-like brains because we have still not learned how to use our whole brain. In fact, our brain is actually out of sync with itself.

We used to believe that our brains did not have the capability of changing or modifying itself after a certain time in our lives. Remember the old saying, "You can't teach an old dog new tricks"? Well, the science of neuroplasticity is now showing us that our brains are "plastic," constantly changing and evolving, and making new network connections.[99] So every human being has the capacity to transform themselves if they want to. We don't have to be stuck at the survival level of our mental evolution. Freedom from stress happens when our brain becomes integrated—when, as shown in chapter 10, all of the major components of the brain are in sync.

Before we explore how the brain works (in the next section), and what role it plays in our dysfunction, let us first look at the next tool for the journey—conscious breathing.

Tool for the Journey 2
Conscious Breathing

Whatever crisis you are going through, come back to the present moment. Anchor yourself with the breath. This will be difficult as your thoughts will be highly charged and will want to pull you into them. Accept what is happening to your thoughts and surrender to them, but keep coming back to your anchor, your breath... the present moment.

When we are stressed or under pressure, our breath is shallow. Shallow breathing is a definite giveaway that you are operating from your survival mode. Taking a few conscious breaths relaxes us immediately, and shifts us out of this primitive, survival state of mind. When we breathe consciously, we start to calm our stress center (the amygdala), and that starts to lower our anxiety. As a result, our mind becomes calm, bringing us to the present, and gives us a few moments before we respond to the situation that we think is causing stress.

Thinking takes place on the left side of our brain and silence is the state of the right side of our brain. Our automatic breathing is a function of our subconscious mind residing in our primitive brain—which has access to our innate intelligence. When we are aware of our breath, we are consciously connecting directly to this intelligence... our natural state of being.

Try this: Close your eyes. As thoughts go through your head, be aware of the left side of your head. Still keeping your eyes closed, take a couple of conscious breaths. Your mind will drop into the present moment and become silent. You have now shifted to the right side of the brain. That is because *conscious breaths take us deeper into our subconscious mind—just below the level of thoughts where we are calm but alert.*

It is that simple to shift your consciousness from your noisy mind chattering left-brain, to your silent, alert right-brain. A conscious breath will stop the worrying thoughts dead in their tracks, and you become completely aware and in the present moment for the duration of the breath. This is how powerful conscious breathing can be to bring you into the *now*. And this can be done anywhere and anytime.

And so we can use our conscious breath as an anchor. It will always drop us into the present moment where we are alert and relaxed. In a way, *this state of mind is only a conscious breath away.* Conscious breathing is the oldest and the most powerful tool we have to slow and stop the thinking mind and to move us into a calm and alert higher state of mind, where peace resides. *Just remember, that the breath is only a tool—what is important is the state of awareness that the breath drops us into.*

Breathing exercise: Become completely aware of your breathing. Feel the breath as it comes in through your nostrils and, follow the breath as it makes its way into the depth of your belly. Don't think of or visualize the breath as it is coming in—but feel it. Then continue feeling the breath on its return journey and as it leaves your nostrils. That's it. It's that simple. Be completely aware of the breath going in and going out. Don't try and control the breath. We are not training or controlling the breath, as is done in some yoga practices. Here we are simply working with our normal breathing.

Part III
Working of the Brain

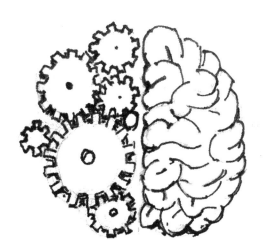

Chapter 10

The Four-in-One Brain

"Awakening, flow, freedom, unity and synthesis are not "all in the mind," after all. They are in the brain as well. Something in conscious functioning is capable of profound change. The subjective accounts have been correlated with concrete evidence of physical change: higher levels of integration in the brain itself, more efficient processing, different "harmonics" of the brain's electrical rhythms, shifts in perceptual ability."[100]
   Marilyn Ferguson, (1938-2008), author and speaker

Thousands of years ago, the eastern mystics had figured out how the mind worked and how to transcend its limits in order *to rediscover their natural state of being.* They did this by intently observing their minds over the years through meditative practices, without ever understanding the structure of the brain. As we saw in chapter 2, the brain is the physical structure through which consciousness manifests the mind.

So understanding the detailed structure of the brain is not essential if we want to know how to get in touch with our natural state of being. However, having some knowledge of how the brain works will help us understand:[101]
1. Why our behaviors, emotions, and thinking are out-of-sync,
2. How stress triggers our survival mechanism,
3. How this instinctive survival mechanism hijacks our higher-functioning brain,
4. How our ego becomes so powerful,
5. Why our rational-mind can take us to the moon, but it cannot solve the problem of stress,
6. Why we need to connect with, and utilize more of our intuitive, often maligned, right-hemisphere brain, and harness its true potential,
7. And what we need to do to regain our natural state of being.

We have four brains (Figure 8) in our head reflecting the evolution of humans over millions of years. These four interconnected sub-brains are built one on top of the other, just like a multi-story structure. Together, they form the conscious and the subconscious levels of the mind:
1. The first brain, the foundation on which the other brains have evolved, is called the "reptilian brain." This brain is instinctive and powerful and is focused on our survival and continuity as a species. It is where our instinctual subconscious mind is located.
2. The second brain to evolve was the "mammalian or mid-brain." This brain, which is also called the "limbic system," is home to our early warning system; the same one that triggers our survival mechanism when we are faced with a perceived or hostile situation. It is also where we find our emotional, subconscious mind.
3. The third and the fourth sub-brains are housed in one brain structure and were the last to evolve. This combined

brain structure is known as the "*new mammalian* brain" or the "neocortex." It is divided into the left and the right brain spheres or cerebral cortices and is further sectioned into the four distinct lobes. The neocortex developed in two stages over time—the first part—the primate or the intellectual brain, which makes up most of the neocortex and the newest addition—the prefrontal cortex, which is just behind our forehead. This highly evolved sub-brain is the home to our inner world, our mind, and our higher cognitive or executive functions. It is referred to as the "seat of our conscious awareness," and is considered the fourth brain.[102]

The Four-in-One Brain

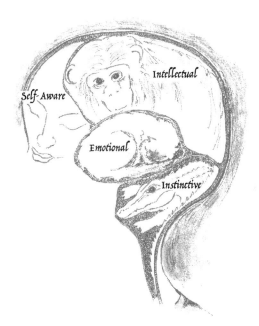

Figure 8. *Whichever of these brains is in control depends on how "conscious" we are. When all these sub-brains are integrated, and in sync with each other, the self-aware brain or the prefrontal cortex takes us beyond our everyday survival living. We then transcend our ego and become fully human.*

Each of the four sub-brains has a mind and intelligence of its own and acts independently of the others, often in a contradictory manner. In other words, the sub-brains are not "in sync" with each other. For most of us, they are integrated neither horizontally (across the left and the right hemispheres), nor vertically (from the prefrontal cortex down to the reptilian brain). And so, the activities of the sub-brains are not aligned and harmonized with one another. As a result, we experience conflicts in behavior, emotions, and thinking... and so we are not in harmony with ourselves and with others. In most cases, our instinctive survival (fight or flight) mechanisms are so powerful and automatic, that they often overwhelm, and even hijack, the higher cognitive brain functions.

Let's look at the sub-brains in some detail.[103]

Chapter 11

The Survival Brain

"Decisions are easy for a dinosaur. If it's food, eat it. If it's an enemy, kill it or run away. Every creature is either dealt with immediately or ignored. More than anything else, reptiles can't wait... Dinosaur Brain thinking is always short-term, with high emotional involvement."[104]

Albert J. Bernstein, author

The "survival brain," also known as the primordial or the reptilian brain, is the first of the four sub-brains. We share its basic functions with the reptiles (think lizards and alligators) and other mammals (like our pets and whales, for example). This primordial brain evolved approximately 400 million years ago and is the foundation over which the other brains developed. It is the simplest of the brains, but also the most powerful. The reptile brain which was designed for survival and continuity consists of the brain stem (which controls and regulates automatic life functions like breathing and blood circulation), and the cerebellum (which orients our body in space and facilitates our involuntary movements).

The primordial brain is not conscious. It reacts instinctively and automatically at a subconscious level to the inputs from our senses. It is driven by our instincts and automatic behaviors, habits, and beliefs (our conditioning), which have become hardwired in our memory and whose roots go deep into our subconscious. It has no emotions and, as we saw in chapter 9, is motivated by the fear of the unknown and the desire for more. The reptilian brain's main purpose is to satisfy what the humanist psychologist Abraham Maslow (famous for his hierarchy of needs motivational model), called our basic physical survival needs—for food, shelter, security, and continuity.[105] Every time the reptilian brain feels threatened, whether the threat is real or even imagined (for example when we are stressed), it will make us fight, run away or hide from the situation. In some cases, we will freeze and not know what to do. In other words, we will experience a mental block—just like a deer caught in the headlights of the car at night!

Even though we have our more evolved neocortex or the human brain, many of us have allowed ourselves to be caught up, and even trapped, in the reptilian brain's survival mode of fear and desire. As we also saw in chapter 9, when we are stressed, we can be completely engrossed in trying to survive, and so, there is no peace—only struggle. To us, life is serious. We are consumed by greed for power, possessions, and sex. As a result, we are selfish, manipulative, and insensitive to the feelings of others or what is called the "dark triad" of personality (narcissism, Machiavellianism, and psychopathy—"a triple whammy of nastiness").[106] And these personality traits are reflected in our society as a dog-eat-dog, survival-of-the-fittest mentality.

Chapter 11 The Survival Brain

Thus, we form an impression of a scary world and one of scarcity. The only things that we are concerned with are our own welfare, our personal safety, and security. And by "our" I mean family, friends, country, and so on—nothing else matters. As a result, we tend not to trust anyone and fear everyone and everything.

We are always afraid and anxious and hence, stressed out. We are never satisfied or contented with anything for long. We always fear that we don't have enough, and we won't be able to get enough and so, our desire is insatiable.

Our primitive brain's power lies in its ability to perform routine and automatic behaviors and habits. It implements them efficiently and effectively when it interacts, or more accurately, reacts, to our environment. Since this sub-brain is motivated by fear, it does not like change and does everything possible to keep everything the same. This is why change is so difficult... but not impossible.

Chapter 12

The Emotional Brain

"Reason may override our emotions, but it rarely changes our real feelings about an issue. Our emotions allow us to bypass conscious deliberation of an issue, and thus to respond quickly based on almost innate general categorizations of incoming information. This may lead to irrational fears and foolish behavior: Often we don't consciously know why we feel as we do about something or someone."[107]

Robert Sylwester, Emeritus Professor of Education at the University of Oregon

Our second sub-brain is called the mammalian or emotional brain. Also known as the limbic system, this brain developed on top of our reptilian brain. It is the smallest of the four sub-brains and evolved around 250 million years ago. The limbic system adds the emotional component to the sensory input information that we receive through the brain stem (or reptilian brain). It tells us whether the things that we perceive are threatening or not. It also processes various emotions such as fear, anger, and pain. And when you combine the emotional and survival brains, we gain the ability to react instinctively, but with emotions. So in a way, this emotional brain fine-tunes our instincts for survival. The integration of these two sub-brains fulfills our emotional and social needs according to Maslow's hierarchy of needs. We share this capability with mammals such as dogs and elephants.

When my daughter Faheema was quite young, she knew exactly which of my emotional buttons to push to get what she wanted or to drive me crazy before I became wise to what she was doing. Years later, she would tell me, "Dad, it was way too easy to get you going!" Young children are good at triggering these emotions in adults. As Dr. Jill Bolte Taylor, a brain scientist, says in, My Stroke of Insight,

"When we are newborns, these cells [of the limbic system] become wired together in response to sensory stimulation. It is interesting to note that although our limbic system functions throughout our lifetime, it does not mature. As a result, when our emotional "buttons" are pushed, we retain the ability to react to incoming stimulation as though we were two-year-old, even when we are adults."[108]

Daniel Goleman, the author of *Working with Emotional Intelligence*, coined a term for emotional outburst when it was out of proportion to the perceived threat. He called it the "amygdala hijack."[109]

The Mammalian brain (or the limbic system) is the home to the amygdala, our emotional center. And as discussed in the earlier chapters, our amygdala acts as an early warning system that triggers our fight or flight reaction and takes us into the survival mode. The purpose of the amygdala is to assess all

Chapter 12 The Emotional Brain

incoming sensory information and filter out situations that are threatening. And so, every situation we encounter has already been emotionally evaluated by the limbic system, and decision made as to whether it is a threat to survival or not, and what needs to be done. The decision is always instantaneous. Let us see how this constant emotional assessment of incoming data affects us.[110]

1. Unconscious Decisions: Emotional evaluations of incoming sensory data are done *unconsciously* without any input from the conscious mind. The conscious mind, in most instances, may not even be aware of the need for a decision to be made (see chapter 6).
2. Emotional Decisions: We cannot separate emotions from reason/logic because the limbic system is connected directly to the neocortex, and everything must pass through the emotional filter of the limbic system. So even if we try to keep our feelings from our thinking process—it is impossible to do so. Emotions are already part of the decision-making process even before we start to think about a decision.
3. Feeling Beings: Since the emotional brain evolved before the thinking brain, we are "feeling beings who think," instead of "thinking beings who feel," and yet many of us steadfastly believe that *feelings* do not play a part in our decision-making process. Emotions and feelings are intimately connected and are often used interchangeably, but there is a marked difference between them. As we saw above, emotions are physical states triggered by the amygdala in the limbic system to assess incoming sensory information. Feelings come afterward. They are mental states formed by our emotions but are influenced by our experiences and conditioning and experienced in our intuitive right brain.
4. Feelings Above Reason: In many cases, our feelings can override our rational left-brain.

As we saw in chapter 9, the amygdala's filtering mechanism does not differentiate between external threats, like encountering a bear in the forest, and potential threats (like worrying) created by the framework of our conditioned mind. When we say we are conscious of everything that is going on in our lives, in reality, we are not. As we also saw in chapter 5, over 95% of what is going on in our minds is the result of the subconscious processing. We don't even have a choice in the matter. As our habits, beliefs, attitudes, and experiences are different from each other, different people may perceive different things as "threats." Sometimes we may be afraid of something, and say that it is silly to be afraid of it, but the fear is an automatic response to a belief or an experience that we may have had.

Becoming aware of threats to our physical being is good for survival, but continually reacting to "potential" threats can have a negative impact on our lives; we may say and do things that we later regret. And the *amygdala does not forget*. It retains all memories of what it considers as threats—everything that makes us anxious and fearful and then responds to these potential threats in the same manner as the retained memory response. That is why new things or new experiences are always threatening to us, and we stop taking risks. This way of responding then becomes a vicious cycle of the "same old, same old" from which we cannot step out. And, with this ingrained response mechanism, we meet the challenges of our daily living.

In the limbic system, our experiences begin to get stored as memories, and we remember events that gave us pleasure (immediate gratification) and those events that were painful. Hence, we do everything possible to move toward pleasure and away from pain. This instinct, of being drawn to pleasure and repelled by pain, is the carrot-and-stick approach to motivation in today's terms—rewarding and or punishing to encourage specific behavior. This instinct is also what determines our moods. We

Chapter 12 The Emotional Brain

feel good or bad because we are affected by what is going on in our environment.

Children are born with fully functional and operational reptilian and limbic sub-brains. And so the early years of our life (up to seven or eight years old) are spent in the subconscious world of the instinctive reptilian and the emotional mammalian brains. As a result, as we saw in chapter 3, everything that we acquire and learn from others when we are young gets firmly implanted in our subconscious memory... *without the critical scrutiny of the conscious brain.* This lack of oversight is because the conscious brain or the neocortex is still in the early stages of development and hence we do not have a chance to consciously evaluate the downloaded information—because we are not even aware of it. This powerful process of subliminal learning of our childhood—our beliefs, attitudes, assumptions and so on (our conditioning) has a tremendous impact on us. It shapes our lives and defines our personality. Once our personality has been established, it is very difficult to change or modify the programming from our early years. Then, our lives unfold, not according to what we consciously want but according to these programmed (other people's) beliefs, attitudes, and behaviors. In other words, *we are not in control of our own lives.*

Chapter 13

The Conscious Brain

"We should not pretend to understand the world only by the intellect; we apprehend it just as much by feeling. Therefore, the judgment of the intellect is, at best, only the half of truth, and must, if it be honest, also come to an understanding of its inadequacy."[111]
C.G. Jung, (1875-1961), Swiss psychiatrist who founded analytical psychology

The conscious human brain is the largest and the most recent brain. It is called the neocortex or the *new mammalian* brain, and formed on top of the two older brains (reptilian and mammalian), covering them. It evolved in stages some three million years ago with the primates and became more complex in human beings. The neocortex is divided into the left, and right hemispheres, and a bundle of nerves called the corpus callosum connects the two halves. These hemispheres are further divided into four pairs of lobes or sections responsible for a variety of functions.

Three pairs of lobes are contained in the posterior or the back cortex, which covers most of the top and back of the head. It includes the *parietal lobes* (responsible for feeling, sensing, movement, and orientation), the *temporal lobes* (responsible for hearing and memory), and the *occipital lobes* (responsible for visual processing). The posterior cortex, allows us to experience and visualize our external world through our senses, and provides us with our orientation and physical place within it. As Daniel Siegel, author of Mindsight describes it, "The posterior cortex is the master mapmaker of our physical experience, generating our perceptions of the outer world—through the five senses—and also keeping track of the location and movement of our physical body through touch and motion perception."[112]

The fourth pair of lobes (the frontal lobes) is contained within the frontal cortex which covers the front part of the brain. It gives us access to our inner world. Within, and part of this frontal lobes, and just behind our forehead, is the prefrontal cortex—sometimes referred to as the fourth brain. This region of the brain is *the seat of our awareness* and is *in essence of what makes us human.*

The Primate (Intellectual) Brain

We share the combination of the two primitive brains and the neocortex (primate brain) with primates such as monkeys, gorillas, and apes, but it is much more highly developed and complex in humans. This primate brain is the intellectual, rational brain that relies on personal interest and logical reasoning.[113] It is the home of the ego-self and the voice in the head (which is restless and chattering like a monkey and is often called the "monkey mind").

Chapter 13 The Conscious Brain

The Prefrontal Cortex (seat of our awareness)

"When the frontal lobe [the prefrontal cortex] is in action, we exhibit our highest, most elevated level of consciousness, our self-awareness and our ability to observe reality... The concept of "self," which is the highest form of understanding that the conscious mind can possess, is in the frontal lobe... In other words, if we can use the frontal lobe and control it, we can know and control ourselves and our future. To what greater achievement can we aspire?"[114]

Joe Dispenza, author, lecturer and corporate consultant

The prefrontal cortex has access to and controls all the other sub-brains. And as such, it is in the center of everything that is happening in our inner and outer worlds. The prefrontal cortex regulates and controls our subconscious emotions and impulses and inhibits inappropriate thought and behavior. This part of the brain is the home of our mind and our higher cognitive functions such as focusing, planning, reasoning, creating, decision-making, and communication. Unlike in our primitive survival and emotional brains, in which the primary purpose is survival, the prefrontal cortex does not believe in the status quo. It "allows us to supersede the stimulus-response, action-reaction, cause-effect patterns we unconsciously live by day to day."[115]

Being Fully Human and Creative

As long we are alive, living in our everyday ego consciousness, and doing the same things over and over again, the primitive brains are accomplishing their purpose. But the prefrontal cortex is different. It is the center for our intention, our will, our focus, and our attention. When the prefrontal cortex, especially the middle prefrontal cortex, is fully developed and engaged, it has the ability to pull us beyond the stress and suffering of our everyday survival living *by integrating all our brains* (horizontally across the left and right hemispheres) and vertically (from the prefrontal cortex right down to the brain stem). As a result, we transcend the ego and become *aware that we are aware,* and we operate from our natural state of being–with insight, intuition, creativity, and a heightened sense of awareness. When this transcendence occurs, we finally realize what it means to be fully human and creative.[116]

An easy way to visualize how the various sub-brains are interconnected and interrelated to each other is to use the hand model (Figures 9-1, 9-2, 9-3, 9-4) of the brain developed by Dr. Daniel Siegel[117] and adapted here to reflect what we have been discussing above.

Hand Model of the Brain

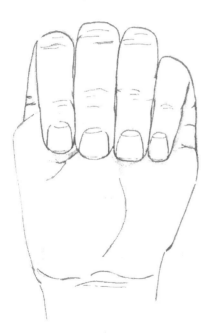

Figure 9-1. *Make a fist with the thumb tucked inside. The front of the folded fingers facing you is the front of the head, and the back of the hand then represents the back of the head.*

Chapter 13 The Conscious Brain

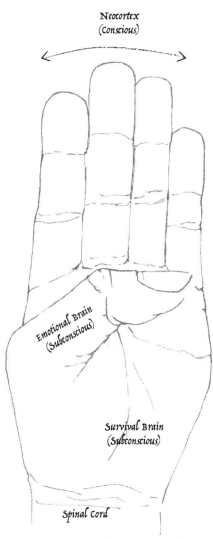

Figure 9-2. *Open the hand with the thumb still tucked in. The fingers represent the neocortex, the thumb is the emotional brain (limbic system), the palm is the survival (reptilian) brain, and your wrist is the spinal cord coming into the brain stem at the base of the skull.*

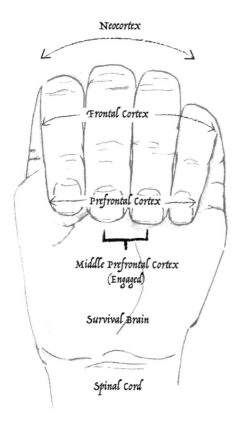

Figure 9-3. *Fold the fingers (neocortex) over the thumb again so that the fingertips touch the palm. The neocortex is divided into the left and the right brain hemispheres (not shown) and completely covers both the subconscious primitive brains. Now the prefrontal cortex, represented by the fingertips, especially the middle prefrontal cortex, which is behind your eyes in the forehead, is in touch with all the sub-brains and is fully engaged. The brain is wholly integrated both horizontally (the left and the right hemispheres) and vertically (the reptilian brain, the emotional brain, the cerebral cortex, and the prefrontal cortex).*

Chapter 13 The Conscious Brain

Psychologist Abraham Maslow describes this process of transcending the ego in his theory of human motivation. His framework of the *hierarchy of needs* (or *our innate urge to expand and grow*) provides a blueprint for realigning the sub-brains and finding our natural state of being. He represented this theory of motivation as an internally driven six-level pyramid (Figure 10), moving from our basic needs at the base, to our highest needs at the top. As our basic needs are met, we are pulled up the hierarchy through the first four levels of needs by the unconscious, internally driven process of instincts and conditioning that we saw earlier. And so, we move from the

Maslow's Hierarchy of Needs

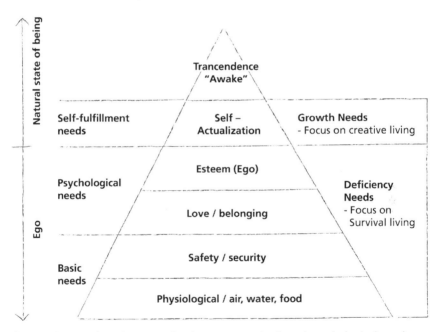

Figure 10. *Even though many of us have met our basic and psychological needs, we are reluctant to explore the higher growth needs and realize our full potential. And so, we spend our lives trying to survive the best way we can... and in the process, we create suffering for ourselves and others.*

physiological and safety (or survival) basic urges to the psychological belonging and esteem-fulfillment needs of the ego. Up to this fourth level of satisfying the needs of the ego, our focus is entirely on survival.

But once we have met our survival needs, (which Maslow calls deficiency needs), we are ready to achieve self-actualization and fulfill our potential. In other words, we can now become the person that we always had the potential to be, once we have moved beyond our survival or deficiency needs. We can only do this by consciously accessing our right intuitive brain again (horizontal integration of the two brain hemispheres) and *becoming self-aware*. After this integration happens, we begin to live in the state of creativity. Then, as all our sub-brains realign and work in harmony, we have an inner urge to reconnect to our highest need... our natural state of being—something that is beyond the ego consciousness. Maslow called this reconnection with our natural state of being, self-transcendence (or enlightenment). Once our internal reference point changes from the ego to the natural state of being, we become "awake" and fully human, living in creativity.[118]

If these higher-level growth needs are "wired" within us and becoming fully human is our destiny, then why are we still stuck in the animal and ego levels of survival where there is so much suffering, even though we have a self-aware brain that can help us?

Because, for many of us, the middle prefrontal cortex (Figure 9-4) has not fully developed. And so we find ourselves living in the ego consciousness of the survival mode at the mercy of our primitive brains and the voice in our heads. It is not that the prefrontal cortex never gets engaged. It does. Once in a while when our mind is calm and clear, and we are happy and content

Chapter 13 The Conscious Brain

or compassionate and generous, we are in our natural state of being, but unfortunately these moments don't last.

However, this doesn't mean that we do not have the potential to overcome our egos and our primitive brain thinking and behaving. We do. The key to overcoming these challenges and making our natural state of being permanent, again, lies in the prefrontal cortex—capitalizing on what is already there for us to use and to develop further.

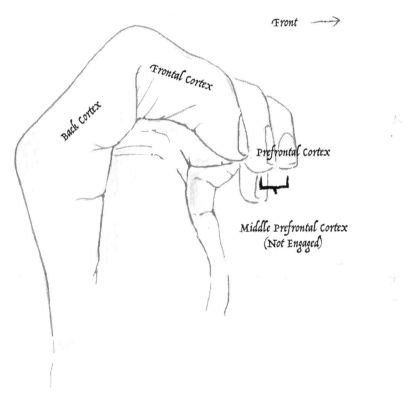

Figure 9-4. *For many of us, the middle prefrontal cortex is not fully developed, and so most of the time our sub-brains are out of sync.*

A series of different studies have shown that our prefrontal cortex is hardwired for altruistic behavior and it can override our selfish actions.[119] But when we are generous and give to charities or other institutions in our egotistical state, it is because we expect a return for our generosity—a tax receipt to offset our income, our name on the new wing at our community hospital, a chance to meet someone who we think is important and so on. But "giving completely for its own sake—with absolutely zero expectation of pleasure or another reward in return—is rare."[120] That is, unless we become aware of this natural ability, and engage it.

In one study, scientists using a Functional Magnetic Resonance Imaging (fMRI) provided volunteers with money and a list of charities. They were then told that they could: 1) choose to donate to the charities of their choice, 2) not donate to the charities, or 3) keep the money for themselves after the completion of the study. Scientists found that for volunteers who gave to charities experienced a rewarding feeling— "giving is actually inherently rewarding: The brain churns out a pleasurable response when we engage in it."[121]

In another study, volunteers were asked to take part in a bargaining game. Then using a weak transcranial magnetic stimulation (TMS), scientists were able to switch off a part of the prefrontal cortex making the subjects in the study, "selfish and egotistical."[122]

In yet another study, Bill Harbaugh, a University of Oregon economist, working with law students, found that many people gave to charities "because they expect some tangible reward—if not a monetary one, then a social one."[123]

So, while it is true that we are hardwired to give, and feel good about it, our *conditioning* dictates "what we do with our generous thoughts and inclinations... [and] we also have power over whether to take advantage of those natural capacities or let them wither away."[124] Hence the challenge that we have is to find a way to engage the prefrontal cortex on a continuous basis so that we can have permanent access to our natural state of being.

Interestingly, our "frontal lobes are the last part of the brain to develop."[125] They start developing when we are around seven or eight years old and do not reach maturation until we are in our mid-twenties and for some people even much later in life, if ever. This late development of the prefrontal cortex is the reason why most young people exhibit such, "notoriously selfish behavior."[126] Once, this region of the brain is developed, we then have the ability to question our subconscious conditioning. But, most of us don't do that. And that's because we get busy with our education, work, and family or we don't think there is anything wrong with our conditioned habits and behaviors—*we believe it is normal.* And, even if we wanted to change or modify our conditioning, we don't know how to do it. As we saw in chapter 5, by the time we are in our thirties, most of us are psychologically complete and remain so throughout our lives.

Though the frontal lobes are the last to develop, they are the first to degenerate with prolonged stress in our later years. This deterioration of the frontal lobes does not affect our intellect, but "it degrades areas responsible for inhibiting irrelevant or inappropriate thoughts... [and] older adults are more likely to be socially insensitive across a variety of domains... [and] simply have greater difficulty suppressing prejudices than younger adults do."[127] What this means is that many of the things that we learned subconsciously as children, such as our prejudices, biases, and other attitudes, beliefs, and behaviors, which we have tried to hide or overcome, will resurface in our later years. And that is why a couple of weeks of sensitivity training for changing of these beliefs or at least becoming more sensitive of our attitudes and biases (as is the practice in the workplace now) does not generally work.

In the next chapter, we will explore how the left and the right hemispheres of the brain process information and how these two sides of brain complement each other.

Chapter 14

The Famous Left and Right Brains

"The left side encompasses everything reason can conceive of. The right side is a realm beyond reason. As individuals, we have to strive to maintain a balance between heightened reason and creative chaos (what quantum physics discovers as they break down matter and electrons)."[128]

Musetude Trust website

Organization of the Cerebral Hemispheres

The cerebral cortex (or the neocortex) of the brain is divided into two halves—the left-brain hemisphere and the right-brain hemisphere. A large number of nerve fibers known as the corpus callosum facilitates communication between the two hemispheres.

A lot of research has been done over the years on how the left and the right sides of the brain process information. It began with the split-brain experiments of psychologist Dr. Roger Sperry in the 1970s and continued with the work on the psychology of consciousness by psychologist Dr. Robert Ornstein and others. Dr. Sperry, who won a Nobel Prize for his work on "split-brain" patients, cut the corpus callosum in patients who suffered epilepsy to prevent the seizures from traveling from one hemisphere to the other hemisphere of the brain. By cutting the corpus callosum, he made the two hemispheres act like two separate brains. These two brains essentially created two minds, or as Dr. Ornstein put it, "two modes of consciousness which simultaneously coexist within each one of us."[129] Each mind has a separate functionality or specialization. The left hemisphere of the brain is the home to the rational, logical, and analytical mind, while the right hemisphere accommodates the holistic and intuitive mind. In other words, we have two distinct ways of looking at the world; dualistically—meaning we split everything we see into "either-or" perspective, and non-dualistically—where everything is viewed from a holistic or integrated perspective (Figure 11).

It wasn't until Dr. Jill Taylor, a brain scientist who watched and experienced her left-brain hemisphere shut down (as a result of a massive stroke), that anyone was able to confirm "the psychological or personality differences contained within these two structures [brain hemispheres]."[130] In her book, *My Stroke of Insight*, Taylor discusses the functions and the characteristics of the left and right hemispheres of the brain and the role that the right hemisphere plays in what she describes as "Nirvana,"[131] or what is often called *spiritual awakening*. Taylor says her "stroke of insight was that at the core of my right hemisphere consciousness is a character that is directly connected to my feeling of deep inner peace. It is completely committed to the expression of

Chapter 14 The Famous Left and Right Brains

peace, joy, and compassion in the world."[132]

The Famous Left and Right Brains (Two modes of consciousness—two different ways of perceiving the world)

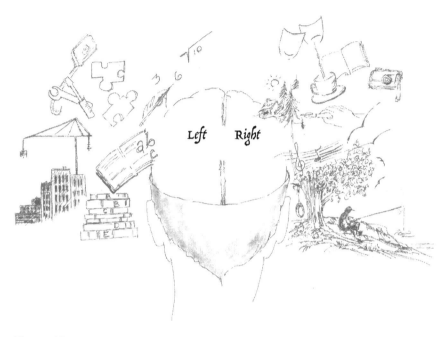

Figure 11

Left Brain

- *Focus on the outer world*
- *Rational and detail-oriented*
- *Things happen in sequence, one thing at a time*
- *The this OR that, dualist point of view. It can't be both*
- *Noisy brain—home of the ego and the mind chatter*
- *"Doing" consciousness*

Right Brain

- *Focus on the inner world*
- *Intuitive and holistic*
- *Everything happens at the same time right here, right now*
- *The this AND that, non-dualistic approach. It connects everything*
- *Silent brain—directly connected to the innate intelligence*
- *"Being" consciousness*

Taylor describes, that as the stroke was silencing her ego (the everyday consciousness associated with the left hemisphere), her consciousness shifted to her active right hemisphere. She further states that, with this shift in consciousness, she went from "the doing-consciousness of my left brain to the being-consciousness of my right brain... all I could perceive was right here, right now, and it was beautiful."[133] She describes this sense of liberation and transformative experience as timelessness, present moment awareness, peace, connectedness to the universe, and the absence of thoughts. And she believes that, "the experience of Nirvana exists in the consciousness of our right hemisphere, and that at any moment, we can choose to hook into that part of the brain."[134] As we saw earlier, spiritual awakening or enlightenment is simply the expansion of our consciousness and the rediscovery of our original, natural state of being.

Many of us are already aware that we are frequently pulled in different directions when we are trying to make a decision or solve a problem. How many times has our head said something and our heart or gut-feeling says something else?

It is interesting to note that this dual nature of the mind has been mentioned in the early Chinese texts and other literature where the right hand, controlled by the left brain hemisphere, is associated with the rational, male, yang, assertive, light or "macho" qualities and characteristics. In contrast, the left hand, controlled by the right brain hemisphere, is associated with mystical or intuitive, dark, female, yin or receptive qualities and characteristics.[135]

In other words, all these characteristics are present in every human being, but because of our conditioning and education, most of us only exhibit characteristics that correspond to our gender. As we saw earlier, to be fully human, we need to integrate both our left and right brain hemispheres or our masculine and feminine qualities (Figure 12). Richard Rohr, author of *Eager to Love: The Alternative Way of Francis of Assisi*, describes bringing together of our male and female principles as, "a combination of lightness of heart and firmness of foot at the same time... the lightness of heart comes from contact with deep feminine intuition and with consciousness itself; the firmness of foot emerges when that feminine principle integrates with the mature masculine soul and moves forward with confidence into the outer world."[136]

Yin and Yang

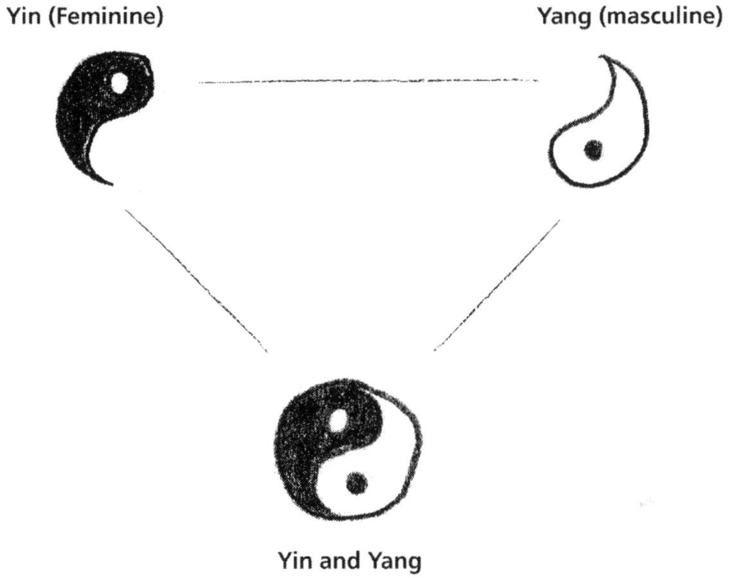

Yin (Feminine)   Yang (masculine)

Yin and Yang

Figure 12 *The two opposing but complementary forces within us—two sides of the same coin.*

The Brain's Left Hemisphere

"Your belief carries more power than your reality."[137]
                    Bruce Lipton, cell biologist and lecturer

As we saw in chapter 3, the left-brain hemisphere develops later than its right-brain hemisphere counterpart. It is associated with rational knowledge, the intellect, and specializes predominantly in areas usually considered scientific, such as logic, linearity, numbers, sequence, analysis, linguistics, and other similar activities. The left-brain hemisphere, using the intellect, deconstructs present-moment, big-picture perception of the world (received by the right hemisphere) into smaller chunks of mental concepts of what we see. For example, we use the word "tree" to describe the tree that we see. In this way, we can make sense of the external, multidimensional world that we see, where everything is happening at the same time. While the use of mental concepts is helpful in understanding the world, it is limited because the word "tree" is not the actual tree that we see—it is just a mental concept, an abstract image in our mind. The problem is that we often mistake the word "tree" for a real tree, and we end up believing in the mental concepts as reality. And so, we become stuck within an illusion—a virtual world of mental concepts that we have created, and that we take for real. This illusionary world then acts as a screen between us and what is happening outside of us.

The left hemisphere's knowledge is based on our subconscious programming, our previous experiences, and memories embedded in its recesses. It uses this knowledge to operate. This knowledge then conditions our consciousness and in turn interprets what we see, or more likely, what we choose to see, as "real."

The rational left-brain brain is the world of the ego-self, mental concepts, the voice in the head, and the intellect. It is

Chapter 14 The Famous Left and Right Brains

efficient, and detail oriented and emphasizes the masculine principles. It is very rigid and runs our lives "by the book," so there is no place for common sense or intuition. For example, when you take your car to a mechanic, he or she will take the car for a test drive and may know intuitively what the problem is but will disregard his or her intuition and go through a set procedure to check for the problem. Another mechanic will also take the car for a test drive, know intuitively what the problem is and fix it. The left brain looks at life with an "OR" or a dualistic point of view.[138] It divides the world into this or that, black or white, right or wrong... but what we perceive cannot be in between these polar opposites. And so the rational mind loves to pigeonhole everything and everyone, in order to make it easy for us to generalize and understand.

Here in the left hemisphere things happen in a sequence, one thing at a time, and so time is created as past, present, and future. In this state, the rational mind's focus is on the external, physical world of space and time, the world of our senses. It looks for happiness outside of itself in the external world. It wants to pursue more of and bigger and better "objects." It then rationalizes that this indulgence of these material objects will make us happy.

The rational brain's primary concern is on the survival of the physical body, and hence our attention is continuously directed to the well-being of the body—how it's doing, how it looks, and so on. And so the rational brain thrives on its separateness and individuality and tends to isolate the person from other people.

As we will see in the next chapter, our society is based on this mode of consciousness, on rational and analytical knowledge. We are a verbal and intellectual society, and our emphasis is on the intellectual and scientific way of thinking rather than that of the arts and humanities. When people refer to their minds as computers, they are referring to their thinking mind—the rational, analytical left-hemisphere brain. For many people, the intuitive right-hemisphere brain seems completely irrational and useless in working with and understanding the world. And that's because the right brain does not have any language and analytical capabilities, and is unable to focus on or understand details. It looks at things all together and all at once in a holistic, non-dualistic manner.

The brain normally operates in silence—all the neurons firing away quietly. However, the left-brain hemisphere has become noisy because the voice in the head has taken over and monopolized the rational mind's functioning. Hence we have become anxious, fearful, lonely, and unhappy, continuously generating the fast-paced beta brain waves, which result in sustained chronic stress over time.

As the rational mind's focus is on the outside world, it looks for the cause(s) of stress in our external environment. For example, we rationalize that stress is caused by working long hours, so we conclude that the solution to reducing stress must be to work shorter hours. As we saw earlier, this approach does not resolve stress because the problem of stress does not reside outside of our internal world. And because we don't understand this, we end up trying to manage and cope with stress with rationalized, outside-world solutions.

The Brain's Right Hemisphere

"Our right hemisphere is all about this present moment. It's all about 'right here, right now.' Our right hemisphere thinks in pictures and it learns kinesthetically through the movement of our bodies. Information, in the form of energy, streams in simultaneously through all of our sensory systems. And then it explodes into this enormous collage of what this present moment looks like, what this present moment smells like and tastes like, what it feels like and what it sounds like."[139]

Dr. Jill Taylor, brain scientist, and author

Chapter 14 The Famous Left and Right Brains

The right hemisphere is associated with intuitive knowledge and specializes predominantly in areas relating to our inner world, as opposed to our external environment. This intuitive knowledge has to do with the knowledge of the self, our inner world of the mind, consciousness, and awareness—our feminine principles. It is personal knowledge as opposed to intellectual knowledge of the rational, masculine brain. The intuitive brain is the world in which outside sensations come at us all at the same time, in this moment, here and now. As we saw in the example in chapter 5, when we were watching the traffic at an intersection, we were fully aware of all the sights, smells and sounds surrounding us. Immediately, we sense and know what is happening all around us. There are no borders between objects as such, and the objects tend to merge into each other. Everything is connected as a whole. Everything is possible when it comes to the right brain because there is no ego to restrict it. It is nonverbal, spontaneous, and creative, where time and space are infinite. Our right hemisphere is connected to the innate intelligence or wisdom of our *being* and encompasses the world of feelings, peace, insights, and present moment awareness—and also what are known as flow and peak experiences.

Maslow described peak experiences as heightened moments of awareness. Flow experiences are similar to peak experiences but tend to last longer. We will be looking at these altered states of the mind in much more detail in chapter 23, in the section on Touchpoints of Sanity.

The intuitive right-brain looks for happiness within itself, and that's because it knows that everything is within. It operates in silence. Right brain activities are associated with the alpha brain waves that make us calm and alert.

This right-brain hemisphere is what I call the silent brain or quiet brain. It is the big-picture, holistic brain that gives us an overall perspective, where ideas are born, where dreams are made, where imagination soars, and where we have access to our true self—the wisdom and intelligence of the universe. This wisdom is new knowledge that comes in an instant, in this moment, and in quantum leaps. In other words, it comes as a sudden insight.

The right brain looks at life with an "AND," non-dualistic perspective and connects everything.[140] It provides a holistic view, and so we see similarities, interrelationships, interdependencies, and patterns, which are, in essence, insights. We cannot see these kinds of connections or how things are related when we are focusing on the details, as does the rational left-brain.

The right-brain hemisphere allows us to understand things intuitively and immediately, unlike the intellectual knowledge of the left-brain hemisphere, which comes from learning and accumulation of knowledge. There is intuitive understanding because the right brain is intimately linked to the primitive areas of the brain and the body and has access to the innate intelligence of our being—of who we really are underneath it all. This kind of knowing or intuition is what is commonly known as "our gut feeling."

The intuitive feeling brain fosters compassion, and intimate closeness, unlike the rational brain which cultivates separation through mental concepts or thought-forms. The intuitive brain "is the seat of our emotional and social selves."[141] We tend to think of the right-brain hemisphere as the "heart," our emotional being, or as some rationally minded people would say, "touchy-feely." The intuitive brain has not been fully explored because it has not been deemed useful for our survival or understanding of the world. That's because it does not have verbal and analytical capabilities. In fact, people tend to discount its value because they believe it is irrational and that nonverbal communication is not important. And so, inadvertently, we reject our feminine

Chapter 14 The Famous Left and Right Brains

principles and intuitions, the very characteristics we need to balance our rational, masculine mind.

Since the right hemisphere's focus is on our inner world, we have to go within ourselves to find the cause of stress, as well as the source of happiness, love, and compassion. What we find is that we create all of these states.

The Working of the Brain

How do the rational and the intuitive states of consciousness work within us? How does the brain change from one state to another state and back again?

When we are learning something new, our right brain is active, and our rational mind is "turned off."[142] In this state, we are alert, attentive and relaxed—the perfect state for learning. This new information is then internalized and stored as memories by our left hemisphere, which facilitates the processing of known, familiar concepts. This processing of information happens while our intuitive brain is "turned off." This turning on and off of the two brain hemispheres is a continuous process. In other words, our brain is constantly making new neural connections as it is learning and adapting to our environment "through dual-brain processing."[143] In day-to-day activities, we alternate between these two modes of consciousness—if we are singing, our left hemisphere, which has the verbal center, is active, and our right hemisphere remains quiet. When we are drawing, our creative right-hemisphere is active, while our left hemisphere is off.

In many of us, our creativity is overpowered by logic and conformity, and we become conditioned because we stopped learning new things long ago. As a result, we rely on the information (creative memories) that we gathered as children. As we saw earlier in chapter 3, Gopnik put it this way, "Babies are explorers and adults are exploiters." The problem that most of us have when we are engaged in an activity is that the voice of the ego, a left hemisphere phenomenon, never really turns off. And so, we are *never fully attentive to anything we do.* In other words, we are never fully present in the here and now, where the activity is taking place. As a result, the ego is "attached" to everything we do.

Where Did This Emphasis on the Left Brain Come From?

In the next chapter, we will see how the ego, which is just mental concepts (i.e., not even real), became so dominant and how it makes our lives miserable, blocking us from our true self—our natural state of being.

Chapter 15

The Right Brain—Missing in Action

"I think therefore I exist"[144]
Rene Descartes, (1596-1650), French philosopher, and mathematician

    This famous statement by Rene Descartes has had a profound impact on western thought. Not only did we begin to equate our identity with our thinking mind, the ego-self, instead of with the whole organism, but it was also the beginning of the emphasis on the rational mode of knowledge. And so began the skewed, lopsided development of the left-brain, intellectual, scientific mode of thinking. With this way of thinking, the focus was on the external world of objects and things, the world of our senses—a world of matter that we can touch, feel, and see.

The inner subjective world of thoughts, feelings, and intuition was considered irrational and not necessary, and so we gradually lost touch with our feelings and the intuitive wisdom of our right brain.

As Marilyn Ferguson, author of *The Aquarian Conspiracy*, said, "Without the benefit of a scalpel, we perform split-brain surgery on ourselves. We isolate heart and mind. Cut off from the fantasy, dreams, intuitions, and holistic processes of the right brain, the left is sterile. And the right brain, cut off from integration with its organizing partner, keeps recycling its emotional charge… [creating]… a kind of cosmic homesickness."[145]

In the process of this skewed development of the left brain, as we saw earlier, we reinforced the ego's importance, and as a result, the voice in the head has taken over the mind. If survival were our intent, which for most of us seems to be the case, then the rational mind would be adequate for that purpose. However, as we have seen, stress, struggle, and the mind chatter then become our constant companions. But as we saw in chapter 13, our aspiration is to operate from our natural state of being and evolve into fully realized and creative human beings. That is our destiny!

It took over 300 years after Descartes made that famous statement for his error in thinking to be rectified. The scientists, who were working on the new science of quantum physics in the 1930s, discovered that both the rational and the intuitive knowledge were needed to understand and explain the bizarre findings of quantum physics.[146]

Before we get into how we can integrate the hemispheres and sub-brains, I would like to take you through the next chapter, which deals with the science behind it all. You may ask what science has to do with our natural state of being or consciousness. There are two answers to this question. First, I have been talking

Chapter 15 The Right Brain Missing in Action

about the natural state of being in many areas of the book. *For me, this state of consciousness is real because I live it every moment.* But the questions you may have, are "Does this state actually exist, and if it does, can science prove it?" Quantum physics demonstrates that not only does this state of consciousness exist but it also shows that it is our original consciousness or our natural state of being—the one that has been covered up by our everyday ego consciousness. The second reason I want to talk about science is to show you where many of our everyday problems got their start. We started to talk about the lopsided development of the left brain (briefly) when we discussed Descartes, but that was only the beginning...

The next tool for the Journey is about understanding our brain waves. Understanding how different brain waves are related to different states of mind will help us to relax at will. Learning to sit in silence and becoming familiar with our breath (two tools we have already encountered), together with knowing how to relax, are the key components of our inner journey of creativity. These three techniques form the foundation on which we will build all our other practices. Even though they seem simple, the techniques are extremely powerful and will have a tremendous impact on your life.

Tool for the Journey 3

Understanding Brain Waves

"Do you have the patience to wait till your mind settles and the water is clear? Can you remain unmoving till the right action arises by itself?"[147]

Lao-Tzu, author of the Tao Te Ching

As we saw earlier in Chapter 3, most of us are only aware of two states of mind—the active or awake beta state and the asleep delta state. We tend to swing between these two states. For example, we are completely stressed during the day, and then come home drained of energy, and fall into an exhausted sleep. Sometimes, sleep becomes difficult because the mind is still running on fast beta waves. Many of us struggle to relax because we only know how to be active. We don't yet know how to consciously shift between the different states of mind (Figure 13) and slow the brain activity to a state that will allow us to rest or fall asleep. Relaxation is a skill that we need to learn and practice. Once we know what it feels like, it becomes easier to relax anywhere and anytime that we want.

Gateway into the Subconscious

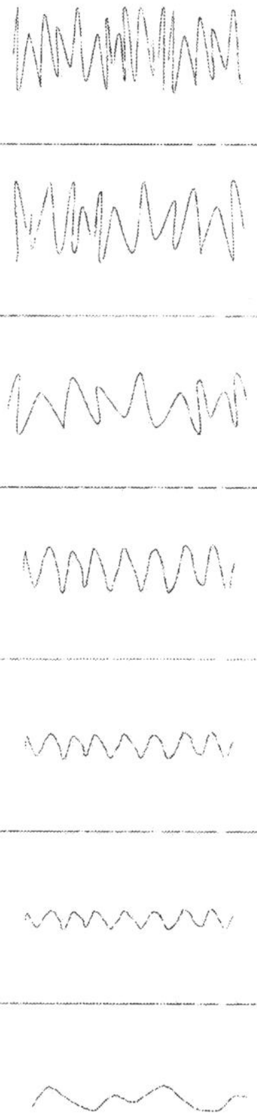

	Brain Waves		State of Mind
Conscious Mind	Lambda 100 - 200Hz		- higher state of consciousness - extremely high functioning - compassionate
	Gamma 50 - 100Hz		- higher state of consciousness - peak mental state - calm and intense focus (flow)
	Beta 13 - 50Hz		- alert - mind chatter - stressed
	Alpha 8 - 13Hz		- alert - no thoughts - calm
Subconscious Mind	Theta 4 - 8Hz		- drowsy - no thoughts - vivid imagination
	Delta 0.5 - 4Hz		- deep sleep
	Epsilon < 0.5Hz		- higher consciousness - extremely high functioning - compassionate

Figure 13 *The different states of mind we encounter as we descend into our mind. If we understand how our brain waves work and learn to control them, we can control the state of our minds. We will be able to change the way we think, feel, and act. These are very broad descriptions of the brain-wave frequencies and states of mind. The whole science of the brain-wave frequencies is quite complicated.*

Tool 3 Understanding the Brain Waves

Beta Waves (Conscious State)—13 to 50 cycles per second

These high-frequency waves are produced when we are wide awake, conscious, and thinking. This state is associated with our left-brain intellectual activity when our attention is focused externally. The higher the beta brain frequency, the more stressed out we are.

Lower beta levels are associated with a focused mental activity and tend to overlap with the higher alpha brain waves.

Alpha Waves (Creative State)—8 to 13 cycles per second

This state is associated with our right-brain activities, in a realm where there is no ego and no space and time constraints. Its focus is on the internal world, our inner consciousness, or our natural state of being. It is the state of now in which we are connected to the creative realm. As Joe Dispenza says in *Breaking the Habit of Being Yourself*, "Alpha serves as the bridge between the conscious mind and the subconscious mind."[148] The slower alpha waves are produced when we are in a relaxed, but awake state. We can bring on this state by simply closing our eyes and taking a few conscious breaths. In this state, we are still aware of our external world, but closing the eyes reduces the amount of incoming sensory information. Our focus turns inward, our brain beta waves begin to slow, and the right brain then starts to become active. The mind chatter begins to subside and might even come to a stop. When both brain hemispheres are at the same frequency, a point where the low beta waves and the high alpha waves overlap, both brain hemispheres are working at par—together. Inner creativity (or meditation) can bring us to this stage. Now we are both physically and mentally relaxed but alert... *in the ideal state for creativity*. Once we understand how to get to this state, we won't even have to close our eyes—just becoming conscious of our breath will bring us into this realm.

This realm is that sweet spot, "an awake brain on idle, the cells firing in unison."[149] In this state, which is our natural state of being, we are both alert and relaxed. This state seems to be a paradox—how can we be alert and relaxed at the same time? We go into and out of our natural state of being regularly, but most of us are not conscious or aware of it and cannot bring this state on consciously when we want it. We know only the hyperactive (stressed) beta state, and if we try to relax, we tend to either become bored and distracted, or our brain frequency slows down further to the point where we feel drowsy and fall asleep.

Theta Waves (Twilight State between wakefulness and deep sleep)—4 to 8 cycles per second.

As we start to relax more, we can go deeper into our subconscious mind and reach the theta frequency state. Here we are alert and conscious but the body is very relaxed, and in fact, has literally gone to sleep. For most of us, this experience does not last long before we fall into sleep. In fact, we don't even notice this state. One minute we are awake, and the next minute we are fast asleep. But with practice, we can stay alert and relaxed and watch the body fall asleep. If we can achieve this state of being mentally awake and physically asleep, we can consciously enter our subconscious realm, which is a place of creativity, vivid imagination, intuition, and profound insights.

Delta Waves (Deep Sleep State)—0.5 to 4 cycles per second

This delta state is the state of deep subconscious dreamless sleep that restores us every night. Very few people are aware at this level, but this state can also be achieved at very deep levels of meditation.

Tool 3 Understanding the Brain Waves

Gamma, Lambda, and Epsilon Waves (Higher States of Consciousness)

There are three other kinds of brain waves which have been identified recently. Very high-frequency gamma waves (50 to 100 cycles per second), even higher frequency lambda waves (100 to 200 cycles per second) and extremely low-frequency epsilon waves (below 0.5 cycles per second—even slower than the delta or sleep waves). These are not found in most of us but have been recently discovered in long-term meditators. Very little is known about them except that they are associated with lucid dreaming, out of body experiences, emotional calmness, compassion, and insights which produce expanded or higher states of consciousness (our natural state of being). As we will see in chapter 25, the interesting thing is that these states of consciousness exist for the long-term meditators, even when they are *not meditating.* Their *brains have physically changed* in terms of how they view and experience the world.[150]

Part IV
The Science and Art of Transformation

Chapter 16

The Science of Wholeness

"Matter as well as mind evolved out of a common cosmic womb: the energy-field of the quantum vacuum. The interaction of our mind and consciousness with the quantum vacuum links us with other minds around us, as well as with the biosphere of the planet. It "opens" our mind to society, nature and the universe."[151]
   Ervin Laszlo, founder of systems philosophy and general evolution theory

   Many of us, as far back as we can remember, have only known, or are accustomed to, the concept of our everyday ego consciousness (i.e., our present state of conditioning or superficial self). How, then, do we know that our natural state of being, or as the physicists call it, the non-local state of consciousness (compared to the local state of consciousness, which is the ego) exists? We can try to think about this state of being, even imagine what it would be like, or maybe talk to someone who has experienced it, but is there any way that we can verify, for ourselves, if this state actually exists?[152]

One way to do this is to experience it directly. What this means is looking inward, within ourselves, and experiencing the different states of mind that we encounter, until we uncover that natural state of being. Here, the focus turns inward to the exploration of an intangible consciousness that is hard to prove and explain. However, this process can be difficult for most of us because we have first to accept, or at least sense, that this state may actually exist, and then have the confidence (and the commitment) that the journey we are undertaking will actually take us there. Such a leap of faith, without any proof, can be difficult to make just because someone, even if that someone was a saint or a sage, said that this state exists.

Fortunately, *we do have scientific proof* that such a state really exists. The fascinating discoveries of quantum physics show us that *our natural state of consciousness not only exists but we can access that state now or any time that we desire.*[153]

Chapter 17

We Are Machines

"I don't need the Pope to tell me how the world functions. I can find that out for myself, because to me, the world is just a machine... I consider the human body as nothing but a machine. A healthy man is like a well-made clock. A sick man is like an ill-made clock."[154]

Rene Descartes

Until the last few decades, consciousness was something scientists did not like talking about, something they wanted to keep as far away from science as possible. They did not want to contaminate pure, hard, science with an intangible concept like consciousness. And when they did talk about it, it was as a brain phenomenon, meaning that the brain created consciousness and when we died, consciousness died with the brain.

CALM BRAIN, POWERFUL MIND

To these scientists, the *focus was on the external world*, which they said operated like a giant predictable mechanical machine made of matter. The person who was instrumental in perceiving the world in this way was Rene Descartes, who, as we saw in chapter 15, was famous for his "I think therefore I exist" statement. He brought about the *dualistic way* of looking at the world when he separated reality (our world) into matter and mind. Descartes was only interested in the physical or materialistic aspect of the world, which he believed was the domain of science. He thought that our external world, the one that we perceive with our senses, was solid and made of matter. That includes large objects like the moon, or smaller objects like a human being, a baseball or even a toothpick.

Matter was a substance that had mass and occupied space. He believed that under the surface (or at its core) these objects were solid and permanent elementary particles or atoms of matter. For example, a playing marble would contain millions of tiny solid pieces (i.e., particles or atoms) of marbles. Material interactions of these solid atoms would determine everything. An external force or collision would be the only way these solid atoms could be affected. In other words, if you want to move a particle, you would have to either strike it or have another particle collide with it. These elementary particles were considered the building blocks of the universe, and the objects could be physically measured and quantified.

On the other hand, Descartes had no interest in the mind, (our inner world) and left the domain of the mind to "God and religion."[155] He believed that the internal, subjective world of our thoughts, feelings, and emotions—our mind—was non-matter because it could not be perceived with our senses; it was intangible and hence difficult to measure and quantify. And so, to these scientists, it was a world where matter and mind were

Chapter 17 We are Machines

separate. They didn't interact and were not related to each other. In other words, each entity, mind, and matter, did its own thing.

According to this "classical" view of science, the world's movements are continuous, flowing from the past to the future. Objects follow the laws of cause and effect, and the world is predetermined and predictive, governed by the laws of nature derived by Newton and others. One of the key assumptions of classical science is that the observer (the scientist conducting an experiment or taking a measurement) does not impact the experiment in any way. In other words, the scientist is impartial, objective and separate from what is being observed (or measured), and their consciousness does not affect or impact the observation.

Three hundred years of classical scientific thinking has had a profound impact on our society. A little later, we will look at the implications of this scientific, materialistic, and mechanistic way of perceiving the world, and how it has affected us.

Chapter 18

A Paradigm Shift—Science Discovers Consciousness

"At the subatomic level, there is a continual exchange of matter and energy between my hand and this wood, between the wood and the air and even between you and me. I mean a real exchange of photons and electrons. Ultimately, whether we like it or not, we're all part of one inseparable web of relationships."[156]

Fritjof Capra, physicist and author

Classical or Newtonian science was based on the study of large objects (that could be seen or imagined) in nature. In contrast, the new science of quantum physics, which had its beginnings in the early twentieth century, is the study of the subatomic world... the world of the very, very small. It "is based on the notion of the quanta—discrete quantities [or packets] of energy."[157] Exploration of the subatomic world only became possible with the discovery of x-rays and other sophisticated measuring equipment. These devices allowed scientists to penetrate and examine the deep layers of matter.

As we saw in the last chapter, classical scientists believed that the elementary particles of matter were atoms which were hard and solid, and occupied space. These atoms were thought to be the building blocks of the universe. Modern X-rays, however, revealed a completely different world. In this new world of quantum physics, not only did the atoms consist of even smaller particles but the atoms themselves were mostly empty space consisting of tiny electrons moving around a central nucleus.

No one has ever seen atoms, let alone elementary particles. The atom has a nucleus at its center with electrons whirling endlessly around it (in orbits or shells). These orbits are not the uniform and circular type that we see around the planet Saturn. Instead, they are clouds of waves where the electrons could be anywhere within those clouds. These wave formations are not like the kind of sound, light or water waves that we are familiar with. We are not able to sense them because they are mathematical formulations or abstractions. The electrons disappear from one orbit and reappear in another orbit—instantly jumping over the space between orbits. These abrupt changes or transitions are called "quantum jumps." When the electrons will jump, or where they will reappear, cannot be predicted.

The nucleus of the atom consists of even smaller particles called protons and neutrons. The electrons, protons, and neutrons are referred to as subatomic particles. The number of protons in the nucleus will determine the type of element and the atomic number. For example, lead has 82 protons while iron has only 26.

Chapter 18 A Paradigm Shift

You may be wondering about the size of these subatomic particles. Gary Zukav, author of *The Dancing Wu Li Masters*, explains,

"If a baseball were the size of the earth, its atoms would be about the size of grapes... to see the nucleus of an atom, the atom would have to be as high as a fourteen-storey building... the nucleus... would [then] be about the size of a grain of salt... [and] the electrons revolving around this nucleus would be about as massive as dust particles."[158]

Astonishingly, these electrons are traveling a fair distance away from the nucleus. The nucleus is so small that the atom is mostly "empty space." "If we use a basketball to represent the nucleus of a hydrogen atom, the electron circling it would be about twenty miles [thirty-two kilometers] away—and everything in between would be empty. So as you look around, remember that what really is there are tiny, tiny points of matter surrounded by nothing... That supposed 'emptiness' is not empty at all: it contains enormous quantities of subtle, powerful energy."[159]

A Classical Newtonian and a Quantum Atom

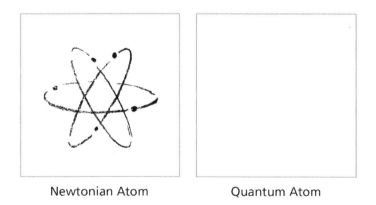

Newtonian Atom   Quantum Atom

Figure 14. *A paradigm shift from a solid matter classical atom to an "emptiness" energy field of potentiality of the quantum atom.*

Suddenly, the old foundation of classical science was shaken. That's because the classical scientists, as we saw in the last chapter, had always assumed that these subatomic particles were made of solid matter (that occupied space). Now, the quantum physicists were discovering *energy* rather than solid matter at the subatomic level (Figure 14). While the laws of classical science still apply to the objects of our world (from baseballs to rockets), they neither work nor can they explain, the phenomena going on at the subatomic level.

The subatomic universe is a field of *energy and vibrations*, where energy and matter exist, not as definite somethings but rather as *tendencies to happen*. In other words, they are waves of possibilities, or as Lynn McTaggart, author of *Intention Experiment* describes "... tiny clouds of probability... [where] every subatomic particle is not a solid and stable thing, but exists simply as a potential of any one of its future selves—or what is known by physicists as a 'superposition,' or sum of all probabilities, like a person staring at himself in a hall of mirrors."[160] (Figure 15).

Hall of Mirrors

Figure 15. *Superposition: Every subatomic particle exists in multiple states at the same time, just as we see countless images of ourselves stretching to infinity in a hall of mirrors.*

Chapter 18 A Paradigm Shift

The subatomic world, exists as a web of interconnections and interrelationships of millions and millions of subatomic particles, as one organic, living, conscious and sentient being. This world is alive, vibrant, and seems chaotic. Particles are destroyed, and particles are created, and they appear from nowhere and disappear into nothingness (into "empty" space). At the subatomic level, there is no difference between matter and energy. *Everything is happening right here and right now.* It is a world of possibilities beyond our sensory perceptions—a *non-sensory reality* beyond space and time as we know... and called by many names—intelligence, quantum consciousness or non-local consciousness. This non-sensory reality is the same *consciousness* that we discussed in chapter 2.

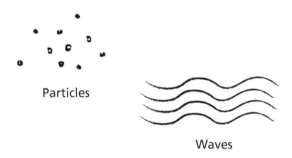

Figure 16. *Particles and waves*

In the subatomic world, these subatomic particles have a dual nature (or physical characteristics)—*they exist as particles or waves* at the same time (Figure 16). A particle is a solid object that occupies space. A wave is a non-fixed force-field that is spread out over an area. So when we describe the particle as a wave, it can be anywhere in that wave formation with its position described by probability fields (defined as the chances of the particle being at any particular point within the wave formation).

So, physicists work out the probability (or chances) of finding the particle in a specific location at a certain time within the wave formation. Both particle and wave properties are needed to define the characteristics of subatomic particles. The very act of measuring or observing these subatomic particles will affect and change them... from a wave-formation into a particle. The observer then becomes the influencer of what is seen. This interesting phenomenon is called "The Observer Effect," and will be discussed more a little later in the chapter.

So what does this mean? It means that a realm of *infinite possibilities (wave formations) already exists in our consciousness.* Any one of those infinite possibilities or choices can become our reality. All we need to do is to choose *one of the possibilities* in order to create the reality that we desire. The Observer Effect states that the mere act of observing will collapse the wave formation into one particular particle (object)—one choice, position or reality determined by our intention. As Amit Goswami says in *Quantum Creativity*, "This consciousness chooses one facet out of a many-faceted wave of possibility and collapses it to one particular facet; for the electron [particle]... this means one particular position." To *collapse* simply means to *materialize.* And Goswami explains this concept with the following simple analogy using the picture (Figure 17) of "My wife and my mother-in-law," below:

> "When we see one image—the young woman or the old—and then shift our perspective of looking to see the other image, we are not doing something to the picture. The possibility of seeing both meanings is already there in our mind. We are just recognizing and choosing one of our own possibilities."

Chapter 18 A Paradigm Shift

Figure 17. *"My wife and my mother-in-law."*[161]

What does all this mean when we are looking at an ordinary everyday object like a toothpick? Let's bring in Gary Zukav again: "[The toothpick is made of] wood... wood is made of fibers... wood fibers... are actually patterns of cells. Cells, under magnification, are revealed to be patterns of molecules. Molecules, under higher magnification, discovered to be patterns of atoms, and, lastly, atoms have turned out to be patterns of subatomic particles. In other words, "matter" is actually a series of *patterns out of focus*. The search for the ultimate stuff of the universe ends with the discovery that there *isn't any*. If there is an ultimate stuff of the universe, it is pure energy, but subatomic particles are not "made of" energy; they are energy... At the subatomic level, there is no longer a clear distinction between what is and what happens, between the actor and the action. At the subatomic level, the dancer and the dance are one."[162] In other words, the observer (the one who is observing) and the observed (the object of observation) have become "entangled"—they have become one. We will look at the phenomenon of entanglement in the next chapter.

Observer Effect —the role of consciousness in shaping our reality

As we saw in chapter 17, and according to classical scientists, when it came to observing nature or measuring the properties of objects, the observer (the person making the observation) was always objective and impartial and did not affect the object that was being observed or measured. In other words, we (or our consciousness) did not influence or alter our reality. That meant there was a duality in the act of observation—the observer (the subject or "I") was separate and independent from the object (the observed).

However, quantum physicists have found that *we do indeed affect our reality*. One of the fascinating experiments in quantum physics demonstrates how the act of observation affects what is being observed. It's called "the double-slit experiment." The experiment consists of a device that emits electron particles (or light waves) directed at two screens, one behind the other. The front screen has parallel slits for the passage of particles or waves, and the rear screen records the results.

A beam of light is aimed at the front screen. Light waves go through the slits and form a typical wave pattern on the rear screen (similar to water or sound wave patterns).

Interestingly, when the electron gun was used to shoot electrons (particles) through the parallel slits, the results on screen two indicated a pattern typical of *wave* behavior. That would suggest that the electrons (particles) were acting like waves as they went through the slits of the front screen.

However, when the above experiment was repeated using a detector (a measuring device) to find out which of the slits the electrons were going through to create the wave-like pattern, the

Chapter 18 A Paradigm Shift

resulting pattern on the screen was completely unexpected. The pattern was particle-like, not wave-like observed in the earlier experiment. This result implied that the electrons were going through the slits as individual particles and not in a wave formation. So by putting in a measuring device, the experimenter (or the observer) changed the behavior of the electrons—from a wave to a particle.

No matter what the scientists did, the electrons always sensed their presence and changed their behavior—from a wave to a particle. The experimenters tried to trick the electrons by placing the detector unit behind the front screen (i.e., after the slits). This meant that the scientists were trying to take a reading after the electrons had already gone through the slits. But this made no difference—the electrons knew they were being watched and so changed their behavior before entering the slits even though the measuring device was placed after the slits. It was as if the electrons knew someone was watching and decided to change their behavior after the event had already taken place.

And so quantum physicists found that no matter what precautions are taken to separate the observer, from the object being measured, there is no such thing as being objective—we can never be objective—*we are always part of the observation and can never eliminate ourselves from it.*[163]

Most importantly, not only do we affect the outcome of what is being observed, but we can change the outcome of an event *after* it has taken place. This implies that even *our intentions affect the outcome.* Quantum physics "suggests not only that the observer brings the observed into being, but also that nothing in the universe exists as an actual "thing" independently of our perception of it.... [this] implies that reality is not fixed, but fluid, or mutable, and hence... [everything is] open to influence."[164] In the subatomic universe, as we saw earlier, the *observer and the observed have become one.*

Hence, quantum physics has brought about a paradigm shift in the way we view the world. It focuses on consciousness, which is the foundation of all being, rather than matter. So instead of saying that our reality is made up of matter surrounded by inert or dead space (as many scientists believe), we are now finding that the space is not inert but is consciousness... and matter is one of its manifestations. We have gone from a science of things to a science of nothing or *no-thing*, and the implications are staggering. The focus on consciousness changes the way we perceive the world—from seeing the world as nothing more than a machine, to a world that is alive and throbbing with life. Mystics and sages of the ancient wisdom traditions have talked about many of the discoveries of quantum physics for centuries. We will look at the parallels between the findings of quantum physics and mysticism in chapter 22.

Chapter 19

Quantum Billiards

"I think I can safely say that nobody understands quantum mechanics."[165]

Richard Feynman, theoretical physicist (1918-1988)

If you are struggling to understand quantum physics and its implications, you are not alone. Even Richard Feynman, a Noble Prize winner for his work in quantum physics, didn't understand it. Let me try and explain some general differences between the prevailing classical "materialistic" theory of perceiving the world, and what quantum physics is saying about how we see reality. We will use a game of billiards to demonstrate.

Billiards (Figure 18) is a game played on a rectangular, cloth-covered slate stone table with raised rubber cushioned edges along the sides and six pockets (four in each corner and one in the middle of each long side). Using the point of a long cue stick, the player strikes the solid white billiard ball (called the cue ball) and shoots it toward the 15 numbered billiard balls to knock them into the pockets. The balls bounce off the cushioned edges in a predictable, geometric manner.

Figure 18. *Billiard table*

As we saw in the last chapter, all material objects, including billiard balls, are made up of subatomic particles. In this world of the very small, we don't talk about individual particles. Instead, we look at "group of particles," because there are millions of them. For our hypothetical billiard game, let us assume that we can see and follow individual subatomic particles. This assumption is quite a stretch of the imagination, but I want to show you some of the fascinating and weird discoveries of the "Now you see it. Now you don't" science of quantum physics.[166]

Classical Billiards in the World of the Very Small

As we saw in chapter 17, classical science says that if we reduce the size of the billiard ball to that of its subatomic components, the tiny subatomic billiard balls (particles) would

Chapter 19 Quantum Billiards

still retain all the properties, characteristics, and behaviors of the regular billiard balls. What this means is that the particles would behave in the same way, no matter the size of the object. Physical laws would govern the actions and behavior of the subatomic particles—so in theory, everything could be predicted. Hence, the game would play out in precisely the same manner that it would be played in our physical world.

Therefore, classical science predicts that depending on how we strike the cue ball, and where the cue ball hits the billiard ball:

1. We can predict exactly where both the balls will end up because their outcomes are predetermined. Their trajectories can be accurately calculated because they follow a specific course of action governed by the physical laws. For example, the ball will go from point A to point B and then to point C—in a sequential and continuous movement.
2. We can make the billiard ball bounce off the cushion edge in exactly the desired angle.
3. We can hit the cue ball, and we can see its effect on both the cue ball and the numbered (object) ball (that it strikes) through the law of cause and effect. Logic also dictates that the cue ball cannot influence or interfere with the actions of the object ball in any way unless it physically touches the ball. As a result, we can calculate what happens to each ball based on their behaviors as individual and separate entities.

Quantum Billiards in the World of the Very Small.

Quantum physics says that if we play billiards at the quantum level, the outcome will be very different compared to the classical science viewpoint.[167] It will take us away from the predictive outcome of our everyday world to the creative chaos of the quantum world. It becomes a game of chance and probability because we can never be sure of the outcome. And also, the game cannot be played out in two dimensions like regular billiards on a flat table surface, because the quantum world of the very small is *multidimensional.*

Here are some of the strange properties and characteristics that will be exhibited when the cue ball strikes the object (numbered) ball:

1. When we strike the object ball, the person looking at it from the other end of the table does not see the ball traveling toward them in a straight line but instead sees the ball "smearing" across the billiard table like a wave.[168] The ball loses its shape as its edges are blurred. When this happens, we cannot tell whether the ball is a particle or a wave or even determine its actual position on the table.

As we saw in the previous chapter, particles exhibit a dual nature in the quantum subatomic world—they exist as particles or waves at the same time. We need both these properties to define the characteristics of the subatomic particles. In fact, these microscopic particles can exist in many different states (called superposition) and can behave in many different ways at the same time—for example, if the particles are not observed, they will exist in all states at the same time as wave forms, but will settle into a single state when observed. It is like having the different phases of water—sold (ice), liquid (water) and gas (vapor)—all existing in a container at the same time. As soon as we open the container to see what is inside, these multiple states of water will collapse into a single physical state. It could be ice, water or vapor. We can't tell which of these states it will be until we look inside the container. And that applies to our quantum billiard game—we cannot actually determine the exact position of the ball. The best we can say is that the ball is "mostly here (and) partially somewhere else."[169] Hence, when we strike the ball, we cannot know exactly what the outcome will be because our single shot will have multiple possible outcomes... just like a game of chance. And that is why

Chapter 19 Quantum Billiards

quantum physicists always talk about probabilities and possibilities.

This superposition (subatomic particles existing in multiple states) is hard to comprehend with our rational, logical mind because in our everyday physical world, we are used to a thing being either a particle (an object like a billiard ball) or a wave (like water waves), but not both at the same time. Our language is inadequate in trying to describe and understand what is going on. We need the "irrational" or intuitive, holistic side of our brains to understand and make sense of this phenomenon. To simplify the language, some quantum physicists describe the dual characteristics of the subatomic particle as "wave-particles."[170]

2. After the cue ball and the object ball interact and then separate, the cue ball is still able to influence the behavior of the object ball, without touching it again. The balls seem to be able to communicate with each other. It doesn't matter how far apart they are. Even if one of the balls were at the other end of the room (or, for that matter, on the other side of the world), the other ball would still be able to influence it. This phenomenon is "analogous to a set of twins being separated at birth, but retaining identical interests and telepathic connection forever."[171] The balls have become what the scientists call "entangled," acting as if they were one entity. Einstein aptly named this phenomenon as "spooky action at a distance."[172]

3. Unlike in our everyday world of billiards, where everything happens in a sequential, continuous and flowing manner, the movement is discontinuous in quantum billiards. The ball does not go from point A to point B and then to point C—instead, it jumps from place to place, bypassing the space existing in between. Once it jumps, you can't predict where it will land. It could land on the billiard table, or we might find it somewhere else in the room. This discontinuous movement is called a

"quantum jump or leap," and it's instantaneous—it just happens. And what happens is always new.

4. When you hit the ball against the cushion edges expecting it to bounce back, the ball will seem to go through the cushion and reappear on the other side. This quantum phenomenon is called "tunneling."[173] The encircling cushion cannot contain the balls on the billiard table. They can end up anywhere in the room, mixing with particles from other objects, including our subatomic particles.

5. There is no cause and effect relationship in quantum billiards. In the subatomic world of quantum billiards, everything is happening at the same time, in the here and now... in this present moment.

Even though the discoveries of quantum physics have brought about a radically new way to view the world, many people, including classical scientists, are still reluctant to let go of their mechanistic view of the world which has dominated our scientific thinking for over three hundred years. Let us look at the implications of this mechanistic viewpoint before we look at how quantum physics has brought about a shift in our collective consciousness.

Chapter 20

Our Mechanistic World

"Are we machines that fooled themselves into thinking we had consciousness, or are we consciousness that built a machine so that it could experience the world (a world that is just ourselves in another guise)?"[174]

Deepak Chopra, author and speaker

We Are Just Machines, Plain and Simple

The mechanistic, materialist way of thinking is that we are just machines, completely rational and objective living in a dead universe. Even though we know from experience that we are conscious living organisms, to the classical scientists, there is no place in our lives for our intangible, subjective inner-world of consciousness, feelings, emotions, and intuition. That's because they believe that we don't require these "things" for our survival. In other words, they consider matter to be inanimate and unconscious. They look at consciousness as a brain phenomenon and feelings and emotions as just chemicals and electrical impulses in the brain. When the brain dies, consciousness dies with it. As Richard Dawkins, author of *The God Delusion*, says, we are just "lumbering robots with brains genetically programmed computers"[175] The scientists' goal then, is to find ways to make us more and more powerful, thinking, rational and objective machines.

The problem then becomes that *if we think of ourselves as machines, we will behave like machines*, and not care about other people or the environment because, to us, everything is unconscious, nonliving, and therefore, disposable. In other words, our primary purpose then becomes one of survival—in the world in which we find ourselves, in the best way we can.

One of the other outcomes of the mechanistic worldview, or more accurately, the cornerstone of the materialist philosophy, is the emphasis on the material things, and how they supposedly "make us happy"—how much we can *collect, consume, and ultimately waste*. This has become our way of life.

As Victor Lebow, the twentieth-century economist and retail analyst said in 1955, just after the end of the Second World War, "Our enormously productive economy demands that we make consumption our way of life, that we convert the buying and use of goods into rituals, that we seek our spiritual satisfactions, our ego satisfactions, in consumption. The measure of social status, of social acceptance, of prestige, is now to be found in our consumptive patterns... we need things to be consumed, burned up, worn out, replaced and discarded at an ever increasing pace."[176]

Chapter 20 Our Mechanistic World

And so, as our focus turns to the external world, we look for happiness through external things and objects that only give us temporary satisfaction. That's because these things are not permanent. Material things provide fleeting contentment to the ego, prompting us to look for more stuff resulting in a search that never ends. Pleasure and satisfaction are only related to our sensual pleasure—which is elusive. We forget that "The only thing constant is change."[177] *Everything else in life is temporary.*

Rational Thinking and the Ego

In this classical or materialist mindset, we believe that our internal reference point, the ego, is our real self. We then focus all our energies on working with our ego to survive—by making it stronger, faster, efficient and effective. This strategy seems to be the only way to help us manage the daily stresses and struggles we experience in our lives. *And so, we try and survive the best way that we can and don't ask whether we can change ourselves so that we do not suffer anymore.*

If this view of the world reminds us of the workings of the left-brain hemisphere, it's not a coincidence. The architect of this worldview was Descartes. And as we saw earlier, he set the stage for the left-brain, rational-mind, male-dominated society with its emphasis on science and technology. And so the ego influenced rational mind deals with, and perceives the world of matter through our senses; in other words, we look at reality from the classical science viewpoint.

Under the watch of the classical scientists, the ego and rational mind emerged as all-powerful. To these scientists, and by extension to our society (because our society is modeled after this materialistic approach to reality mindset), there is no allowance for our natural state of being or the non-local state of consciousness. In other words, we are completely egocentric with our focus on the external environment. There is only one way to see the world, and that's from our ego's point of view. Over the last three hundred years, human evolution has stalled because we've only concentrated on evolving our ability to think, practically forgetting about our intuitive capabilities. Human evolution, in reality, depends on the complete use of both hemispheres of the brain, not just the rational side. We need both intuitive wisdom and analytical intelligence to really help us eliminate our mental suffering and to elevate ourselves into a more advanced, creative state of living.

Transformation Is Not Possible

According to classical science, everything in the world is predetermined and predictive—including us. As such, we cannot bring about a transformation in ourselves, even if we wanted to. Whatever genes we've inherited from our parents, together with our conditioning, determines who we are, and who we are going to be. Hence, we only have a limited choice (i.e., free will) to make superficial changes in our lives that many self-help books advocate. This change is within the framework of our conditioning—just tweaking our programming, as we saw earlier. And so we start to believe that we have no control over our lives. We then become victims of our environment. We think that external events affect us and that we are powerless to do anything outside of trying to accommodate our external environment. A perfect example is stress—we tend to blame external factors for our stress, and so we make minor changes in our lives by, say, learning coping mechanisms, like time management.

What is the difference between change and transformation? Change is an *incremental* or step-by-step improvement of our ego. In other words, change makes us more efficient and effective in the art-of-survival. Transformation, on the other hand, is *radical*. It is *a quantum leap* out of the ego's survival mode and into our creative, natural state of being—*nothing of our old self remains*.

Chapter 20 Our Mechanistic World

Utilizing this old, mechanistic science, allowed us to make great advances in science and technology transforming our external world and, in the process, making our lives more comfortable. However, this materialistic mindset has *done nothing to transform us*. Instead, as we saw in chapter 7, this way of life has accentuated our neurosis making living in survival mode, our default state-of-mind. We've become powerful, stressed-out, computing machines with hardly any feelings—and in the process, we move further away from our natural state of being.

Moreover, we keep creating new technologies at a faster rate than we can comprehend or realize their implications on society. To make matters worse, the rational way of thinking that is creating all this technology does not seem to be able to control it anymore. As Samuel Arbesman, Senior Adjunct Fellow at the University of Colorado observed, "Our machines, while subject to rational rules, are now too complicated to understand... intellectual surrender in the face of increasing complexity seems too extreme and even a bit cowardly, but what should we replace it with if we can't understand our creations anymore?"[178] And as we also saw in chapter 1, when we begin to lose control of our creations, can we even begin to understand, or predict, their impact on us?

We have worked out flight paths, gravitational pulls, trajectories for space crafts and landed man on the moon with precision, but we haven't been able to solve the problem of stress—our mental suffering. Yes, our materialistic thinking can come up with all sorts of phenomenal drugs to counter the effects of stress, but this way of thinking cannot help us eliminate it. Stress is a problem that the thinking, rational mind will never be able to solve because the intellect on its own cannot help us calm our fears and anxieties which create stress—we can medicate ourselves, but we can't think our way through fears and anxieties.

Chapter 21

The Holographic World

"If an atom is 99.99999 percent energy and 0.00001 percent physical substance, then I'm actually more nothing than something! So why do I keep my attention on that small percentage of the physical world when I am so much more? Is defining my present reality by what I perceive with my senses the biggest limitation I have?"[179]

Joe Dispenza

Existence of Consciousness

In an interesting study, two people were asked to meditate together holding the thought or intention that they would be able to communicate with each other through their minds—known as "non-locally" (without the use of any devices, signals, or senses...

and outside of space-time). They were further asked to maintain this meditative state of mind throughout the experiment. After twenty minutes, they were separated, put into Faraday chambers (isolated and electromagnetically impervious rooms), and hooked up to EEG machines to record their brain's electrical activity in the form of brain waves. One person was then shown a series of light flashes and the EEG machine recorded the effect of these flashes as specific brain-wave patterns. In the meantime, the EEG machine of the second person (who had not seen the light flashes), was recording similar brain-wave patterns. In other words, these two people were communicating *directly* without the use of any electromagnetic signals.[180]

In our everyday world of space and time (i.e., our ego consciousness state), we need our senses, or some kind of connection or signal, in order for two people to communicate. When two objects, in this case, the two minds, *become entangled through intention*, we no longer have two separate entities. *They have, through quantum entanglement, become one consciousness beyond the limits of space and time*—eliminating the need for any sensory or signaling communication. Communication is now direct and instantaneous. Both these people had transcended the ego state throughout the experiment, and they were operating from their non-local consciousness. This direct, or signal-less communication is how telepathy works, and *the non-local consciousness is our natural state of being*. According to quantum physicist Amit Goswami,

> "This state [our natural state of being] is beautifully described by three simple words in Sanskrit—Sat Chit Ananda—or Existence Consciousness Bliss. It is the state of being awake—it is when consciousness becomes aware of itself that is when one has moved beyond the ego consciousness. Bliss is our natural state."[181]

Chapter 21 The Holographic World

Everything in our physical world begins from this non-local state of consciousness—an invisible vibrating energy field of the subatomic world. This energy brings the subatomic particles together to create atoms ... that then combine to form molecules... and then cells and so on, up to the physical objects such as we find in our surroundings and ourselves. This chain of events is how reality comes into being. Another way to look at consciousness is to see it as a hologram. A hologram is a three-dimensional image created by splitting a light beam into two beams and bouncing them off of two mirrors to an intersection point. What's interesting is that every single 3-D building block of the hologram (no matter how small, or in what position of the hologram) *contains all the information of the entire hologram.* The universe works in a similar manner—since everything in the universe is a web of interconnections and interrelationships, each element or "particle" within the universe carries all the information of every other element of "particle" of the universe. In other words, you and I have all the information of the whole universe right in our consciousness.[182] It's just that we haven't yet learned how to access all this information.

The Persian poet and Sufi Mahmud Shabistari wrote about this web of interconnectedness some eight hundred years ago:

"Every particle of the world is a mirror,
In each atom lies the blazing light of a thousand suns.
Cleave the heart of a rain-drop, a hundred pure oceans will flow forth.
Look closely at a grain of sand, the seed of a thousand beings can be seen."[183]

... or what William Blake meant when he wrote "Auguries of Innocence" some three hundred years ago:

*"To see a World in a Grain of Sand
And a Heaven in a Wild Flower,
Hold Infinity in the palm of your hand
And Eternity in an hour"*[184]

Let's see how this non-local state of consciousness unfolds (or can unfold) within us. In our physical world of space and time we appear as separate entities, but in fact, we are more than the physical forms. On the surface, we all look physically different and can perceive ourselves and others with our five senses. What we see is the physical body, which is made of matter. If we go within, just below the surface, we encounter our mind, the home of the ego-self—our memories, thoughts, feelings, and emotions. These are intangible mental creations. They are virtual—not solid but are still matter nonetheless. Going even deeper beyond this layer of thoughts (our mind) there is nothing or *no-thing* as we know it—only an invisible vibrating quantum energy field. This field is infinite, eternal space, that is very much alive, alert and aware. It is our consciousness or our natural state of being. In this dimension beyond space and time, we are a web of interconnections and inter-dependencies with one another. We are part of the whole, or as we saw in chapters 18 and 19, we are *entangled*. In reality, *we are all one*—just *different manifestations of the same energy*. We have *no independent existence*. In other words, everything in the universe defines everything else.

If this is the reality, why don't we see it as such? Why is our sense of perception so distorted? That is because this way of observing is beyond the limit of our existing senses. Our five senses are only capable of perceiving 0.00001 percent of the visible, physical world that we need for our survival. Using only our five senses for perception is merely living on the surface of our being. We haven't even come close to *touching* our center—forget about *living* from our center of being.

Chapter 21 The Holographic World

And so our perception, the way we see the world, is just an illusion. It is not that the world is not real—it is, but what we see is only a tiny fraction of reality... one that is almost negligible—and we assume that this is all there is. We will explore this idea in more detail in the next chapter. In order to move beyond this "survival mode of perception" (as we saw in chapter 13), we need to develop an enhanced way of perceiving.

The importance of the whole brain
"A different model of learning [is required]... Technical training is easy compared to developing emotional intelligence. Our entire system of education is geared to cognitive skills... Capacities like empathy or flexibility differ crucially from cognitive abilities; they draw on different areas of the brain... For intellectual skills, the classroom is an appropriate setting... For behavior change... life itself is the true arena for learning, and this takes practice over an extended period of time. One common mistake... is trying to instill an emotional competence... using the same techniques that effectively teach how to create a business plan."[185]

Daniel Goleman, psychologist, and author

How can we describe a world that lies both beyond our sensory perceptions and space and time? We can't—it's not possible. The difficulty lies in the limitation of our everyday language. We developed our language to describe, explain, and understand our everyday world of matter made of separate entities, or objects, in space and time. This worldview is based on our rational mind and our senses.

And so, when the founding fathers of quantum physics discovered the subatomic universe at the beginning of the twentieth century, they had difficulties in explaining what they had found. They realized that the rational mind of scientific, intellectual thinking was inadequate to describe the newly discovered world of the very small. They needed to look at the findings from another perspective or an expanded consciousness of the intuitive mind in order to make sense of what they were observing. In other words, they needed to utilize the functionality of the "whole-brain" to understand and describe reality.

And so to accomplish this understanding, there was a reconciliation between the rational and the intuitive minds, which had gone through the Descartes split some three hundred years earlier.[186] For many years, it was only the quantum physicists and a few scientists, who began to use these findings in their own fields. It was they who acknowledged the *importance of whole-brain thinking* in their work.

It wasn't until about three decades ago that many people began to recognize the need for what Daniel Goleman, author of *Emotional Intelligence: Why It Can Matter More Than IQ,* calls the emotional intelligence (EQ). He describes how the EQ of our intuitive right-brain is needed to balance our rational brain's cognitive skills. According to Dr. Goleman, "emotional intelligence refers to the capacity for recognizing our own feelings and those of others, for motivating ourselves, and for managing emotions well in ourselves and our relationships… [and]… the five basic emotional and social competencies [are] self-awareness… self-regulation… motivation… empathy… [and] social skills."[187] In other words, *EQ is our ability to manage our feelings and emotions so that our survival mechanisms don't overwhelm our rational mind when we are anxious or stressed.* These "EQ" attributes are some of the characteristics of our natural state of being and the initial, but very important, skills required to begin the integration process of the *whole* brain.

Chapter 21 The Holographic World

Transformation is possible

"Focused thought has the power to literally affect anything, from the growth rate of plants, to the direction that fish swam in a bowl, to the manner in which cells divide in a petri dish, to the synchronization of separately automated systems and the chemical reactions in one's body...human thought can literally transform the physical world."[188]

Dan Brown, author of The Da Vinci Code

According to quantum physics, not only can we transform ourselves, but, we can do it now. Our world is not predetermined, as we have been led to believe by our classical way of thinking. We have a choice as to how we want our lives to turn out. One of the most astounding and fascinating findings of quantum physics we saw in chapter 18, is that not only do the subatomic particles change behavior if they know they are being watched, but the change is instantaneous—in quantum jumps. When we are not watching, the particles behave as invisible waves or energy fields, and when we look, they become particles of matter. So their behavior depends on our mind (or thoughts). In other words, matter (or for that matter, anything) materializes from an invisible field of energy when it knows we are looking for it. But before it emerges, matter exists everywhere in this energy field as *an infinite number of possibilities.*

Hence, the act of observation is powerful, and because of that our thoughts and feelings are also powerful. We change what we focus on or pay attention to. If we observe our thoughts, we can change them too. The *mind manifests matter* because as the scientists say, mind and matter are *entangled*. Hence we are intimately connected with the world around us, and we affect it all the time. That what we choose to focus our attention on can materialize in our own world. In fact, because matter, before it comes into being, exists in an infinite number of possibilities, we can create any reality that we care to choose. Every experience we have was one of the many possibilities before one of these possibilities is actualized in that experience. And so if we want to transform ourselves, we only need to make different choices. We have the *freedom* to choose, but once we have chosen, there is only one outcome.

So what comes next depends on what we do now. We have control over how the next moment will unfold. Even if we don't think we are doing anything or deciding anything, we are still choosing through our subconscious preconditioning. We let our conditioning (our early childhood programming) decide this moment and so the next moment will then be more of the same. However, when we are in the now, the present moment, we have an opportunity to change the outcome of that moment. Being in the present moment breaks the cycle of our preconditioned responses. Previously, we never had "time" to stop and be in the now, because we were always running from our past, skipping over the now, and jumping directly to the future... thinking (and hoping) that the future would be different (better) than the past.

In other words, what we were in the past, we are today, and we will perpetuate the same thoughts, habits, and beliefs tomorrow—because we keep thinking and doing the same things over and over again. And so, we keep re-creating the same reality, assuming that tomorrow is going to be different. But how can it be? The future is just a continuation of the past. If you don't change the now, this moment, the future will be the same as the past. Then we allow our life to unfold exactly according to our stored programming, and as Gandhi said in chapter 3, these stored beliefs and habits then become our destiny. Until and unless we become *aware of this*, and make *conscious choices*, our every decision will be influenced by our previous conditioning. The choices we then make will lose their power to change us. In fact, as we operate more and more from (preconditioned) habit, we

Chapter 21 The Holographic World

lose our ability to be creative—because all that we are doing is manifesting our old, habitual responses. And, so, the power to change our reality lies in our *observation of the way that we think.*

Why don't we see that our thoughts create our world... our reality? It's because our chaotic mind scatters our intentions. When we are *focused*, with *clear intentions*, we can *make things happen*. And as we saw in introduction II, *intention is focused, directed, or targeted thought*. And *thought is energy* that can be focused like a laser to *change physical matter*.[189] But most of the time, our minds are chaotic, sending mixed messages to our non-local consciousness, the world of possibilities from which everything is actualized. Focused thought not constrained by mind chatter happens when the mind is calm and clear—when we are in our natural state of being.

Unfortunately, many of us believe that the *world* affects us, and this way of thinking has caused us so much grief and anxiety. It has made us victims of the effects of our environment. However, *we are not helpless*. Up to now, we have blamed our external circumstances for causing stress because we believed we could not control these events. But the new science shows that *we have an enormous power to control our environment*. Instead of being mere observers or participants, *we are actually creators in our world. Our every look, touch, word or thought has an impact on our surroundings*. We cannot claim ignorance anymore, or as Bruce Lipton says, "You are personally responsible for everything in your life, *once you become aware* that you are personally responsible for everything in your life."[190]

The four fundamental principles of quantum physics have now shown us a way to bring about this transformation in us—to rediscover our natural state of being. The principle of non-locality confirms the existence of our natural state of being. The observer effect says that when we are in this natural state, we can change our reality. Accessing this state requires the use of our whole brain, The principle of discontinuity (or the process of quantum jumps) tells us how we can access this state using creative thought, gaps between thoughts, insight or intuition. As Amit Goswami points out, "Discontinuity [is] the discovery of something new of value in thought… [or]… a quantum leap of Aha! insight."[191]

The subatomic universe that the quantum physicists have discovered behaves very much like the consciousness that the mystics of the East and West have been talking about for centuries. In the next chapter, we look at the parallels between science and mysticism.

Chapter 22

Science and Mysticism

"I see science and mysticism as two complementary manifestations of the human mind; of its rational and intuitive faculties. The modern physicist experiences the world through extreme specialization of the rational mind; The mystic through an extreme specialization of the intuitive mind. The two approaches are entirely different and involve far more than a certain view of the physical world. However, they are complementary... both are necessary, supplementing one another for a fuller understanding of the world... Science does not need mysticism and mysticism does not need science; but men and women need both. Mystical experience is necessary to understand the deepest nature of things, and science is essential for modern life"[192]

Fritjof Capra

Some of the leading scientists of the twentieth century who were involved in the exploration of the atomic and subatomic world also happened to be interested in mysticism and Eastern philosophies. They found many parallels between the nature of reality that they had uncovered and the reality experienced by the mystics and sages. As we saw in the introduction, a mystic is anyone who undertakes the inner journey to experience his or her true nature. And so when these scientists realized that the scientific intellectual thinking was inadequate to explain this non-sensory universe, they turned to the mystical worldview to help them understand their weird and unusual findings.

Some similarities between science and mysticism:[193]

1. Nature of reality: Science and mysticism approach the task of understanding the nature of things or ultimate reality, from two very different but complementary ways—as we saw in the above quote by physicist Fritjof Capra. Both of these approaches require the scientist and the mystic to break through barriers that screen the ultimate reality. The physicist explores the physical world of matter using the rational mind and sophisticated instruments in order to break through and penetrate the different levels of matter. The mystic (or sage), on the other hand, has to break through the mental barrier of the ego. He or she uses meditation and other techniques (like conscious breathing and chanting) to silence the noisy mind and bring about a shift in consciousness—this is to access the deeper brain structures and penetrate into the different levels of the mind.

2. Consciousness: Both the physicist and the mystic came across a non-sensory world in their respective explorations. In fact, the physicists are now confirming what the mystics discovered thousands of years ago. They have shown, through scientific experimentation, that a

Chapter 22 Science and Mysticism

non-local state of consciousness exists at the subatomic level of matter. As we saw in chapter 18, this universe is alive and vibrant and is made up of energy and vibrations. It is a unified energy field of potentialities and possibilities. Everything is integrated (interconnected, interrelated, and interdependent) into one organic, fluid, and undifferentiated living being. There no dualism—everything comes into being from the same dimension. In other words, *everything is just a different manifestation of the same invisible vibrating quantum energy field.*

Mystics found the same non-local universe through a direct way of perceiving the mind. They called it the "void" because it is formless and empty... but not empty in the sense that there is nothing in it—there is—and it is consciousness (the same invisible vibrating quantum energy field of quantum physics). As physicist Amit Goswami pointed out in the introduction I, this state is "the ground of all being." It is the cradle of creativity or potentialities, from which all forms arise and into which all forms disappear. This "void" is where all thought and duality end. It is always changing, flowing and transforming. It is the source of life.

In fact, if the quantum physicists were to look into the human body using their measuring instruments, they would come to the non-local consciousness that the mystics perceive through the subtler levels of mind. This non-local consciousness manifests in us as our natural state of being.

3. The role of consciousness in shaping our reality. As we saw in the last chapter, we affect and change what we pay attention to or observe. Hence, observation is the key in both the subatomic world of matter and in the mystical experiences—that is, *our consciousness affects our reality.* In quantum physics, this phenomenon is called the "Observer Effect." Not only does our consciousness bring

what we are observing into being but that nothing exists independent of our perception of it.

Furthermore, as we also saw in the last chapter, the quantum physicists found that at the subatomic level, it is difficult to distinguish between the observer and the observed because they are entangled—they have become one. The mystics go beyond this state and reach a point in their meditation when the subject merges with the object, and only the act of observation or as they would say, pure awareness, remains. They have now transcended their ego-self and reside in their natural state of being.

4. The challenge of explaining the non-sensory world. Just as the mystics have difficulty expressing what they experience through meditation (because the experience transcends the realm of thought and language), the quantum physicists have similar problems explaining the non-sensory world of matter using the rational mind.

And so, there is a more fundamental reality that we cannot perceive but which affects everything that we see and do. *Hanyashingyo*, the Buddhist *Wisdom and Heart Sutra*, which was written almost 2,000 years ago, sums this as follows: "That which can be seen has no form, and that which cannot be seen has form."[194]

Quantum physicists have now confirmed what the mystics and sages have always said: that our perception, the way we see the physical world as mechanical and dualistic, is an *illusion* or *maya*. This distorted sense of reality happens in three ways:

1. We see things and objects as separate from one another—they are not. At the quantum level, all things exist in a web of connections. They are entangled (interconnected and interdependent on one another) and are part of the whole… one organic being. In other words, everything in the universe affects everything else.

Chapter 22 Science and Mysticism

2. We see objects as forms, matter or solids—they are not. At the core (quantum level), there is "nothing" (no-thing). It is a non-physical realm, called by many names—intelligence, energy, or simply consciousness. This consciousness is our reality from which everything comes and into which everything returns.

3. Virtual world. We live in a virtual world constructed from words, ideas and images, and so we lose contact with the real things. This is fine for communication amongst us, but soon the mental concepts become our reality.

Transcending the superficial self (the ego) and identifying with the ultimate reality (the natural state of being), is called liberation, awakening, or enlightenment. And as we will see later, this experience of transcendence produces pure awareness or clarity—a state in which we experience the world without the screens or filters of our mental concepts. With practice, we can achieve and maintain this state of awareness in our daily lives.

Centuries ago, many mystics acquired this knowledge of the ultimate reality after many years (or even lifetimes) of searching. They would leave their families, travel long distances to be with their gurus, and go through difficult initiation processes. Today, this is not only unfeasible, but it is virtually impossible to do in modern society.

However, in recent years some teachers like J. Krishnamurti, Eckhart Tolle, and Sri Nisargadatta Maharaj have shown us that we can access this "natural state of being" in the here and now and, as will see, the process need not take long—if we are earnest in our desire for transcendence.[195]

We have now completed our preparation and laid the groundwork for the next stage in our journey. But before we move on to the next section on "the process of transformation," let us explore the next tool for the journey—the art of observation.

Tool for the Journey 4
The Art of Observation

At the beginning of the book, I included an epigram from the Book of Exhortations, as quoted by José Saramago in his novel *Blindness*: "If you can see, look... If you can look, observe..."[196] I have also talked about the importance of observation in the work we are doing. So what does "to see," "to look," and "to observe" mean? Each of these ways of perceiving (Figures 19-1, 19-2, 19-3) depends on our level of awareness. In other words, how conscious we are.

The Art of Observation

To SEE

Figure 19-1

1. To "see" is the first level of observation. It is the act of seeing the world from the ego's conditioned point of view. This conditioning which includes our filters limits our ability to be aware of everything that is going on in what we see. In other

words, our perception is biased and dualistic—we split everything we see in terms of *I like, I don't like, this is good, or this is not good*. In this way of seeing, we are unconscious or blind to what is actually going on around us. As a result, we experience life situations as a series of stressful events and get trapped in the survival mode of existence—without any way out. As we saw in chapter 20, our rational brain on its own, cannot help us because it doesn't know how to get us out of the survival mindset. This rational brain and the ego-based way of perceiving is how most of us see. It is the only way we have known and are familiar with.

If you can *see*, learn to *look*.

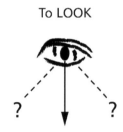

Figure 19-2

2. To "look" is the next level of observation or awareness. To shift to this level of expanded awareness, we need to pay attention to things. We start by focusing on what we are seeing as if we are studying it. There is some purpose in this activity. Now, we are looking from the internal reference point of our natural state of being. As well it adds a holistic or unitive perspective to what we are looking at, instead of the dualist viewpoint of the ego (in seeing). We also begin to see connections and patterns between individual objects. This way of perceiving (what I call "intentional looking") only lasts as long as we are concentrating on that particular object. With this holistic or non-dualistic perspective, we are now able to step back from the problem and see the solution. Struggle

starts to diminish with this expanded awareness. We are completely present for the moment that we are concentrating on the object of our attention. This *right-brain skill of observing* is not taught in our educational system, which as we saw earlier, is geared to teaching the rational mode of knowledge acquisition.

If you can *look*, learn to *observe*.

Figure 19-3

3. To "observe" is to achieve the final state of observation, beyond the expanded awareness of focused looking. In this state, our rational and holistic minds are working together in harmony. We shift to pure (unbounded) awareness, our natural state of being. When we observe, we are mindful, aware, and using our inner senses. It is as if we are seeing things for the first time (without the influence of past knowledge). It is pure observation, looking without judgment and bias. As we saw in the introduction, it is seeing with "a new organ" of perception... seeing with "new eyes." It is a non-dualist mode of perception—just seeing the facts. Now there are no problems, only challenges, which we view as opportunities for growth. We have become *enlightened* to a new way of perceiving; we are now one with our environment.

The following example of driving on the highway will help clarify the differences between the three states of seeing, looking and observing.

To see—we are driving but not aware of anything in particular. We are on autopilot, lost in our thoughts. Then we realize that we need to stop for a break.

To look—now we begin to pay attention because of our need to find the next rest area, a travel plaza or a service stop. As a result, our awareness expands as we pay attention and become more present. Once we find what we are looking for, we revert to our ordinary way of seeing.

To observe—in this state, we are completely aware of everything going on around us as we are driving—the oncoming traffic, the cars traveling behind us, the speed at which we are traveling, the distance to the next rest area and the police car waiting behind some trees to nab speeders. Our awareness has expanded to include everything—it is as if we have become one with everything around us.

Learn to observe and achieve *a higher state of awareness.* Just as we refresh a computer browser page to update its content for the most updated information available, we need to refresh or renew our "old tired conditioned eyes" and learn to see the world around us again at each moment without filters or judgment. In other words, *look at everything as if you are seeing it for the first time.*

Here are a couple of things you can do to increase your awareness.
- Walk in nature. Assume you don't have a language. How would you perceive everything? You would observe without any comments, judging, naming, and so on. You would look at people and your surroundings with complete silence or awareness. In other words, you shift to your natural state of being which is the background

Tool 4 The Art of Observation

upon which everything you perceive appears. Bring this type of awareness to everything you encounter. Observe so intently that you feel you are becoming one with the object(s) of your observation. You are then completely silent and alert to what is going on around you. In reality, this method of *observation is effortless*. If you are making an effort, then you are trying too hard—just relax into effortless observation and the resulting awareness.

- Practice changing the way you see things. Instead of looking at the objects, look at the spaces between the objects. There is *silence* in these spaces. Space or silence is the background, the canvas on which the objects appear, and it's our natural state of being (our consciousness). We must direct our attention to these spaces in order to be able to observe the silence within them. As soon as we do that, our mind becomes quiet, and we become aware of the silence. When stressed, we only hear the noises in our mind, and they drown out the silence of the space. Our mind becomes quiet when we *shift our focus* to the space between two objects. We are then able to notice the silence of the space.

What we just discussed is an interesting paradox. The mind needs to be quiet to observe the silence or space between two objects, but the mind cannot do so when it is noisy. That's because the voice in the head is distracting. We resolve this paradox by *deciding to focus on the space* and in doing so, automatically silencing the mind—and *noticing the silence of the space*. It's just a shift in attention, but it works. Try it, and you'll see what I mean.

Part V Process of Transformation

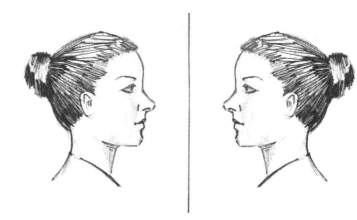

Chapter 23

Touchpoints of Sanity

"From the moment you came into the world of being, a ladder was placed before you that you might escape."[197]

Rumi

Escape from what? Rumi means to escape from suffering—from the mental noise that is causing so much anxiety and turmoil in our lives, so much stress that it is making it difficult to live happy and satisfying lives. What is the ladder that will help us escape from our misery? It's one of transformation, one that allows us to climb out of our everyday state of ego consciousness and expand into our natural state of being, that of pure consciousness.

But while many of us are not yet aware of this ability to climb out of our misery, we all encounter occasional moments of escape, where we find joy, clarity, and happiness. These moments can range from watching a sunset to playing with our child, where we are not thinking of anything other than paying attention to what is happening right in front of us—at that moment. If it were not these occasional, but precious, periods of happiness, many people might become depressed, or even insane. I call these sporadic moments of joy, "touchpoints of sanity." As the name suggests, these touchpoints give us a chance to experience *sanity* by climbing our ladder into our natural state of being—beyond the realm of our streaming thoughts and our ego-self. It doesn't matter that these touchpoints can be fleeting. However strong the web of mental structure our ego has built to prevent access to this state of mind, the wall is still porous. It cannot stop the light of our natural state from shining through and brightening our lives regularly… even if it is for just a few minutes at a time. These openings provide a slight shift in our everyday consciousness when we are able to "touch" our true self, and they leave their mark on us. We are not the same anymore. We are now enlightened by that experience.

    I view touchpoints of sanity as mini ladders or "gaps of enlightenment," of present moment awareness that allows us to climb out of our ego-consciousness into the naturals state of being. The gap creates space in the mind where thoughts cannot survive. Think of this space as a gap between two thoughts, in a constant stream of thoughts. The present moment (the now) is the jump-off point into an uncharted area—our natural state of being, and it opens up new horizons for us. Every time we find ourselves in the now, the ego's grip on our mind is loosened, and we have insights into the nature of things. The concept of being *in the now* is already ingrained in many people's psyches because of the work of the modern-day spiritual teachers. The challenge is that this idea is still a concept for many of us, one that is not yet fully developed to bring it to fruition. We will discover, however,

Chapter 23 Touch Points of Sanity

how to access this wonderful, present-moment state of being, in the next few chapters.

Many of us stumble into these touchpoints not knowing what they mean. We experience an "aha!" moment or two, or a few minutes of clarity, happiness, or peace, and, before we know it, these experiences are gone. These touchpoints of sanity soon fade into pleasant memories, as we are drawn back into our stress-laden lives of survival living. These precious moments of sanity remind us, if we are lucky, that there is more to life than what we see and experience on a daily basis. Sometimes we want to re-live memories through our thoughts, but this is not the same thing as experiencing them in real life. This is because memories are mental concepts, mere verbal descriptions representing the moments of experience, but they are not the real thing.

However, if we choose to understand, feel, and experience the touchpoints fully as they occur, we can heighten our awareness of them and lengthen each touchpoint experience. With practice, we can catch these moments every time they happen. Once we become receptive to these incidents by paying attention to them, we tend to experience them more often. The more time we spend in these present-moment experiences, the more sensitive we become to the opportunities for the transformation they offer. These touchpoints have the power to change our lives in ways we can't even imagine. They can shift our consciousness to a higher state in an instant. For some of us though, even if the touchpoints were wide-open doors, inviting us to enter, we would not want to go through them out of fear of what lies beyond these doors—the unknown.

These touchpoints go by different names but they all give us access to our natural state of being—gaps of enlightenment, *bardo*, thin places, flow moments, peak experiences, and insights. Let's look at these in more detail.

Gaps

"Between stimulus and response, there is a space. In that space lies our freedom and our power to choose our response. In our response lies our growth and our happiness."[198]

Author unknown

These gaps of space/silence are everywhere if we care to look. They exist between two streaming thoughts—when the first thought passes and the next thought hasn't yet arisen, or between two breaths—the instant after inhalation and before exhalation. Visually, we can experience this idea by focusing on the space between two pieces of furniture in a room. Sometimes, the mind becomes quiet (creates a gap) when we are awestruck by the breathtaking view of a beautiful sunset. All these examples of silence and space are aspects of our natural state of being—our consciousness.

Bardo

"The word "bardo" is commonly used to denote the intermediate state between death and rebirth, but in reality bardos are occurring continuously throughout both life and death, and are junctures when the possibility of liberation, or enlightenment, is heightened."[199]

Sogyal Rinpoche, Buddhist teacher, and author

Bardo is a Tibetan word meaning "gap" or "in the middle." These bardos are powerful moments that occur throughout our lives. Similar to gaps, they are in-between spaces of *present moment awareness* or "nowness." They can be of short duration, like a moment between thoughts or breaths, as we saw above, or they can extend over longer periods, like flow and peak experiences, which we will discuss a little later.

Chapter 23 Touch Points of Sanity

Thin Places

"Thin places," the Celts call this space,
 Both seen and unseen,
 Where the door between the world
 And the next is cracked open for a moment
 And the light is not all on the other side."[200]
   Sharlande Sledge, Baptist pastor, and author

Many times, when we find ourselves near an ancient sacred site, or even when we are walking in a certain part of a city, we are overwhelmed by a sense of peace. In Irish spirituality, these places are called "thin places," where the veil separating heaven and earth is so thin that the two worlds meet. As a result, the place feels sacred and peaceful because our everyday ego identity that we have nurtured and maintained all these years suddenly gets stripped away revealing our true natural self, albeit only for a moment or two. As Eric Weiner, travel writer and the author of *Man Seeks God*, writes, "Travel to thin places…disorient[s]. It confuses. We lose our bearings and find new ones. Or not. Either way, we are jolted out of old ways of seeing the world. Thin places relax us, yes, but they also transform us—or, more accurately, unmask us. In thin places, we become our more essential selves… Maybe thin places offer glimpses not of heaven but of earth as it really is, unencumbered. Unmasked."[201]

These thin places are usually associated with physical places in nature—sites like mausoleums of saints, some ancient mosques and churches, and forests. However, these transforming experiences are not only confined to physical spaces. They, just like other gaps, exist everywhere and can be experienced at any time, as we saw above.

Peak Experiences
"Think of the most wonderful experience of your life: the happiest moments, ecstatic moments, moments of rapture, perhaps from being in love, or from listening to music or suddenly 'being hit' by a book or painting, or from some creative moment."[202]
Abraham Maslow, (1908-1970), psychologist, and author

Peak experiences, according to Maslow, are *transpersonal experiences* that take us into an altered state of mind, our natural state of being, where time and space have no meaning, and where we feel as one with the universe. For a brief moment or even for extended periods, peak experiences make us unbelievably happy and alive. They help us realize that there is more to life than our everyday struggle for survival. So in a way, peak experiences are much more impactful than gap experiences. They block out thoughts and chatter to quiet our mind—allowing us to access our natural state of being. And so we are enlightened in that moment. We are ecstatic, and the moment is pure bliss. However, this state cannot be sustained for long as thoughts come rushing in, and the feeling is lost. Our thoughts attempt to memorize the experience for recollection at a later time, but the intensity of the peak experience cannot be replicated from memory—it must be in real time... *in the now.*

Many of us experience these peak experiences, but some people tend to encounter them more often. Maslow wanted to try and reproduce these peak experiences so that anyone could experience them without going through, what he called spiritual training. Maslow believed that peak experiences were human experiences and not spiritual. So he studied the thoughts, actions and characteristics of saints, sages, and other fully realized or "self-actualized" individuals and came up with a list of attributes or characteristics that defined a self-actualized person. Maslow described a self-actualized person as someone who achieves their

Chapter 23 Touch Points of Sanity

full potential and thus has a greater tendency to experience these peak moments. He suggested that there were a number of ways to encourage self-actualization, some of which were:

- By completely immersing ourselves in whatever we are doing,
- By becoming spontaneous, honest, and comfortable with uncertainty,
- By paying attention to our intuition and
- By having a sense of humor.[203]

Flow Moments

"People in flow often make the difficult look easy, an external appearance that mirrors what is happening in their brain. Flow poses a neural paradox: we can be engaged in an exceptionally demanding task, and yet our brain is operating with a minimal level of activity or expenditure of energy. The reason seems to be that when we are bored and apathetic, or frenzied with anxiety, our brain activity is diffused; the brain itself is at a high level of activation, albeit poorly focused, with brain cells firing in far-flung and irrelevant ways. But during flow, the brain appears efficient and precise in its pattern of firing. The result is an overall lowering of cortical arousal—even though the person may be engaged in an extremely challenging task."[204]

Daniel Goleman

Flow experiences were first identified and studied extensively, by psychologist Mihaly Csikszentmihalyi (pronounced "Me-hi Chicksent-me-hiee"). He came up with several conditions that define the state of flow. He called these conditions Optimal Experiences:

1. Being completely absorbed by the activity that is undertaken (and this usually happens when we like what

we are doing, and know it is something that we can do well),
2. Have a feeling of breaking through our normal day-to-day reality, and into another state of consciousness, where our senses are heightened and where we feel alive, alert and have a sense of well-being—in other words, we are completely involved with life,
3. Where we are so completely focused on what is happening in the here and now that we lose track of time,
4. Doing the activity seems effortless—as if it is being done by itself.[205]

These optimal flow experiences are similar to Maslow's peak experiences except they tend to last much, much longer. The state of flow is achieved when a person's mind or body is pushed to its limits in a voluntary effort to accomplish something difficult and worthwhile. It has also been described as being "in the zone," "on a roll," "wired in," "in the groove," "on fire," "centered," or "losing ourselves in the moment."

Csikszentmihalyi also found that even if we are able to master flow in one area of our lives, the conditions of flow might not be achievable or transferrable to everything else that we do. He gives examples of people like "Bobby Fischer, the chess genius, [who] appeared helplessly inept except when his mind was on chess" and "Picasso, [who] enjoyed painting but as soon as he lay down his brushes he turned into a rather unpleasant man."[206]

This inability to sustain the flow conditions in our everyday lives is the problem that many creative people face because they tend to straddle two worlds—the ordinary world of the ego and the creative world of flow. It's as if these people are touched by some unseen power while they are creating, performing or writing. But as soon as they are away from their elements, most of them fall back into their ego minds—with the same life problems, issues, and turmoil, like the rest of us.

Chapter 23 Touch Points of Sanity

Here are some other examples of how people describe flow experiences.

The multi-talented singer-songwriter Michael Jackson described the intense flow experience that overcame him when he was on the stage performing: "On many occasions when I am dancing, I've felt touched by something sacred. In those moments I've felt my spirit soar and become one with everything that exists... I keep dancing and dancing... and dancing, until there is only... the dance."[207]

Musician Carlos Santana, who pioneered Latin rock, described his band's flow experience this way: "We know that a two-hour or three-hour concert is going to feel like fifteen seconds, because the first thing that happens when something spiritual assaults the place [is that] time disappears, gravity disappears, issues disappear."[208]

Flow experiences can be very addictive. That's because our normal day-to-day lives seem dull in comparison. Getting into the state at will can be difficult. Many try to recreate the experience from memory, but as with peak experiences, feelings from memories cannot give us comparable sensations. The addictive nature of these experiences is why people engage in dangerous activities like free-form rock climbing (achieving flow through the risk of harness-free climbing), long distance running (pushing past pain to achieve "runner's high"), or high speed drag racing (delicately balancing risk, control and attainment of maximum speed).

Csikszentmihalyi said that we should do challenging activities in multiple areas of our life in order to turn our life into a "unified flow experience." But this is not easy. He says it can take years to develop expertise in the various aspects of life in order to trigger flow experiences—not everyone can do it. His suggestion of making the mind more complex to achieve the state of flow would entrench the ego deeper and hence difficult to dislodge. This is not what we need. We need to move beyond the limitations of the ego.

If you have experienced flow, then you have already experienced your true state. In fact, enlightenment is nothing more than these flow moments strung together to create a permanent state of flow. Enlightenment is being in a continuous state of flow, not only when we are doing a difficult task, but also in everything we do—even what we consider routine things like washing dishes or working on a factory assembly line. When we are in flow, we are completely present to everything that is happening around us, and fully involved in whatever we are doing.

Insights

"There is a force within that gives you life—Seek that.
In your body there lies a priceless jewel—Seek that.
Oh, wandering Sufi,
if you are in search of the greatest treasure,
don't look outside,
Look within, and seek That."[209]

Rumi

Many of us don't know where insights come from or how they come about, but we experience them almost daily—from finding a misplaced item to remembering a forgotten name, to solving a difficult problem. If we think about a problem and then put it aside for a while, the intuitive, natural state of being, takes over and at some point, generates an intuitive understanding of the problem. Suddenly, we have the answer—"an aha! moment." It is a flash of inspiration that may last for just a moment. As we saw in chapter 15, the intuitive mode of knowledge creation works by integrating things, finding relationships and interconnections. It sees the whole picture and pulls information from everywhere unlike the rational mind, whose focus is narrow and specialized.

It seems magical when these insights can just pop into our heads out of the blue, but they result from the creative process that we are already familiar with. Our inner creative process involves preparation (learning everything about the problem), incubation (putting aside the problem and doing something else, "the aha! moment" (the insight), and implementation (using the insight to solve the problem). The creative process brings together rational knowledge (the first and the last steps of the process), and intuitive knowledge (the second and the third steps).[210] This creative process uses both hemispheres of the brain. We think it is something special and that only a few people have access to. But this state is always available to us, at any time, except when the constant chatter of the ego obstructs it.

Gaps, insight, flow, and peak experiences are nothing more than small doses of the wisdom of our natural state of being, attempting to break through our ego conditioning. Even though we only have limited or momentary access to these snippets of wisdom, they do bring relief from the turmoil and struggles of our ego-driven lives.

Let's see how we can make this a permanent state using inner creativity just discussed. The internal process of self-discovery is a continuous process. It goes deeper into the mind and uncovers layers of misperceptions, beliefs, and attitudes of our conditioning until we finally get in touch with our natural state of being. As insights come forth, we start living through our natural state. Our outer world begins to change. Actually, the world remains the same, but the way we perceive it changes because "insight is joy; so as life becomes more and more conducive to insight, we become happier."[211]

This process of inner creativity combines the principles of quantum physics and the meditative and practices of the mystics, to synchronize and integrate our brains. That, in turn, brings about a quantum jump, or a transformational shift, in our consciousness. You are already familiar with the techniques (beginner's mind, sitting in silence, conscious breathing, and learning how to relax) that will form the foundation on which we will build all the other practices. Now we can begin our climb up the mountain...

Chapter 24

Mountain—The Climb

"I am a servant of whoever will not at each stage imagine that he has arrived at the end of his goal. Many a stage has to be left behind before the traveler reaches his destination."[212]

Rumi

Cultivating the Right Side of the Brain

The mantra of extreme altitude mountain climbing is *"pole, pole,"* (pronounced polay, polay), the Swahili words for "slowly, slowly" or "step by step." And so, our attention is drawn to each step that we take. Walking very slowly is not only a powerful strategy to help the body to conserve energy and acclimatize to the altitude as oxygen levels decrease, but it also forces our minds to slow down. It lowers our brain wave frequency from the high beta levels of our everyday stressful living to the calm alertness of the upper alpha levels, thus readying us for the journey.

As we focus our attention on each step that we take, we relax and delve into the present moment, in the here and now.... where life is unfolding. This focus on the present moment is what is called *mindfulness*. To be mindful is to be aware of everything that is happening in this moment, without judgment. Buddhist monk and teacher, Bhante Henepola Gunaratana, explains mindfulness this way, "If you are remembering your second-grade teacher, that is memory. When you become aware that you are remembering your second-grade teacher, that is mindfulness. If you then conceptualize the process and say to yourself, 'Oh, I am remembering,' that is thinking."[213]

Each step then becomes important, not the act of reaching the summit. Mindfulness and other meditation practices restructure our brain, silence our mind chatter and shift our awareness to the right brain hemisphere so that we can begin the process of integrating our brain. We learn that when we are mindful, it is difficult to be *anxious or fearful* on our journey. That's because we are now completely present and paying attention to things moment-by-moment as we calmly walk our way through or around the obstacles on our path. Our attention is focused on our steps and the path—not looking up the mountain and being overwhelmed by what lies ahead.

As we saw earlier, most of us have a very short attention span that keeps shifting from past memories to future expectations and occasionally drops into the here and now. It is not that we are not mindful at all. We are. But we are unconscious or unaware that we are mindful when we are actually mindful. The difference now is that we are conscious of the process of being mindful. When we are not attentive, large chunks of our lives go by without the awareness, and the benefits, of the experience. It might be difficult to be mindful all the time, but as soon as you become

Chapter 24 Mountain—The Climb

aware that your attention has drifted away, you can gently bring it back to the present moment. Remember, we are not trying to conquer, assault or attack the mountain—or our environment, as most people try to do. That is how our rational mind works. What we are doing is learning how to work, and be in complete harmony, with our environment because, as saw in chapter 21, we are intimately connected with the world around us, and are always affecting it, whether we realize it or not.

Here is a simple technique to help us shift our awareness from the rational act of thinking to the intuitive act of feeling as we climb. This technique is especially good for those of us who are very rational minded.

Even though the voice in the head is confined to the rational left-brain hemisphere, its noise seems to engulf the whole brain and does not allow us to feel what is going on around us. As you climb, walk as if you do not have any mind chatter. Then try and feel your way around by letting your body take you where it wants to. Soon you will be feeling things, rather than thinking about them. After a while, you will be able to move more easily between your rational and intuitive minds. As you climb higher (and your practice gets deeper), you come to realize that you are neither your rational mind (the home of the ego), nor your intuitive mind, but something beyond that. You are your natural state of being—your essence. And that includes both the rational and the intuitive minds. The rational and the intuitive minds can be developed, but *our natural state of being is what we have been, what we are, and what we will always be.* It is just that we have lost sight of this state because we have allowed our ego-self to take over our lives.

With sustained attention and focus, many of us may also experience the meditative state of flow as we climb. In this state, we feel completely alert, relaxed and ascend with minimal effort. The body and mind working in sync. It is as if the act of climbing is being done by itself. This is what Lao-Tzu, the Taoist philosopher and the author of the classic *Tao te Ching*, meant when he said, *wei wu wei* or "doing-not-doing" or *effortless effort*.[214]

Mindfulness is a powerful way to expand our attention in all areas of our lives. With practice, we can extend this present moment awareness into many moments of awareness. If we are alert in this moment, then we should also be alert in the next moment, because this moment unfolds into the next moment. And if we are not alert, we can always find the reason why we are not alert. It is our thoughts that intrude and take us away from the present. When we are aware, mindful and alert, we begin to be able to "observe" our thoughts and stop the negative thoughts before they spiral out of control. When we are mindful, we disrupt our usual conditioned way of responding to our "problems."

With mindfulness, we also learn to be alone and silent and begin to enjoy our own company. Yes, we talk to people in our team, but for most of the climb, we are on our own with our mind. Most people don't like their own company. They are easily bored with themselves and look for things to do. *If we learn to be quiet and alone with our mind, and enjoy it, we will never experience boredom or loneliness.*

As our mind starts to quiet down, we begin to feel lighter and more energetic. When our mind becomes calm, clear, and alert, our capacity to learn and observe increases. We start to pay attention to everything in our environment—the rocks, the flowers, the porters and the scenery. We also begin to have fun and actually enjoy the journey. This way of looking at life is the lighter side of the intuitive, right brain. It knows how to have fun, how to be creative and enjoy life... if we allow it! To the right brain, reaching the summit will happen, but the enjoyment of the journey is what is important. On the other hand, the rational left

Chapter 24 Mountain—The Climb

brain, which is the home of the ego, is "serious," and wants to complete the task of climbing as soon as possible so that it can go and climb other "mountains." The reason for this is because the ego looks at the act of reaching the summit as an achievement, and focuses on the endpoint, rather than the journey—and the experience.

The Role of Guides

"If you wish to know the road up the mountain, Ask the man who goes back and forth on it."[215]

Zenrin, The Gospel According to Zen

Guides have reached the summit and have returned to guide other travelers on the path through unknown or uncharted territory. It is said that when the student is ready, the master will appear. And that is very true. Guides are not just gurus and masters but can be "ordinary" people we meet every day. It could be our cleaner, our mechanic, our gardener, our teacher—or even a stranger. Once we decide that we want to start the journey, teachers will appear just when we need guidance to help us reach the next stage. Sometimes even a guiding word or a smile of encouragement will trigger something within us. Other times, the teacher may be in the form of a book that we have read many times before, but only now becomes apparent because of our need for this information.

The Art of Letting Go

"Life is what you make it. Accept what you cannot change, change what you cannot accept... unlike most people diagnosed with a terminal illness, I accepted that I had ALS (amyotrophic lateral

sclerosis [or Lou Gehrig's disease]) immediately and I proceeded to live life the only way I know how."²¹⁶

Steven Wells, who has ALS

Another mantra of extreme altitude mountain climbing to help us get acclimatized is "to climb high and sleep low." Just as acclimatization is the key to slowing us down when we are climbing the outer mountain, to let the body get used to the lower oxygen levels, *the art of letting go* is the key to ascending the inner mountain.

If we climb too high too fast, our bodies and minds will not be able to adapt to sudden changes, and we will become disoriented. Our inability to adjust to the decreasing oxygen levels will force us to descend back to the lower camp to rest or in some cases, even force us to abandon the climb.

And so, we climb higher up the mountain to acclimatize to the new oxygen levels and then descend to the next camp to rest, rejuvenate and prepare for the next stage of the journey. We also do this to "digest" and integrate what we have learned and share our newfound experiences and knowledge with others. Our journey into the mind is a gradual process of transformation so that we can become accustomed to the increasingly expanded consciousness. In the process of inner creativity, there is the *doing phase* and the *being phase* where we just let go of what we have been doing and turn our attention to something else. This process of letting go allows our subconscious to continue doing the work, while we do something else.

Letting go is a critical ability to develop. We need to travel light on our journey. Traveling light applies not only to the physical items we carry in our backpack but also to the emotional baggage that the voice in the head makes us lift. This is a heavy load to bear. It holds us back because when the mind is entangled in worries, it consumes a lot of our energy. What is worry? It is the non-acceptance of what is happening right now. The difficulty

Chapter 24 Mountain—The Climb

is that we are always hoping that things should be different than they are.

The voice in the head is only interested in thinking about what life could have been or should be. So in its virtual fantasy world, the weather on the mountain should be perfect for the climb, the tents, and the sleeping gear should be warmer. Or in our everyday world, there should not be any traffic jams, no line-ups at the checkout counters at the grocery stores, no one should cut us off when we are driving, and everyone should be happy. But these thoughts are not reality. This way of perceiving the world is living in our mind. We are so wrapped up in our mind chatter that we cannot accept the fact of what is really happening, and in the process forget to fully experience what life has to offer in this moment of time.

So learn to accept things as they are without wanting to change them. Start with small things or, for that matter, take this moment and see how it unfolds. As Eckhart Tolle says, "Single out this moment... allow this moment to be as it is."[217] When we say yes to what is, we hit against the "now," and we are then directly in touch with what is really happening. What we accept is transcendent—we go beyond thoughts and the mind chatter. What we resist or fight against sticks around in our mind long after the incident or situation has occurred. When we transcend our thoughts, we learn not to fight to change something that has already happened or what is happening right now. We keep moving and say to ourselves, "What can I do now?" or "Where do I go from here?" The journey then becomes easier—there is no resistance anymore.

Progress on the Journey

"Change can be so constant that you don't even feel a difference until there is one. It can be so slow that you don't know whether your life is better or worse until it is or it could just blow you away, make you something different in an instant."[218]

George Monroe (character), Life as a House

Because of our different backgrounds, our conditioned mental state and the way we have prepared for the journey, progress can vary from person to person. We all don't progress at the same rate, so comparing ourselves with others (a survival instinct) is meaningless and useless. Progress is usually associated with our rational, ego way of thinking because we are always working toward a goal. Our ego wants to know how we are doing in comparison to others. For example, on the outer mountain, we know we are progressing because we ascend from a lower camp to a higher camp.

For the inner mountain, however, progress is much more subtle. Self-realization is not a goal to be reached, and it is neither "an accomplishment nor an achievement. It is you realized something that has already been around."[219] We have to progress at our own pace. After we have climbed for a while, we realize that we cannot make rapid progress, but each and every step becomes important because it moves us closer to the next stage. The important thing is to be focused and to make the effort. And sometimes we may find ourselves struggling. So stop and rest as often as you want. But we are always progressing because the work that we are doing is expanding our consciousness and so changes are happening, but they may be difficult to perceive.

Before we tackle the next stage of the journey, let us take a break and look at the power, the benefits and the practice of meditation that will take us to the summit.

Chapter 25

The Science and the Power of Meditation

"Yesterday I was clever, so I wanted to change the world. Today I am wise, so I am changing myself."[220]

Rumi

In this chapter, we will look at the science and the power of meditation to change us and in the process, bring about a transformational shift in our awareness. Long-time practitioners of meditation understand its many benefits and power. Numerous scientific studies highlighting the benefits of meditation have been published over the last forty to fifty years, but it is only in the last two to three decades that these studies have become more freely available to the general public.

Many people associate the practice of meditation, especially mindfulness meditation, with stress reduction. While this is true, this benefit is limited and only a small, albeit significant benefit of meditation. As we will see below, meditation has been scientifically proven to bring about fundamental, verifiable, and measurable structural changes to our brain. It does this by synchronizing and integrating our sub-brains, and by making our whole brain coherent. Meditation has the ability to overwrite our subconscious programming and help us break free from our autopilot mode of past programming. It makes our brain function in a unified and holistic manner bringing about a different way of perceiving the world—from our *natural way of being*. As the brain transforms, our life follows suit. We move away from our survival limiting mindset and begin to live a conscious, creative life. Eventually, nothing of the old thinking remains—it is a complete psychological revolution. As Krishnamurti, the Indian mystic, said, "Inward or psychological revolution implies a complete transformation, not only of the conscious mind but of the unconscious as well."[221]

Meditation achieves a complete psychological revolution by accessing all parts of the brain to create new neurons and connections. As we saw earlier in chapter 13, the brain never stops growing, changing, and adapting to our environment. The brain's ability to keep evolving throughout our lives is what neuroplasticity is all about—"the ability to rewire and create new neural circuits at any age."[222] The rate of change depends on the *kind of thoughts that we think every day.*[223]

How does just sitting quietly and meditating bring about all these changes? The benefits for different types of meditation techniques may vary slightly, but in general, here are some of the key outcomes.

Chapter 25 The Science and the Power of Meditation

Brain Integration—Horizontal Synchronization and Vertical Integration

The brain's nerve cells are interconnected and interdependent on one another. They transmit information through the generation of electrical fields (or brain waves) which can be measured using an electroencephalogram (EEG). Because brain waves are electrical energy fields, they are governed by the principles of quantum physics, and hence, exhibit properties such as entanglement, wave/particle duality, and superposition. "Your brain waves are simply the superposition of the multitude of electrical states being formed by your nervous system."[224] Superposition simply means that all our various brain waves that exist at any particular moment merge into one dominant and most energy efficient wavelength depending on what we are doing. As we saw in chapter 3, each type of brain wave is associated with a specific mental state. For example, our waking state is dominated by beta brain waves while delta waves dominate our sleep state. Alpha, theta or gamma brain waves produce variations of a meditative state.

When we close our eyes to begin a sitting meditation, over eighty percent of the incoming sensory information from our external environment stops. That allows the brain to quiet down as the faster beta waves of our noisy chattering conscious left brain, which processed this external information, start to slow down. At the same time, as our awareness (attention) turns inward to our thoughts, the slower alpha waves that dominate our calmer subconscious right brain start to speed up. At some point, these waves merge into alpha/beta waves... also called high alpha waves. In other words, when we meditate regularly our everyday wandering, anxious, and fearful, all about— "me" mind, which the neuroscientists say is our neural brain default mode network (or DMN), slowly gets deactivated. Flooding our brain with the merged alpha/beta waves clears away the "noise of the depressive past and the anxious future" and creates a state of *present moment awareness*—our *natural state of being*.[225] Eventually, our old DMN is cleared away, and this natural state becomes our *new default mode of operation*.

When this stage is reached, the merged alpha/beta waves are harmonized and in sync with each other and become coherent. In quantum physics terms, the energies of the two different waves have become entangled. The merged waves spread across the rational left and the intuitive right brain hemispheres creating what is known as *horizontal synchronization*. "This increased coordination of the activity of the two sides of the brain, with their known separate functions, may account for the greater creativity observed in meditators in a number of psychological tests."[226]

Meditation has a profound impact on the brain. Not only does it synchronize the two brain hemispheres, but it also integrates all the sub-brains to make the whole brain coherent—optimized and high functioning. And in the process of integration, meditation actually changes the brain's physical structure—the brain cells and their connections. What is truly amazing is that this happens very quickly with just a few weeks of daily practice. Brain imaging techniques have revealed that doing eight weeks of Mindfulness Based Stress Reduction (MBSR) program will actually shrink the amygdala, the old area in the brain that is triggered when we are stressed. At the same time, meditation will increase the thickness of our prefrontal cortex, which, as we saw in chapter 13, is responsible for higher cognitive functions, such as self-control, creativity, awareness, and communication.[227]

The prefrontal cortex/amygdala connection is important because the amygdala responds to fear and emotions. When we are in a survival mindset, that of constant anxiety, fear, and perceived threats, we over activate the amygdala—which then becomes a problem. As we saw in chapter 9, an overactive

Chapter 25 The Science and the Power of Meditation

amygdala overwhelms the prefrontal cortex and hijacks our self-control and thinking process.[228] And, so, meditation works to shrink the amygdala making it less sensitive to *perceived* threats. So doing more meditation results in a better, more structured brain, with more stable prefrontal connections to our sub-brains creating what is known as *vertical integration*. As Lynne McTaggart of the Intention Experiment found, "the effects of meditation definitely were 'dose-dependent': increases in cortical thickness were proportional to the overall amount of time the participant had spent meditating."[229]

It is interesting to point out that there are other ways to thicken the prefrontal cortex, but you do not derive the same calming benefits as with meditation. Playing video games or juggling for example, which require intense focus and concentration, will thicken the prefrontal cortex by making and intensifying connections between brain cells—but the fear, the anxiety and the voice in the head are still there, only being masked by the intense focus on the challenging task at hand. It is only through meditation and the weakening or decoupling of the connections between the conscious brain and the stress center (amygdala) that the mind chatter will start to fade. That is when you begin to feel meditation's calming effects on the brain.[230] It is this decoupling that is able to shift us out of the survival mindset.

When we meditate, we also become more sensitive and aware of our intuition or what is commonly called our "gut instinct." As you may recall, our gut instinct is activated through our primitive, limbic sub-brain. When our left and right brain hemispheres are working in sync (through horizontal synchronization), the information that they process is more integrated, and therefore, more understandable. For example, a vague gut feeling (before horizontal synchronization) now becomes a clear and understandable gut feeling because the mind has become calm, clear and alert. That's because the gut feeling that would normally be felt just by our emotional/intuitive right brain is now felt, and better rationalized, by our horizontally integrated left-brain hemisphere. Thus, the brain now comes into balance with the horizontal synchronization of the left and right brain hemispheres, and the vertical integration between the prefrontal cortex and the limbic sub-brain below. And so as Lynne McTaggart, author of *Intention Experiment: Using Your Thoughts to Change Your Life and the World*, puts it, there is "evidence of activation of the limbic brain—the primitive, so-called" instinctive" part of the brain involved with primitive emotion. Meditation appears to affect not only the brain's reasonable, analytical "upstairs" but also the unconscious and intuitive "downstairs."[231]

Meditation, through horizontal synchronization and vertical integration, also restores the mind-body connection that many of us have lost. It makes thought and action coherent. In other words, it synchronizes what you are thinking and what you are doing. The alpha brain waves which spread from the right to the left hemisphere also start to spread from the back of the brain (where the sensory centers are located) to the prefrontal cortex in the front of the brain. This spreading of the alpha waves results, "in heightened mind-body coordination and a greater integration of thought and actions."[232]

This spreading of the alpha brain waves across the whole of the brain—from ear to ear and from back to front at the same time—is called "alpha coherence"[233] and "is an indication of moments of transcendence or pure consciousness."[234] This state is our natural state of being—the state of the *"awake brain on idle, the cells firing in unison"* as we saw in the tool for the journey section on relaxation. In this state, the mind is calm and alert, and the body is completely relaxed. The left and right hemispheres are in sync, the prefrontal cortex is engaged, and the sub-brains are aligned. The whole brain is integrated and coherent—optimized

Chapter 25 The Science and the Power of Meditation

and high functioning. At this point, the "perceptual and psychological barrier"[235] between ourselves and our environment has been lowered—in other words, our ego's hold on us loosens, our consciousness expands, and we start to feel one with our environment. Another way of looking at the world emerges as the "filter" of the ego drops away, and we are left with our natural state of being. We start to lose track of time. There is a sense of calmness and silence on a background of deep stillness or awareness. This feeling permeates and affects the whole brain.

Usually, we can focus on either the external world (on things out there) or on our inner world of thoughts and emotions—but not both. Very few people can focus on both at the same time. As we saw above, when we transcend, we become one with our environment. Then there is no separation between inner or outer worlds—*it is simply just awareness.* This state is not just a temporary feeling that lasts only during the meditation practice. With continued practice, it becomes part of our everyday living.

The state of transcendence or pure consciousness is what quantum physicists call the *non-local consciousness*. As we saw in the meditation experiment in chapter 21, this is the state that both the meditators had to get to in order for them to be able to communicate with each other. This state is common and available to all human beings. It is a state where we are interconnected with everyone. This way of being is in contrast to our personalized ego state of everyday consciousness where we are essentially isolated from everyone else.

Studies have shown that for non-meditators, this state of alpha coherence occurs "only partially... and only for very brief periods of time"[236] during the normal course of their day. As we saw in chapter 23, we encounter fleeting moments of sanity, joy, and clarity when our prefrontal cortex is engaged, and we are not preoccupied with our worries. However, with just two months of meditation, the brain wave coherence of a novice is similar to that of a person who has been meditating for a long time. In fact, you can change the brain with just eleven hours of meditation.[237] The difference is that a novice meditator cannot sustain brain coherence outside of the meditation session. A long-term meditator's brain-wave coherence can persist throughout the day while that person is engaged in other activities.[238] The calm and alert state has stabilized and becomes his/her default state of mind.

The fact that our natural state of being, stabilizes and becomes our default state with continued practice, is also confirmed by a study of long-term meditators who had practiced mindfulness meditation for 40,000 hours. In fact, brain scans done on these long-term meditators revealed no difference between their resting or normal brain and the brains of people when they were meditating. "At this level of expertise, the prefrontal cortex is no longer bigger than expected. In fact, its size and activity start to decrease again... it's as if that way of thinking has become the default... it is automatic—it doesn't require any concentration."[239]

Meditation and Aging

As we saw in chapter 13, the frontal lobes are the last to develop and the first to degenerate in our later years especially if we have been under chronic stress. A number of studies, examining the link between age and cerebral gray matter, have found that the brains of people who meditate grow bigger and show fewer effects of aging than those who don't. The increase in the thickness of the "parts of the brain that deal with attention and processing sensory input... [was] more pronounced in older than in younger people. That's intriguing because those sections of the human cortex, or thinking cap, normally get thinner as we age... meditation practice can promote cortical plasticity in adults

Chapter 25 The Science and the Power of Meditation

in areas important for cognitive and emotional processing and well-being."[240]

Meditation and Gene Activity

Not only does meditation change our brains on a physical level, but it even affects us at a molecular level—in our very "genes." Biologically speaking, our genes are inherited from our parents. The combination of genes from each parent determines our physical and psychological makeup (height, hair, color, intelligence, personality, etc.,). Genes are contained in protein structures called DNA (deoxyribonucleic acid), and strands of DNA make up the 23 chromosomes found in the nucleus of our cells. It was once thought that our genes were fixed and could not be changed. The ability to change our genes (through meditation) is a significant discovery. Up to the last two to three decades, conventional wisdom said that the genes we were born with would determine our outcome in life. What we are now saying is that meditation has the power to change the expression of genes (turning our genes on or off to change how they function). In other words, *our mind controls our destiny, not our genes!* The impact of our experiences and our lifestyle on gene expression is what the new science of *behavioral epigenetics* is all about. The literal translation of epigenetics means "above or on top of genetics." And **so it is our life** experiences (which is outside of our genes) that determines how our genes are expressed. As Bruce Lipton, cell biologist, says, "The mission of behavioral epigenetic scientist is nothing less to than to figure out how nurture shapes nature. Here, nature refers to gene-controlled characteristics, and nurture refers to the influence of a wide range of life experiences, from social interactions to nutrition to a positive mental attitude."[241]

Studies have shown that meditation slows the wearing down of the telomeres (end caps that protect our chromosomes after cell division) by boosting the production of telomerase (an enzyme which protects and increases the telomere length). This is because meditation eliminates stress by changing how we perceive the world. A positive outlook and way of life lengthen the telomeres while a negative outlook, one laden with anxiety and fear (or stress), wears them down. Prematurely worn telomeres impede cell division and eventually result in cell necrosis (death). They make us age faster and are also associated with many diseases such as heart attacks, hypertension, and dementia. In fact, these studies also found that long-term meditators had longer telomeres than people who didn't meditate.[242]

But you don't have to be a long-term meditator to slow the aging process and lengthen life. Studies have also shown that "even beginners can start protecting their telomeres from the ravages of time and cell division... just 15 minutes' meditation in novices had immediate effects on the expression of many genes, for example increasing the activity of the gene that makes telomerase and reducing the activity of genes involved in inflammatory and stress responses. It's amazing what sitting still with your eyes closed and focusing on your breath can do for your cells."[243]

Studies have also shown that inexperienced meditators can benefit from their very first session, but they need to keep practicing for the changes to accrue and become permanent.[244] As Deepak Chopra, author and speaker, says, "The reason that eight weeks [of meditation] is enough to cause significant changes in the brain is that the underlying circuitry [mind-body connection] that connects mind, genes, and brain operates every second of our lives."[245]

Chapter 25 The Science and the Power of Meditation

Meditation for Anxiety, Depression and Pain

A study done by researchers at John Hopkins University School of Medicine found that the relief provided by thirty minutes of daily mindfulness meditation was comparable to taking antidepressants to alleviate the symptoms of stress, pain, and even depression. Madhav Goyal, the leader of the study, says, "A lot of people have this idea that meditation means sitting down and doing nothing... But that's not true. Meditation is an active training of the mind to increase awareness, and different meditation programs approach this in different ways."[246]

Meditation and the Higher States of Consciousness

As the process of meditation transforms our brains through integration and coherence, and we begin to function from our natural state of being, we have the ability to access, and experience, even higher states of consciousness and perception. But we have to maintain the practice. As we saw above, all the brain waves are simply the superposition of various conscious states, and so the long-term meditators are able to collapse the brain waves of higher states as they progress in their meditation. These higher states of consciousness continuously refine and expand our awareness even when we are not meditating. "Altered physical brain structures allow advanced meditators to experience novel states of consciousness... [They] often report greater feelings of equanimity, patience, and compassion for others—even at times when they're not meditating."[247]

As we saw in the tool for the journey on brainwaves, the normal range of brain wave activity and states of consciousness that most people experience ranges, from delta waves (below 4 Hz—subconscious sleep) to beta waves (50.0Hz—waking consciousness). But the brain wave frequencies of these higher states of consciousness (experienced by long-term meditators) range from very high frequency gamma waves (50 to 100 Hz), even higher frequency lambda waves (100 to 200 Hz) and extremely low frequency epsilon waves (below 0.5 Hz—which are even slower than the delta waves).

In other words, when experienced meditators are operating with this kind of gamma electrical activity in the brain, they are processing information at 80 to 100Hz. This processing speed is two to four times faster than what most of us can do operating from our everyday conscious beta brain frequencies (of between 20-30 Hz).[248] These gamma waves are moving extremely fast—moving from the back of our brain to the front, and from side to side. They cover the whole brain and create what is called *gamma synchrony*. Gamma synchrony is different from the alpha coherence that we saw earlier. Whereas alpha coherence creates a *calm and alert state*, gamma synchrony creates a *calm and intensely focused state,* like when you are in the state of flow. "Gamma synchrony—not relaxation but an intense though serene attention or calm and intense focus... super attentive to whatever it is focused on in that moment of time... [creates an] increase in contentment, bliss, and happiness."[249] With this kind of heightened awareness, long-term meditators feel blessed and are in a constant state of flow. They are creative, happy and perceive the world very differently from everyone else. This state is their enhanced state of being.

In fact, brain scans of monks who were long-term meditators found interesting results. Neuroscientist Richard Davidson did brain scans on famed Buddhist monk Matthieu Ricard (a.k.a. happiest man on earth). He found that, during meditation, Mr. Ricard produced "levels of gamma waves never reported before... the scans also showed excessive activity in his brain's left prefrontal cortex compared to its right counterpart, giving him an abnormally large capacity for happiness and a reduced propensity towards negativity."[250] Davidson found the brains of the monks had structurally changed to "tune into happiness most of the time." He even found that the brains of inexperienced meditators "showed increased activation of the "'happy-thoughts' part of the brain"[251] in as little as eight weeks of mindfulness meditation.

Chapter 26

Witnessing Meditation—At a Distance and Without Entanglement

"Since 95 percent of our behavior is controlled by our subconscious autopilots, not our conscious minds, by definition our lives are physical printouts of the behaviors programmed in our subconscious minds."[252]

Bruce Lipton

The above statement begs the question—how do we undo our subconscious programming that has a certain way of perceiving the world, a certain mindset that controls our actions and behaviors? Before we can undo anything, we have to become aware of how we are living right now. We need to observe, to be mindful of our behaviors and habits. In other words, we need to create a "habit of mindfulness."

As we saw in chapter 24, to be mindful is to be aware of everything that is happening in this very moment, without judgment. In other words, mindfulness is to be aware, to notice, to pay attention moment-by-moment. This way of perceiving is how our true nature observes life. We are not accustomed to paying attention to the present moment, but we need to bring this moment-by-moment awareness to everything that we do. Our mind is perpetually distracted and hardly ever pays attention to what is going on in the here and now. To complicate matters further, our wired world and our always-on portable devices have made the problem even worse. As we saw in the introduction, whatever little attention we can muster is being frittered away by touching, swiping, and tapping on our smartphones two or three times every minute.

And so, we have to learn to control our attention, both in terms of focus and duration. We can do this by practicing formal sitting meditation. This form of practice is useful in developing and training our attention, and then bringing what we have learned to our everyday activities. Initially, it will be difficult to be mindful in our daily lives, because we will not be able to sustain focused attention on anything. However, our power of attention will increase as we keep up the practice of formal sit-down meditation. With continuous training, our attention will expand into awareness, and we will be able to stay focused for longer periods of time. Eventually, a time will come when mindfulness becomes our way of life, our very being.

We will use two different kinds of meditations for our formal sit-down practice—concentration meditation and witnessing meditation. They are used to train our attention and to slow the stream of thoughts down so that it can be observed. In terms of

Chapter 26 Witnessing Meditation

brain science, we are making use of both sides of our brain—the left hemisphere for training our attention and the right hemisphere for observing the mind. Sometimes we try to stop our thoughts by sheer will alone. But this approach seldom works because the harder that we try, the more anxious our mind becomes. A restless chattering mind is one of the characteristics of the ego, and so the ego will resist our attempts to quiet the mind. The only solution for a noisy mind results when we (learn how to) observe it. Our ego doesn't like the attention, because once understood it loses its power and resistance.

Why does meditation work? And what is the difference between concentration and witnessing meditations? Science provides answers to both of these questions.[253]

Meditation works because the *uncertainty principle* of quantum physics states that different physical qualities of an object can never be measured accurately at the same time. That's because when we measure one of the characteristics, the other attributes are affected by our measurement. For example, if we observe an object in motion, we can pay attention to either its content or its direction of travel, but not on both at the same time.

Concentration and witnessing meditations are akin to the analogy of seeing the trees among the forest (or vice versa), where concentration meditation is a granular focus on the "tree" and witnessing meditation is broad picture focus on the "forest."

In concentration meditation, the object of our focus can be our breath, a candle flame, or a mantra. We will use the breath because we have already done some work on it earlier (see the tool for the journey 2). And so, using the uncertainty principle, we pay attention on our breath and not worry about how fast or slow we are breathing.

Concentration is a function of our rational, logical thinking mind. It requires effort, but it is not the effort of tensing or forcing the mind to do something. It is the gentle and natural effort of attention. As we continue to focus on the breath, we notice that the breath starts to slow down. Concurrently, the thoughts begin to slow down as well. We are becoming present-centered and, in the process, we are better able to focus our attention for long periods of time.

The uncertainty principle also holds true for our thoughts. We can observe either the details of thoughts or their flow, but not both.[254] And so, in witnessing meditation, we observe, become aware of, and flow with our thoughts (i.e., forest) but not get caught up in the details of the individual thoughts (i.e., trees). Witnessing meditation is a non-doing activity. Awareness is who we are in essence and becomes available to us when we access our intuitive mind. Not doing anything does not mean we are not doing anything.[255] We are not striving for any particular thing, and so there is no effort exerted. It is being aware of what is happening in our minds and bodies as we relax into ourselves. We are being mindful, alert and aware moment-by-moment. Just like in chapter 24, where we became aware of our steps on our ascent up the mountain, we now become aware of our thoughts inside our brain.

And so, we direct the power of concentration and present-centeredness, to observe the thoughts and penetrate deeper into our mind. This process will help us to break through past patterns of programming and conditioning, in order to get reacquainted with and to rediscover our true self and state of being.

Chapter 26 Witnessing Meditation

Practice

"It is a mistake to think that the sadhana [meditation] cannot be practiced for lack of time. The real cause is agitation of mind."[256]
                    Swami Brahmananda, (1863-1922), Indian mystic

It doesn't take very much effort or time to establish a meditation practice. Here are some simple steps to follow to start practicing sitting meditation.

1. Keep a Regular Schedule: Establish a regular schedule for your meditation practice. The best times to access our subconscious mind and overwrite our past programming are in the mornings when we wake up and, in the evenings, before we go to bed. As we saw in chapter 3 and tool for journey 3 on understanding the brain waves, the half-awake transition state is when the conscious mind has not taken hold yet in the morning after we wake up. This state is where the calm and relaxed theta and alpha waves of the subconscious mind dominate. The half-asleep transition state is when the conscious mind is winding down to get ready for sleep, and we transition into the relaxed alpha/theta subconscious state.

2. Determine How Long You Will Meditate: If you have been practicing conscious breathing and relaxation as we talked about in the tools for the journey, you will have no problem sitting for twenty minutes or more. You can increase this time to forty or forty-five minutes over several weeks as you become comfortable with the meditation process. You can even meditate more than once a day. However, if you are just beginning the practice, start with a five to ten-minute sitting once a day until you get accustomed to sitting quietly for this period of time. After three to four weeks of practice increase the time to twenty, and then to thirty minutes. The whole point is to make this period of meditation a priority—to make it a part of your life. It is interesting to note that

once the benefits of meditation start filtering into your daily life, you will be hooked and it will become a priority for you.

3. Don't Worry About Postures: If you can't sit on the floor, then sit with a straight spine on a chair. The whole idea is that you are comfortable and don't fall asleep while you are beginning to relax. And even if you do fall asleep, it is okay. Don't give yourself a hard time for falling asleep. Find a quiet place where you can be alone and won't be disturbed. A darkened room will help. Try to use the same place every day.

4. Do, Don't Think: *Do* the meditation, but don't *think* about the process or the outcome. In other words, don't have any expectations about achieving a specific end result but be an active participant in the meditation. Also, don't try and take charge of the process. Let it unfold naturally. Meditation is not something you set out to get—like making it to a goal or an achievement. It is something that *happens to us* and is a process of rediscovering our true nature. It is being aware. If you are focused on the result, nothing will happen because you will stay with the mind chatter on the surface of the mind. Just remain aware as consciousness unfolds. Each session will be different.

Sometimes focusing on the breath or the thoughts will be easy and on other occasions, the mind will not settle, no matter what we do. This is the nature of our mind. When this happens, we may think that the meditation is not doing anything, or that we are not doing the practice correctly. We may even get to the point of giving up for the lack of results. But if you recall, in the process of inner creativity (chapter 23), there is a time to practice and a time for incubation—to assimilate the changes that are happening in our brain and getting ready for more changes and insights. Also, as we saw in chapter 25, new neural networks start to replace the old ones, and the brain

Chapter 26 Witnessing Meditation

begins to undergo structural and functional changes. Some of these changes are seen in as little as eleven hours of practice—that is just thirty minutes of meditation a day for twenty-one days.

And as we also saw in chapter 25, the changes in the brain are dose-dependent, meaning that the extent of the changes are proportional to how much we practice. Meditation is a gradual process, so be patient and enjoy the journey!

Concentration meditation is the first step to building and strengthening attention. Once mastered, we move to witnessing meditation, which uses the strength of attention to expand into awareness—our natural state of being.

Concentration Meditation—Conscious Breathing

Sit comfortably, close your eyes, breathe through your nose and become aware of your breath. Breathe naturally. After a few minutes, focus your attention on the tip of your nose, noticing the breath as it gently flows in and out through your nostrils. Usually, when we first do the practice, there will be a tendency to control the breathing when we become aware of it. Don't. Keep breathing naturally, maintaining your attention on your breath. Don't worry that your breath is short or deep or it should be of a specific duration. Just watch the breath calmly.

At the beginning of the practice, your breathing is usually fast and shallow because your mind is active. As we saw in chapter 21, one of the most important principles of quantum physics is the "observer effect"—*whatever you observe, or pay attention to, will change*. This principle applies to everything including our breath and our thoughts. For example, when we start to pay attention to our breath, it starts to change—the breaths become slower and deeper. And the mind begins to calm down, and we begin to relax. That's why we don't need to try and control the breath and make it slower or force the thoughts to slow down—both these things will happen automatically, as we keep paying attention to the breath. If your mind wanders, you have lost your focus on your breath. When you notice your attention wandering to your thoughts, don't try and stop them. Rather, simply bring your attention calmly back to your breath. *Your conscious breathing then becomes your anchor.* Each time that you bring back your mind to your breath, your attention gets stronger. Your mind is becoming more stable, and your awareness expands.

After a period of time (and this will depend on the individual), you'll begin to notice that your breathing becomes so refined and subtle that you may even think that you are not breathing. Don't panic. When you need air, you will breathe. Again, don't worry if your focus is lost because your breathing has become too subtle. Just become more mindful, and you will notice the breath again. The more refined your breath gets (through observation), the more refined your awareness becomes. You begin to experience deep relaxation, and you feel calm and blissful. At this point, you are becoming more present and centered in the moment. Practice twenty minutes a day for a couple of months or until you get to the point where you can maintain your focus on your breath continuously for fifteen to twenty minutes. This is where you want to be. As well, continue to be mindful of your breath throughout the day whatever you are doing.

Now that your breathing is slower, your mind is calmer, your attention is stable, and your thoughts have slowed down, we can begin witnessing meditation.

Chapter 26 Witnessing Meditation

Witnessing Meditation
"The beginning of personal transformation is absurdly easy. We only have to pay attention to the flow of attention itself."[257]

Marilyn Ferguson

Becoming aware of the flow of attention is what witnessing meditation is all about. To begin the process, gently shift your awareness from your breath to your thought process. Thinking thoughts and being aware of thoughts are two different things. In thinking, you are completely involved with the process. Your attention or awareness is tied up with the thoughts. And the chain of thoughts seems to be continuous—one thought after another.

Being aware of the thoughts means being mindful of the thoughts. When you are aware, you step back and watch the thoughts completely detached from them. This kind of observing does not draw you into the thoughts—it is witnessing them from a distance.

Witnessing meditation is all-encompassing.[258] It includes awareness of:

- Our thoughts (the object of our attention);
- Our focus and the power of our concentration (as we direct it toward our thoughts);
- The present-moment centeredness that we developed in the conscious breathing meditation;
- Any distractions around us;
- The loss of our attention and the wandering of our mind.

In other words, our awareness has the ability to be *aware of itself*. You may not be able to be aware of all these things right away when you start your meditation, but with practice, your awareness will expand and become all-inclusive.

In the early stages of the meditation, just become familiar and reacquainted with what is going on in your head—your inner world of thoughts, ideas, mental concepts, beliefs, and emotions. Watch the thoughts as they go across the screen of your mind from *a distance without entanglements.* As these mental formations come and go, follow them without getting trapped in them—just be aware of them and let them go. What this means is that you observe your thoughts without any judgment, reaction, or identification with them in any way. Become an impartial witness to the perpetual chatter in your head. Awareness can then take us deeper into the mind because it does not get bogged down with the details of the thoughts. There is a certain peace and calmness to the process.

Concentration and witnessing meditations work hand-in-hand. If you find that the mind is becoming restless and you are losing awareness, go back to conscious breathing until the mind settles down. Your breath is your anchor, come back to it whenever you need it. Then return to observing your thoughts. This is how the two meditations work together—they support and build upon one another. In the process, we become more present and are able to hold our attention for longer periods of time.

As you continue to watch your thoughts, you will notice a number of things. You will see there are two kinds of thoughts—factual thoughts and worry thoughts. Factual thoughts are reminders of things that need to be done, and of course, you know what worry thoughts are—things that have already happened in the past or might happen in the future.

You'll notice certain patterns in your thinking. The same thoughts may loop around in different combinations as if they are trying to draw your attention. It's as if your mind wants to see which combination of thoughts will grab your attention and initiate a response. You will find that over ninety percent of the thoughts that come to your mind are "recycled." They are the same thoughts you thought the day before. It is not that you continuously think of the same thoughts over and over again. It's

Chapter 26 Witnessing Meditation

that these thoughts never really leave your mind. They are always there in one form or another.

Up to now, you may have assumed that you as the observer and your thoughts, were the same thing—and that you had no control over your thoughts. Now, as you watch your thoughts, you might notice a distinction between you as the observer and the thoughts being observed. This awareness is the beginning of the separation between you the observer, and your thoughts. You start to realize that thoughts are just mental concepts that you create, and you can make them come and go—but you as the observer are always present and aware. You begin to understand that *you are not your thoughts. You are the controller of your thoughts—thoughts do not control you.* There is a distance between you and your thoughts. It feels as though your thoughts are on a movie screen in front of you, and you are observing from the back row of the movie theater. Just as we get drawn into the story unfolding on the screen, we get drawn into the drama of the stories unfolding in our mind.

Once you understand how your thoughts work, you begin to understand how they create our survival mentality. You realize that the voice in the head is nothing more than just thoughts running amok! In a movie theater, if you don't like the movie, you can get up and leave at any point... because you always know that it is just a movie. In the same way, you have the power to engage, or not engage, with the thoughts passing across the screen of your mind. If you happen to engage or pay attention to any one thought, it will drag you into its grasp and personal drama. *So the choice is yours—choose which thoughts to engage in and which thoughts to avoid.*

The *observer effect* also applies to our thoughts. You will notice that with our continued attention to our thoughts, the stream of thought generation and flow starts to slow down. You will also see that the thoughts are not continuous. Each thought is separate, with a beginning and an end—one thought comes to an end, another thought starts. After a while, you will begin to notice a gap developing between the end of one thought and the beginning of the next thought. The gap is a space in which there is *silence* or *pure awareness*. This awareness is our natural state of being. It is our ground state (the background), on which thoughts appear, much like the analogy of the clouds appearing on a canvass of blue sky in chapter 28. And just as more blue is revealed when the clouds become fewer or smaller, thoughts, when they subside, reveal more and more of our true nature or state of being. These gaps of silence are the "touchpoints of sanity" that we discussed earlier. The difference now is that we are consciously creating them by observing our mind through meditation.

The observance of gaps between thoughts is your first indication of, or encounter with, your natural state of being. *This encounter is the beginning of the transformation.* Even though a gap is just a glimpse or feeling of your true self, it will be enough—that is the beginning of your reconnection to your true self. This small glimpse will change you because, for the first time, you will come to know that there is something in you beyond the ego identity that you have been displaying to the world. The shell of the ego is finally beginning to crack.

If you direct your attention to the gap between thoughts, you will notice that you lose the gap as soon as the next thought moves in. If you don't pay attention to this next thought, it fizzles away, and then the gap starts to widen. Often, we are so excited that there is a gap between our thoughts that we immediately verbalize that excitement and say to ourselves, "Wow... the thoughts have stopped," or "There is emptiness." This verbalization restarts the thinking process (and thought generation) just when we are trying to slow down our thoughts. So try to avoid the urge to verbalize. And even if you do

Chapter 26 Witnessing Meditation

verbalize, it is okay. Have patience. After some practice, you will be able to stay with the feeling of emptiness (pure awareness), without thinking any thoughts. The key is *not to desire the gap*, but rather to *just keep directing your attention to that gap*.

Thoughts will start to lessen in frequency and duration until only one or two thoughts go through the mind. A time comes when there are no thoughts, and you are completely aware—this is our natural state of being.

You have now made the quantum leap of the *aha! moment* we talked about in chapter 25. You are going from your everyday ego (your secondary awareness) to your true nature (primary or pure awareness). In other words, you have transcended the ego. The function of meditation is to facilitate this quantum leaping—breaking through the ego identity. As Amit Goswami says, "What you meditate upon is the jump from being "here" in the manifest awareness [ego consciousness] to being "there" in the gaps [original consciousness or pure awareness]."[259]

Chapter 27

Self-Inquiry Meditation—The Undoing of our Personality

"The mind is a wondrous power residing in the Self. It causes all thoughts to arise. Apart from thoughts, there is no such thing as mind. Therefore, thought is the nature of mind. Apart from thoughts, there is no independent entity called the world. In deep sleep there are no thoughts, and there is no world. In the states of waking and dream, there are thoughts, and there is a world also... Just as the spider emits the thread (of the web) out of itself and again withdraws it into itself, likewise the mind projects the world out of itself and again resolves it into itself. When the mind leaves the Self, the world appears. Therefore, when the world appears, the Self does not appear; and when the Self appears (shines) the world does not appear."[260]

Sri Ramana Maharshi, (1879-1950,) Indian mystic

When my daughter Faheema was young, she came to me for help with her class assignment. The assignment question was, "Who am I?" She had to write on a flip chart all the things that defined her. So in the center of the paper, she wrote her name and drew a circle around it with arrows emanating from the center going in all directions. At the end of the arrows, she wrote down everything she could think of about herself—I am a girl, I am a daughter, I am a student, I am a violinist, I am creative, and so on.

Everything she wrote down, including her name, had been given to her by us or others (actually downloaded as her programming because she had no control over it) or resulted from external relationships. All these things that defined her were just labels or mental concepts. In other words, virtual without any reality and built on the foundation of the first conscious "I" thought. This first thought is exactly how our personality (ego) gets its start. As we saw in chapter 3, without this first "I" thought, the other thoughts cannot exist, because, for the ego, everything exists in relation to itself. The ego then becomes our internal reference point or the "I" that we think we are, and everything, according to the ego, revolves around itself. It then talks to itself (remember the voice in the head?) and says, "I want," "I think," "I act," "I like," "I don't like," and so on. This "I-thought" always seems to be there, and so we think it is our permanent state of mind. My daughter, who was seven or eight years old at that time, had enough labels to cover most of the large sheet of paper. If I asked her now, I am sure she would be able to complete many more pages.

The school assignment demonstrates two things—how our ego (our self-image and personality) comes into being, and why many of us mistakenly assume that this ego-self is our true nature (or "I").

Chapter 27 Self-Inquiry Meditation

As we saw in chapter 2, there is a difference between the "I" that we *think* we are and the "I" that we *actually* are. The everyday conditioned ego consciousness is who we think we are. It's made up of "I am this" or "I am that" patterns of identifications, associations, and beliefs that we have accumulated over the course of our lives. The ego, in itself, is not bad. It serves an administrative purpose in our day-to-day activities. It is when the ego takes over and runs our lives with its conditioned way of doing and behaving, that it causes so much grief and pain and, in the process, moves us away from the true self that we are.

The "I" that we actually are is the original consciousness that we are born with, and as we saw in the last chapter, this original consciousness can be experienced in the gap between two thoughts. When we are in this state, our internal reference point is our consciousness or our true nature. It is unconditioned and is always aware and creative. This awareness is where we see things as they are... there is no duality. It is just "I am." It is the background (our ground state) on which our everyday ego consciousness sets up shop. So the ego is a creation of this original consciousness and constricts our awareness altering what we observe through the thought forms.

And so, how can we know that our everyday ego consciousness is not our real self, and once we know, how can we then shift our awareness away from the ego and reclaim our true self?

The Indian sage Ramana Maharshi used to give his disciples the question, "Who am I?" as a meditation.[261] The purpose of this self-inquiry was to gain direct knowledge of our true nature. The meditation targets the first "I-thought," the very foundation of the ego. It shows that this "I-thought" has been propped up by its identifications and associations, and has no independent or separate existence.

By questioning the thoughts, the self-inquiry method isolates the "I-thought" from its identifications. Without its identifications, the ego collapses and ceases to exist as we know it. In other words, to find ourselves (our true nature), we have to destroy our false-self first. This ending of the ego's hold on us is what the mystics and spiritual teachers mean when they say, *"to die before you die."* It is not the physical death that they are talking about but rather the death of the ego. Only after the death of the ego is our true self revealed.

Compared to the witnessing meditation technique we discussed in the last chapter, the self-inquiry method is more difficult because there is no object to focus on (breath, thoughts, etc.). In self-inquiry, we focus on the sense (or feeling) of "I." It is a more direct and effective technique to go beyond the ego. Unlike in the witnessing meditation where we watched as the thoughts began to slow down and gaps of consciousness appeared between the thoughts, in the self-inquiry method, we go after the source of the ego itself—the first "I-thought."

Practice

I recommend that you start this meditation with the conscious breath technique discussed in the last chapter to help you maintain your focus on the sense/feeling of the "I." Practice regularly for twenty to thirty minutes and extend the time when you become comfortable. This self-inquiry meditation can also be done while you are going about your daily activities.

Using conscious breathing, bring yourself to the present moment awareness. Now you are ready for the self-inquiry meditation. Focus your attention on the concept or the idea of "I." Don't think of the "I" but try and feel it. Initially, this may be difficult, but with some practice, it will become easier, and you will be able to feel the "I." If you are still having difficulty maintaining your focus, go back to the conscious breathing

Chapter 27 Self-Inquiry Meditation

meditation. Once you are able to hold your attention for ten to fifteen minutes, come back to do the meditation. Then, with complete attention, silently ask the question "Who am I?" and let go. Don't wait for or expect any answers.

Be careful that you don't make the "Who am I?" question into a mantra that you keep repeating all the time because then the self-inquiry becomes an intellectual exercise. And the response to the question "Who am I?" is definitely not intellectual.

As we saw in chapter 3, the ego, resides in the rational mind and is itself a collection of all its identifications. When we keep asking the question, "Who am I?" it is the rational mind that is asking the question. The ego then supplies the answers—which are all its identifications. The process then becomes a game of endless mental iterations running around in a loop, and it becomes difficult to pin down the ego. In other words, we are asking the ego to eliminate itself, or using Ramana Maharshi's analogy we are asking a policeman (who is a thief) to catch the thief, who is himself.[262]

The answer to the question, "Who am I?" lies in the intuitive side of the brain, in awareness, beyond language. If you did not have a language, and if I ask you, "Who are you?" you would try to *feel* for an answer.

And so, when a thought appears, don't wait to complete the thought. Ask yourself, "Where does this come from?" "To whom did this thought occur?" And the response may be, "To me"; then ask, "Who am I?" No matter how many thoughts come, try to feel for an answer. There will not be any response because the sense of "I" that we are holding in our mind is just a thought, a mental concept, and not the real "I"—and hence, it cannot respond.

By constantly holding on to the sense or feeling of the "I-thought" and self-inquiring every time a thought comes, and getting no answer, thoughts will begin to subside (remember the principle of the observer effect?). In fact, as we continue to focus on the "I-thought," our awareness expands, and we go deeper and deeper into our own inner self. What is happening is that our continued focus on the "I-thought" does not allow the "I-thought" to connect with its identifications. And as we saw earlier, without its identifications, the I-thought cannot exist. Awareness becomes effortless because there are no identities to sustain. Maintaining our different selves or the masks we wear is hard work and requires effort (Figure 20).

The Masks we Wear

Figure 20. *The "I am this, I am that..." collection of all the identities and roles we have accumulated has become the wall of mental concepts that we have built around ourselves which needs to be dismantled. We are the center, the essence and everything else is in the periphery. But until we peel the "masks" or the "makeup" we have applied to ourselves to create our persona, we cannot know ourselves.*

And as thoughts arise and subside, because they have nothing to hold on to, our consciousness begins to shift beyond the ego,

Chapter 27 Self-Inquiry Meditation

revealing our true nature. Initially, there will just be glimpses of this state until the identifications and associations of the ego have been broken. Then our true self will stabilize and become our permanent state of being—just like in the witnessing meditation.

Sri Ramana Maharshi describes the shift of consciousness this way:

"The mind will subside only by means of the enquiry 'Who am I?' The thought 'Who am I?' destroying all other thoughts, will itself finally be destroyed... The moment you start looking for the self and go deeper and deeper, the real Self is waiting there to take you in. Then whatever is done is done by something else and you have no hand in it."[263]

Part VI
Transformation

Chapter 28

Mountain—The Summit

"As attention broadens, brain function slows down and attention flows into awareness. Completely limitless attention and awareness are one and the same... it is the background of all function."[264]
                    Jean Klein, (1912-1998), author and teacher

    The fear and uncertainty of the journey slowly dissipate as we make our way up the mountain. Our doubts vanish as we become more comfortable with the climb. It is as if we relax into ourselves. We are not anxious anymore, and we begin to trust ourselves more and more. As we climb higher, our attention, which was focused on our steps, expands. The mind chatter that was so persistent before we started the climb starts to slow down, and in some cases comes to an end. The mind becomes calm and clear. Slowly, the ego loosens its hold on us, as we see that it is not real. It is just a combination of thoughts and mental concepts of things that are real. Now the rational and the intuitive minds are both beginning to work in harmony.

All the energy that we spent on trying to defend ourselves and to maintain the ego is now freed up for improved perception and expansion of consciousness. Our senses become more acute as we awaken to our environment. The view from a higher altitude is much broader than what we would see at ground level. We see the forest from above rather than the individual trees we passed. That is how our holistic right brain sees compared to the rational mind, which focuses on the details. We realize how limiting our view was before we started our climb. And the more we are able to see, the more we know what needs to be done next. It just comes to us. Our motivation now exudes from within, rather than from the external forces which have been driving us up to now, and we start to emerge out of the survival mode of the ego.

One of the most beautiful and exhilarating parts of the climb is when we break through the cloud cover and see the majestic snow-covered mountaintop on a background of endless blue sky. It's not that there are no more clouds in the sky—there are a few, but they are floating way up over the mountain. This *breakthrough is the turning point* in the journey. We notice that the thunderstorm activity of the rainforest is now taking place below us.

The clouds and the sky is a good analogy to illustrate our dual states of consciousness (Figure 21). Just as the sky lies beyond the cloud cover, in the same way, our natural state of being lies just beyond our ego consciousness. The sky is the background upon which the clouds and other planetary objects happen and is not affected by whatever is going on. Similarly, our natural state of being is the background on which the ego-mind happens and is not affected by the turbulence of our egoic activities and life situations that play out every day.

Our Dual States of Consciousness

Figure 21. *The clouds and the sky—an analogy for our dual states of consciousness. We confuse the cloud cover of our ego conscious with the eternal sky of our natural state of being.*

Nothing affects our true self. But until we get to that state, the persistent ego tries to pull us back into the survival mode.

And so, the last stretch of the climb is extremely difficult and demanding, but we now know what we need to do to reach the top–*take one step at a time and keep focusing on the here and now.* Before we realize it, we are at the summit. The euphoria that we are expecting when we reach the top and finding our true self is not there. Compared to the journey, reaching the peak is anticlimactic, because our natural state of being that was slowly revealing itself throughout the journey, is not something new. It has always been around because we are that state, but we have forgotten it because we were overburdened with "ego stuff." However, when we awaken to this state, our life takes a dramatic turn—a completely different way of perceiving the world comes into being. The mental ego structures that we have lived with all of our lives collapse, and there is just *silence* or *pure awareness*. The dualistic, judgemental way of perceiving the world that we are all familiar with gives way to the non-dualistic, unitive perceptive... and that *opens the whole world to us*.

But most of us have enclosed ourselves in a cloud cover of the ego, never realizing that this is a temporary state of our own making and that our natural state is just around the corner. As we saw earlier, we experience this state of being many times during the day, and even if we are aware of these moments, we cannot seem to be able to sustain it. We have become too familiar with our ego and completely identified with it to break free. As I mentioned earlier, the purpose of this book is to show you how close you are to this natural state of being and what you need to do to rediscover it.

The *journey* is not complete until we return to the base of the mountain, for we cannot stay on the summit for too long. But before we begin our descent, let us see what it feels like to live in our natural state of being.

Chapter 29

The "Unconscious" Person Awakens

"I've heard people say that they cling to their painful thoughts because they're afraid that without them they wouldn't be activists for peace. "If I felt completely peaceful, "they say, "Why would I bother taking action at all?" My answer is "Because that's what love does." To think that we need sadness or outrage to motivate us to do what's right is insane. As if the clearer and happier you get, the less kind you become. As if when someone finds freedom, she just sits around all day with drool running down her chin. My experience is the opposite. Love is action. It's clear, it's kind, it's effortless, and it's irresistible."[265]

Byron Katie, author and teacher of "The Work" method of self-inquiry

What Does Living in Our Natural State of Being Feel Like?

Our life undergoes a complete transformation after transcendence as *our internal reference point shifts from our ego to our true nature. We were unconscious and asleep, and now we are awake. It is as if we are born again and have a second chance to live our life.* As Sogyal Rinpoche, the Tibetan lama who wrote *The Tibetan Book of Living and Dying* said, "[it is] a personal, utterly non-conceptual revelation of what we are, why we are here and how we should act which amounts in the end to nothing less than a new life, a new birth, almost, you could say, a resurrection."[266]

With practice, we will naturally arrive at this state. When we are living from our natural state of being, *there is no such thing as going into meditation. Our whole life actually becomes a meditation.* We watch thoughts and emotions come and go, but we don't cling to them. We let them be. We start to become detached from what is going on around us. Detachment, however, does not mean indifference, withdrawal from life, or apathy (which can be due to boredom or lack of interest). Nor does it mean to renounce or to give up on life. Detachment, in this sense, means that the environment does not affect us anymore. This way of living is very different from when we were dominated by our ego consciousness.

As we saw earlier, when we are in the ego state, we are asleep (unconscious). And because we are asleep, we are not alert, and therefore, we are affected by outer and inner influences. They control us. For example, when we think the weather is bad, we are upset. We see a beautiful car on the street, and we become envious. When a good-looking person walks by, we follow them with our eyes and mind. In essence, we are unconsciously affected by everything and every situation, resulting in a mood that is in a constant state of flux.

Once the wisdom of our true self starts to trickle into our lives, we begin to change in ways that we cannot imagine. The old

Chapter 29 The Unconscious Person Awakens

neural pathways of our conditioned brain slowly disappear. All the beliefs that we have accumulated over our lifetime (our baggage) suddenly collapse, and we realize that now we don't have any predetermined ideas, judgments, or preconceptions about anything anymore. As we saw in chapter 25, a new neural network of a new perspective and a different way of perceiving the world sets in, creating new behaviors and characteristics. Whereas before we lived in an isolated personal world with its fears, anxieties, loneliness, and defenses built by our ego (and afraid to allow anyone in), now our inner world is accessible to everyone. This natural state of being is common to all humankind... because *this is what we are in essence*.

Life becomes simple because we stop adding *layers of interpretation* to whatever we are experiencing. We just experience whatever we are experiencing as it is and in the moment. We now have a better understanding of reality. Now we are in touch with life, whereas previously we looked at life through the screen of mental preconceptions. Now we see things just as they are—the simple facts. We are no longer interested in opinions and theories. They obscure the truth because they are perceptions and guesses about what is real. It is easier to deal with a fact, than an opinion, because a fact is what it is—it is the truth, and therefore verifiable. If we build a story around a fact (and that is what most of us do—embellishing it to support our viewpoint), our attention is diverted to dealing with the story rather than looking at the fact. And as we all know, the stories in our minds have no endings.

As we awaken and as our internal frame of reference shifts from our ego consciousness to our natural state, there are no more "personal" rules, laws, beliefs, expectations, duties, or feelings of guilt to guide, motivate or influence us. In fact, we don't need them because we don't anticipate what will happen anymore—we live life as it unfolds moment-by-moment. We become comfortable with not knowing what is going to happen in the next moment, the next hour or the next day. This focus on the present doesn't mean that we don't plan for things like an appointment with the doctor. Of course, we plan for whatever we need to do, but the focus now shifts from the future to the present, to this moment. *We accept life as it is.* We don't want it to be any different than what it really is. We have completely surrendered ourselves to life. And so we look at the world as if it is new every moment. We will still face challenges, but we deal with them as they come, and we move on. Everything we do is what needs to be done at that point in time, so we carry no regrets about the decisions that we make or the outcome of events. We simply accept what happens and move forward—taking life as it comes, moment-by-moment.

With the shift in consciousness, the world feels lighter, as if a weight has been lifted from us. The emotional baggage of the ego which has weighed us down over the years is gone. There is a confidence and certainty in how we live our lives now, and it affects everything that we do. We love and appreciate everything about ourselves—this is *self-love*. We become quieter and happier, and we tend to smile and laugh a lot. Nothing people say about us (or to us) matters, and we don't waste our energy on mental gymnastics, debates, or arguments with others. When there is no mind chatter, there is no ego. There is now nothing to hold us back and to dampen our spirit. We are liberated. We are free. As an old Zen saying goes, *"no ego, no problem."* With the death of the ego, there is no fear of physical death anymore—because it is the ego that is afraid of dying. We regain our innocence and feel incredibly energized. It is fun to be alive—oh what freedom!

Where there is freedom, there is unconditional love, which wants nothing in return. There is no anger, envy, jealousy, or need in love. We don't expect and want anything from anyone, so there are no disappointments—but our love for the person is

Chapter 29 The Unconscious Person Awakens

unconditional. I have heard many people say that there is no such thing as unconditional love. And, yes, as long as we operate from our ego consciousness, there cannot be unconditional love because, as we have seen, the ego's primary concern is its own survival.

Also, when there is freedom, there is no fear. There is no dependency on anything or anyone. We become observers of life, just witnessing life as it unfolds. I am not talking about the dependence on our doctor to look after our health or the cab driver to take us somewhere. But I am talking about psychological dependence on others (sometimes called codependence or neediness)—on our spouse, our parent, our boss, and so on. This type of dependency creates bondage and fear because the dependence is then a give-and-take/reciprocal relationship, and that causes suffering.

The usual reaction against dependency is to try to become independent, but both dependence and independence are reactions to a need. When we find that we suffer because of our dependence on someone, we try to be independent from that person. And so we create a wall around ourselves. In fact, creating a wall is the ego's way of overcoming dependence. This wall hardens, and before long, we have isolated ourselves from everyone for fear of being hurt again. But unconditional love is different than this. It is true independence. Freedom and unconditional love go hand-in-hand.

Why Is It Difficult to Explain This State of Being?

"The tao that can be told is not the eternal Tao. The name that can be named is not the eternal Name."[267]

Lao-Tzu

Trying to describe what the shift in consciousness feels like is like trying to explain something intangible—for example, the transporting experience of intense, deep laughter. We can describe the experience using words, but the actual sensation is still difficult to explain. A person may understand what you are describing on an intellectual level, but they will only "get it" when they actually *experience* intense, deep laughter.

The difficulty of communicating the experience lies on four levels. First, the experience happens beyond the mind, in the world of intuition and silence, where there is no language. Second, our intellect attempts to translate this intangible experience into thoughts so that we can describe what happens in words. Most of the reality of the experience is lost when we try to explain it using words. Third, a timeless, thought-free existence is simply inconceivable to the person to whom we are describing the experience if that person has never experienced that state. Fourth, everything will be interpreted through the person's conditioning, and as such, will only be understood at a fraction of the depth and breadth of the actual experience.

Release of the Imprisoned Intellect: What Happens to Our Thinking?

"Calmness of mind does not mean you should stop your activity. Real calmness should be found in activity itself."[268]

Shunryu Suzuki

One of the fears that we may have is what might happen if our mind chatter (the voice in the head) stops and our mind is silent. Because we are so identified with our thoughts, we may feel that we are nothing without our mind chatter. Remember Rene Descartes? *(I think therefore I exist)*. What is interesting is that when our mind becomes quiet, our mind chatter disappears, but our *ability* to think does not diminish. As we saw in introduction II, this is similar to our ability to speak. If we decide to keep quiet, even for extended periods, our verbal ability is not

Chapter 29 The Unconscious Person Awakens

affected. We can speak at any time. Thinking and thoughts work the same way. There is no loss of ability—we don't lose our edge. In fact, thinking now becomes more effective because there is no constant mind chatter to distract and dilute its power and focus. The intellect is finally released from the grasp of the ego and is now in *synergistic harmony* with our intuitive mind.

The intuitive mind feels—the rational mind thinks. Thinking is good for our world of science and technology but not for personal relationships. Thinking creates distance between people, while *feeling* brings people together. Also, the intuitive right side of the brain can receive insights from the subconscious mind, but it cannot put them into words. The rational left side of the brain can express the insights in words but does not have the capability of receiving the insights. The rational mind's function is to relate to, and work with, our external world. We need an open connection between the two halves of the brain to understand, describe, and make use of the continuous stream of insights that we receive. And for this to happen, the brain has to be calm and alert—both sides in sync. That is what intelligence/wisdom is all about.

For example, we can use our intellect to write about love, and our rational mind will describe love in the most flowery ways possible. In the end, though, what it describes is still expressed as words or mental conceptions. When we inject feelings and emotions from our experience, the words start to take a life of their own. They become real—now we know what love is. When reason and emotions work together in harmony, then the result is divine. There is nothing like it! This is the intelligence/wisdom of our natural state of being (see Figure 22).

Intellect, Feelings and Intelligence

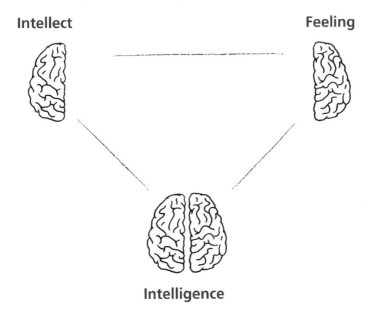

Figure 22. *Intellect is a mental faculty whose roots are shallow. It is rational, logical thought without emotions. It can be trained and sharpened. When it is combined with feelings, it becomes intelligence or wisdom. Intellect without feelings, when combined with the ego, is the cause of much of the suffering in the world.*

Let me give you another example of how the intellect and the intelligence work when we try and answer the question, "What is life?"[269]

The rational mind looks at life as a problem to be solved, just like any other problem of the external world. As we saw in Chapter 14, the rational, logical mind loves breaking things down, so it tries to solve the problem by breaking life into its components and then analyzing them. As soon as you break life down to its individual parts, life is no longer life—it is just a collection of lifeless parts. To the intellect, to understand life is just a matter of analysis and conclusions. The rational mind takes over because breaking things down and analyzing their

Chapter 29 The Unconscious Person Awakens

components is what it is used to doing. The rational mind starts to accumulate knowledge about the parts and then builds on what it finds and finally concludes that it now understands life. This way of gathering information is the method of analysis in which problems of science, engineering, business, etc., are solved. The process is systematic—in other words, the rational mind has to go step-by-step to find and discover, and then build on what it finds.

To the intuitive mind, life can only be known as a whole because the whole is much more than the sum of its parts. So the intuitive mind uses *synthesis,* rather than analysis, to understand life and finds there are no solutions or answers to the question of life. Every day is a new day. You cannot build on any experience that you may have had the previous day. You have to start over again because if you try to relive yesterday's experience, you are reliving a memory, and that memory is dead—it is gone. With the intuitive mind, you have to park all the knowledge that you have accumulated. It is as if you are starting out like a child, curious, and wanting to know and explore—everything becomes a wonder. As you explore, every new thing about life delights you, so you go deeper and deeper. In other words, you have to start with a beginner's mind. This finding and discovering without a "process" is how creativity works. The intuitive mind learns through insights (quantum leaps—or discontinuous learning). Then you use your rational mind to put these insights into forms that can be understood in the everyday world.

When We Are Awake, We Stop Judging

Beyond the mind, there is no duality because we are all one consciousness. In reality, there is nothing good or bad, right or wrong. This duality has been created by our ego and the rational mind. The ego judges and compares everything and then creates mental constructs of reality. That is its function. Good or bad is just our interpretation based on our conditioning.

And so, with the shift in consciousness, we stop judging things as good or bad. We accept people and events as they occur, and as they are. Before the shift, anybody could push our emotional buttons, and we would react mechanically and lose control. Now we don't react anymore. We will know what to say and do, and our response will be out of "awareness." We also don't react to the "faults" of others because we don't focus on their actions anymore. We "see" people from the inside, we see their true nature, and then we understand why they do what they do, why they suffer, and why they make others suffer. This does not mean that we condone their behavior, but now we understand.

Most people are basically good, but some of us have lost touch with our basic goodness. We have become "unconscious" and confused by our survival instincts and our preprogramming or conditioning. As a result, we don't know what we are doing or why we are doing what we are doing. It never occurs to us that what we are doing may be wrong. If we knew, we would not do the things we do to harm others. This is what Eckhart Tolle meant when he said, "There is only one perpetrator of evil on the planet: human unconsciousness."[270]

The Seesaw Between the Everyday Ego Consciousness and Our True Nature

"You should rather be grateful for the weeds you have in your mind, because eventually they will enrich your practice."[271]

Shunryu Suzuki

There is a tendency that when our consciousness shifts, we assume we don't need to practice anymore because we begin to notice some positive changes creeping up into our lives. The quantum jump that brought this shift in consciousness is not the end of the journey, but the beginning. Just because we have

Chapter 29 The Unconscious Person Awakens

gotten to this point does not mean that the inner revolution will continue to unfold automatically. The shift in consciousness has given us the opportunity to bring about a radical and fundamental inner transformation. But we have to sustain it with continued practice and an unwavering intention. So, don't give up on your meditation practice. Sitting meditation acts like a laboratory where we learn and practice skills such as patience, silence, attention, and awareness. We also receive insights which we can apply to our daily living.

Start paying attention to everything that you do. See your life as it unfolds moment-by-moment, and then *you are in touch with life*. All your senses are alert—you can feel it, smell it, hear it, taste it, touch it, and see it. You are then mentally ready for any situation that you encounter. As we have seen, this way of perceiving is different than seeing life through our conditioning or programming—that creates a screen. Our sitting meditation practice will also help us to be mindful during the day.

As your awareness increases, you will be able to be mindful in different situations—no matter how hectic or stressed that you feel. Slowly your natural state of being will stabilize and become permanent.

Operating from our true nature doesn't mean that life situations suddenly become easy. Life situations are what they are, but they won't affect us in the same way as they might have before. We solve problems as they come, and we move on. But we always have to be vigilant in order to make sure that the ego does not get a foothold again.

Sometimes, even though we are vigilant, the ego comes back. It starts out with a small thing, one or two innocent thoughts about something that happened, and before we know it, a cloud of somber mood descends upon us. We get caught in an old thought pattern and are drawn back into the world that we thought that we had left behind. Then we are back into the world of personal drama, and we suffer. Thoughts keep coming, and before long, they have mushroomed. Whatever we try, we cannot seem to quieten the mind—nothing seems to work. This ignoring of the first worry thoughts is what Eckhart Tolle meant when he said, "One small error, one misperception creates a world of suffering."[272]

The best thing under these circumstances is to wait it out—just surrender to what is happening and not fight it. Accept whatever is happening consciously. The ego loves to fight, but as soon as you let go, the ego loses interest and awareness returns shortly afterward. Don't be afraid if you do get caught up in the thought drama once in a while. These kinds of experiences are to learn from because once you awaken, you will never go back to your old self for long—because now you know what the natural state of being feels like. Remember to put the first innocent thought away by not feeding it with attention so that it does not mushroom into suffering!

Another thing that you can do when you get lost in thought is to bring yourself back to the present moment, by anchoring yourself to the breath (tool for the journey 2—conscious breathing). Focusing on your breath will be difficult to do as the thoughts will be highly charged and will want to pull you into their grasp. Accept what is happening and surrender to the mind chatter but keep coming back to your anchor—your breath and the present moment. Conscious breathing stops the mind—one cannot simultaneously breathe consciously and think. When your mind calms down, the right course of action is revealed. Otherwise, you are just reacting to the crisis, that will continue to smolder and occupy your mind.

Chapter 30

Mountain—The Return

"You cannot stay on the summit for ever; you have to come down again... So why bother in the first place? Just this: what is above knows what is below, but what is below does not know what is above. One climbs, one sees. One descends, one sees no longer but one has seen. There is an art to conducting oneself in the lower regions by the memory of what one saw higher up. When one can no longer see, one can at least still know."[273]

Rene Daumal, (1908-1944), author of Mount Analogue

Most people *only plan for the climb* forgetting that we have to return to the everyday world, and the return journey can be quite difficult.[274] It has its obstacles and challenges, but because we have "observed" or "seen," as René Daumal says in the above quote, the descent becomes easier to negotiate, now that we know.

Finally, *we feel comfortable in our skin*. We are integrated and in complete harmony with ourselves and with everything around us. Our masculine and feminine principles are integrated, and our "ways of knowing, sensing, thinking, feeling, intuiting have reached a balance."[275] Our mind becomes calm, and therefore clear, increasing our capacity to learn new things. This is the time when we begin to discover our true potential. Now we can be creative and design the life that we've always wanted. A life that we love, and that makes us happy, and one that will serve humanity with compassion and love. We all have this potential within us, but we've never allowed it to fully manifest because we've spent our time in the survival mode. Now life becomes easy. We always find ourselves in the right place at the right time. It is as if we are flowing *with* life, meeting everyday challenges with minimum effort. This is what it means to be in flow… where we accomplish much with minimum effort. We have truly become "a partner of creation rather than a prisoner of creation."[276] This way of living is what it means to be human.

Now we can understand the three types of forces that shape our lives—instincts, conditioning, and creativity (Figure 23).

1. Instincts: We are born with powerful instincts for survival. We react instinctively, and automatically, to whatever happens in the environment. Fear and desire drive us to satisfy our basic needs.

2. Conditioning: Our conditioning starts on the day we are born. Our caregivers and people around us, who have learned the art of survival from their parents and their experiences, provide us with a framework of beliefs, attitudes, and behaviors on how to think and behave so that we can fit into the society in which we live in. Simply put, we learn to survive.

Chapter 30 Mountain—The Return

3. Creativity: Creativity is a potential force that is within us, and one that must be awakened to move beyond the survival state.

When we are living in survival mode, we are completely focused on trying to survive. And, so, there is only struggle. We are constantly worried about, "What will happen to me?" or "How will I survive?" And, so, there is no time for play or laughter in our lives, because to us, survival is a serious business.

Forces that Shape our Lives

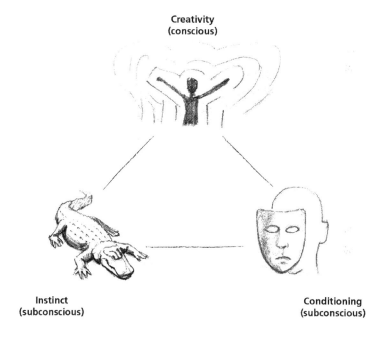

Figure 23. *Most of us only make use of our instincts and our conditioning living our lives, and so we end up reacting to our environment. The creative force is a potential force that is available to all, but we need to awaken it.*

Instinct and conditioning are subconscious forces that make us react to our environment. We don't seem to have any control over what we want to do, except, within the framework of the parameters already set for us by our conditioning. We blame the environment for all our problems, including stress, and for making us unhappy. Creativity is a conscious but latent force, the inner urge to reconnect with our true nature.

We all have a longing for something more than the life we are living, a desire for change. But, as long as we are mired in the what-about-me kind of survival thinking, we will not know how to move forward. Most of us try to use our rational mind to search for a solution, but that is wrong. Thinking will give us better ways to survive, but it will not get us out of the survival cycle. And so we become stuck, spinning our wheels.

But, as we saw in chapter 13, our destiny is not just to survive. Animals survive. We are destined to move beyond survival, to become human, and to live in creativity, our natural state of being (Figure 24). We have the capability and the capacity to transcend to our highest state, but ultimately, it depends on us—on whether we want to make the jump out of survival, or settle and be "happy" living in the survival mode.

When we were children, we were naturally creative (living in our natural state of being), but most of us lost this state of creativity as our conditioning set in. Now, we have to reawaken this third force, the force of creativity, consciously. It doesn't just happen. We do not need a manual for survival—we are born with the instincts for survival, and our caregivers gave us a framework and parameters to live within, to ensure our survival. But living in creativity requires work. The *transformation as we have seen is instantaneous, but we have to lay the groundwork to prepare for this change to unfold.* Unfortunately, for most people, this creativity is never realized again, and it stays dormant for the rest of their lives. I am talking about creative living, not creative endeavors,

Chapter 30 Mountain—The Return

like art, painting, and music. As we saw in chapter 23, many people are creative but don't necessarily know how to live a creative life.

Awakening the force of creativity sounds like something from a Star Wars movie. Actually, George Lucas, the creator of the Star Wars franchise, attributed a spiritual purpose to his movies. He was inspired by Joseph Campbell's mythology, the psychology of Freud and Jung, Zen Buddhism, and other eastern philosophies: "I put Force into the movie in order to try to awaken a certain kind of spirituality in young people—more belief in God than a belief in any particular religious system. I wanted to make it so that young people would begin to ask questions about the mystery."[277]

And, maybe the reason why his movies are so popular, apart from them being fun and exciting to watch is because in some ways they play to our inner yearning for change. But then, most of us don't pay attention to the underlying messages and look at movies as just entertainment, and promptly (or at least after a certain time) forget about them. The inkling for change (that the movies arouse), quickly dissipates, as we get reabsorbed into our busyness. Even though this inner yearning is natural to us, and wants to pull us toward self-actualization, we don't always *see* it because of our entrenched conditioning. Even if we do occasionally see it, we make half-hearted attempts to change or suppress this yearning for change because we are too busy with our day-to-day living. And so we miss the opportunity to emerge from our suffering.

Hence living in survival and living in creativity are not two separate things. They are just two sides of the same coin. How we live comes down to our mindset and what we believe about the nature of suffering.

The Evolution of "Me" (The Integrated Brain)

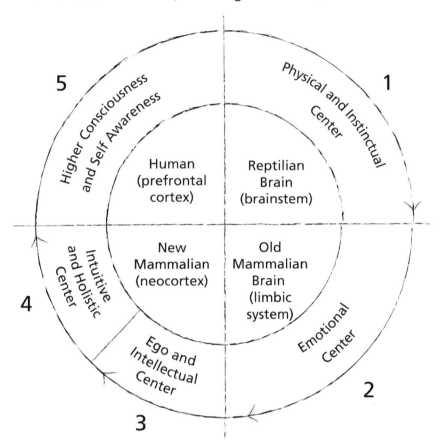

Figure 24. *Most of us find ourselves in the first three levels of inner development, with one of the stages being dominant in our lives, depending on how "conscious" we are and what situation we are facing. We have materialistic tendencies in these states of mind and live in the survival mode with our focus on the external world. Starting with level 4, our attention turns to our inner world and the fulfillment of our growth needs. We are now becoming ready for the transcendence of stage 5.*

Chapter 30 Mountain—The Return

1 Physical and Instinctual Center

It's all about "me." My primary concern is to ensure my body's survival, and so I am driven by fear and desire. I am ruthless and insensitive to the feelings of others.

2 Emotional Center

It is still all about "me," but now I am driven by my likes and dislikes. I have emotional outbursts when I am afraid, or when I don't get what I want. These emotions are out of proportion to the perceived threat. They hijack my thinking brain and downshifts me to my instinctive brain.

3 Ego and Intellectual Center

It is still all about "me," but now I use my ego to leverage my intellect in order to get what I want. Thinking predominates, and I don't have time for feelings. The voice in the head has become all powerful. The "me" now lives in the survival mode, triggered by my constant state of stress.

4 Intuitive and Holistic Center

The "me" has begun to bridge the gap between thinking and feeling. The voice in the head is getting quieter, and the "me" begins to perceive the world differently. It is still about "me," but now it is also about "you."

5 Higher Consciousness and Self Awareness

The "me" has transcended the ego. It is not about "me" or "you" anymore, but it is about us because we are one. All my sub brains have aligned and are integrated and in harmony. The "me" now operates from my natural state of being.

If we believe that we cannot do anything about suffering, then we have consciously decided to live in the survival mode. We avoid living because we fear life. It is like living in a cocoon of our habitual way of doing things and having a fear of venturing outside the walls we have built. We think that if we don't take any risks, everything will stay the same and nothing will disturb us. But *nothing in life is constant (except change itself)*, so everything affects us. As we saw in chapter 7, our responses to life's challenges are not adequate, and we become anxious and afraid—and then stress becomes our constant companion.

If, however, we believe that *only we create suffering* and *only we can eliminate it*, then we are ready for the shift to higher consciousness. We can wait for evolution to take its course, which may take a very long time, or we can evolve consciously now. To move to the next stage and realize our full potential, we have to make it happen by setting off on our own inner journey of transformation.

As we saw in chapter 21, the new science of quantum physics has shown us how we can bring about a transformation in ourselves. It has brought about a shift in the way we view the world. Quantum physics focuses on consciousness rather than matter, on the integration of the brain and creative living, rather than the materialistic world of our stress and survival. Our world is not predetermined, so we have a choice as to how we want our lives to turn out. In other words, the new science is saying that not only can we bring about a change in ourselves, but that change can happen now—at this moment—*if we want to change*. And it shows us how we can free ourselves from the cycle of suffering through quantum leaps of aha! insights, which is how the process of inner creativity works, as we saw on our journey of transformation.

And just as the guides come down the mountain summit to guide other travelers on the path to make the unfamiliar trek, our

Chapter 30 Mountain—The Return

journey is not complete until we come down our "summit" and lend a hand to others who want to undertake the journey. As Jean Klein, author and spiritual teacher, noted, "The ascent is for oneself, the descent for others."[278]

In chapter 3, I quoted Alison Gopnik, who said that "Children are the vibrant, wandering butterflies who transform into caterpillars inching along the grown-up path." To this, I would add: You don't need to stay a caterpillar, suffering, struggling, and surviving. You can turn back into the "vibrant, wandering" butterflies when you rediscover your natural state of being, but now as an adult, you will have the experience of the world, and so you are wise... and you can bring this wisdom to others.

Children are butterflies without knowing that they are. It is their natural state. We can knowingly become butterflies... by rediscovering our natural state of being. I can provide you with the "why to" and "how to," but you have to come up with the "want to." From this moment comes the next—if not now, then when? The next step is up to you!

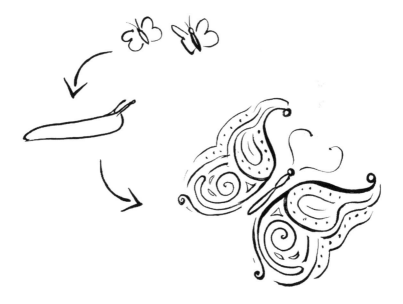

Glossary

1. **Aha! moment:** An insight, sudden realization, or understanding. On our journey, each insight makes the next step a little easier.

2. **Alpha Coherence:** It occurs when the alpha brain waves spread across the whole of the brain during meditation. In this state, the brain is integrated and in sync, and the mind is calm clear and alert. It is a sign of moments of transcendence beyond the ego consciousness.

3. **Alternative States of Consciousness or Reality:** See Higher States of Consciousness.

4. **Altitude:** The height or elevation above sea level. On our journey, we cannot predict the effect of the elevation on us during the physical climb or the effect of the ego on our inner journey. Both of these are out of our control. It is the unknown or uncertainty on our journey or what I call the "trust factor."

5. **Amygdala:** The amygdala, located in the midbrain, acts as an early warning system that triggers our fight or flight reaction and takes us into the survival mode.

6. **Anxiety Gap:** The gap between who we think we are (our ego consciousness) and who we actually are (our original consciousness or our natural state of being). The anxiety gap is directly proportional to how conditioned (or programmed) we are—as our conditioning increases and moves us further from our center, the more superficial and stressed our lives become.

7. **Attention:** The life force that keeps us awake and alert. It is the energy that allows us to focus on whatever we are doing. Attention is inversely related to mind wandering—the more active and insistent the voice in the head, the less attentive we are.

8. **Attitude:** Our mindset—how we think and feel about something or someone, and it is reflected in our behavior. Attitude is something that is under our control, something we can do something about.

9. **Atom:** The smallest unit of matter. It is mostly "empty space" with a nucleus at its center and electrons whirling endlessly around it (in orbits or shells). The nucleus of the atom consists of even smaller particles called protons and neutrons. The electrons, protons, and neutrons are referred to as subatomic particles.

10. **Awareness:** What we are, in essence. Awareness is our original consciousness or our natural state of being, which is our innermost essence, our center, and the deepest level of mind. It is unconditioned and is always awake and alert. See also Original Consciousness.

11. **Awakening:** A shift in consciousness—the separation or disentanglement of awareness from our ego consciousness. This separation can be instantaneous, dramatic, or a gradual process of withdrawal. Awakening is being enlightened to a new way of perceiving reality.

12. **Beginner's Mind:** An "I don't know" mind—like a child' mind—curious, excited, happy, and having fun as it is learning.

13. **Brain Integration:** When all our sub-brains become integrated and are in sync—horizontally (across the left and right hemispheres) and vertically (from the prefrontal cortex right down to the brain stem).

14. **Chronological or Clock Time:** Linear time—past, present, and future. We need clock time to manage our day-to-day activities.

15. **Coherence:** Unity—everything is in balance and comes together in a unified whole.

16. **Classical (Newtonian) Science:** This science is based on the study of large objects (that can be seen or imagined) in nature. It evolved from a mechanistic model of the universe, and its focus is on the external world. It does not work or cannot explain the world of the subatomic particles.

17. **Conditioning:** Our self-memorized framework of habits, social and familial beliefs, attitudes, learned and conditioned behaviors, and responses that mostly come from the first six to seven years of our life. This conditioning which resides in our subconscious mind becomes the center of our personality, the ego-self, and it affects everything we do.

Glossary

18. **Conscious Mind:** Approximately 5% of the total mind is our conscious, analytical, left-brain or thinking (objective) mind. Using sensory perceptions, it's primary focus is on the external world. It is our everyday consciousness and home of the ego.

19. **Consciousness:** It is what we are in essence. See also Original Consciousness.

20. **Creative State:** A stress-free, calm, clear, alert, and aware state—our natural state of being. See also Awareness and Original Consciousness.

21. **Dualistic Thinking:** An "EITHER-OR" or left-brain perspective. We judge everything that we perceive, and so we split the world into "I like," "I don't like," "This is good," "That is bad," and so on. This way of perceiving is how most of us look at reality. Here our internal reference point is the ego.

22. **EEG:** An electroencephalogram (EEG) is a test used to evaluate the electrical activity in the brain.

23. **Ego Consciousness:** Our ordinary, everyday mind or wakeful consciousness—identified with our conditioning. It is our limited or secondary awareness.

24. **Effortless Effort:** Doing by not doing. Doing the activity seems effortless. It is as if the activity is being done by itself—you don't work at it. It happens when the mind is in a state of flow.

25. **Emotional Center:** Our limbic system or the midbrain.

26. **Emotional Intelligence:** Our ability to manage our feelings and emotions so that our survival brain doesn't overwhelm our rational mind when we are stressed.

27. **Empty space:** see Field of Potentiality.

28. **Enlightenment:** Also called spiritual awakening, transcendence, or liberation and is simply the expansion of our consciousness or the rediscovery of our original, natural state of being. It is the shift from our ego-self.

29. **Epigenetics:** The new science of behavioral epigenetics studies the impact of our experiences and lifestyle on gene expression. In other words, how nurture (environmental factors) shapes nature (gene-controlled inherited characteristics).

30. **Esoteric:** Concerned with the inner world of thoughts, emotions, feelings, mind, and consciousness.

31. **Exoteric:** Relates to the outer or superficial world of the five senses.

32. **Field of Potentiality:** No-thing or the 'emptiness' of the quantum atom. That supposed 'emptiness' of the quantum atom is not empty at all—it contains enormous quantities of subtle, powerful energy. It is a world of possibilities beyond our sensory perceptions—a non-sensory reality beyond space and time as we know and called by many names—universal intelligence, presence, consciousness, quantum consciousness, awareness... It is in essence of who we are.

33. **Flow:** An altered state of consciousness in which we are calm, alert, and completely focused. This state is often described as being "in the zone," "on a roll," or "centered." When we are in flow, we are fully present and involved with whatever activity we are doing.

34. **Gamma Synchrony:** This is different from the alpha coherence (above). Whereas alpha coherence creates a calm and alert state of mind, gamma synchrony creates a calm and intense focused state like when you are in the state of flow.

35. **Hierarchy of Needs:** Theory of human motivation in psychology proposed by Abraham Maslow. His framework of the hierarchy of needs (our innate urge to expand and grow) provides a blueprint for realigning the sub-brains and finding our natural state of being. He represented this theory of motivation as an internally driven six-level pyramid moving from our basic needs at the base, to our highest needs at the top.

36. **Higher States of Consciousness:** These states are different enhanced world views and include near-death, out of body, paranormal, peak and flow experiences. These experiences take us out of our everyday, physical reality of space, and time.

Glossary

37. **Hologram:** A three-dimensional image created by splitting a light beam into two beams and bouncing them off of two mirrors to an intersection point. Every single 3-D building block of the hologram (no matter how small, or in what position of the hologram) contains all the information of the entire hologram.

38. **Inner Creativity (or the inner journey) Process:** Inner creativity is a system of change or technology to bring about a transformational shift in us by decreasing what I call the "Anxiety Gap"—the gap between who we think we are and who we actually are. It is a four-stage process and involves preparation (learning everything about the problem), incubation (putting the problem aside and doing something else, in other words bringing thinking on the problem to an end), "aha! moment" (an insight) and implementation (solving the problem with the insight).

39. **Intention:** The targeted or focused thought that sets the course and gives us the energy to embark on the journey we are planning to undertake.

40. **Intellect:** Analytical intelligence—It is rational and logical. There is no emotion or creativity in the intellect.

41. **Illusion (maya):** A distorted sense of reality. It is the abstraction of the world that we have created that we take for the real world.

42. **Loneliness:** That feeling of emptiness within us. Loneliness is not the failure to connect with others, as many believe. It is the failure to connect with ourselves.

43. **Matter:** A substance that has mass and occupies space.

44. **Meditation:** There are many techniques of meditation, but the essence of meditation is the training of our attention and awareness so that we are fully present in the moment. It does this by restructuring the brain, organizing the mind and making the mind, calm, alert, resilient, and creative. In the process, meditation triggers a transformation of consciousness within us that will change our lives.

45. **Mind:** Consciousness can have different manifestations in the universe, but, in the physical brain, it appears as, what we call, the mind. There

are, however, many levels of mind, but the two most important ones are our original consciousness or the deepest level of mind and our ego consciousness or the top-most or superficial mind.

46. **Mindfulness:** To be mindful is to be aware of everything that is happening in this moment, without judgment, resistance, or holding. It is moment-by-moment attention.

47. **Mysticism:** The practice of going within ourselves to experience our original consciousness—the ultimate reality, which is beyond our sensory and intellectual experience. A mystic is anyone who undertakes this journey.

48. **Natural State of Being:** Our essential or true self—our Buddha nature. See also Awareness and Original Consciousness.

49. **Neuroplasticity:** The brain's ability to rewire and create new neural circuits at any age in response to experience and training.

50. **Non-Dualistic Thinking:** An "AND" perspective. It provides a holistic view, and so we see similarities, interrelationships, interdependencies, and patterns, which are, in essence, insights. Here our internal reference point is awareness or our natural state of being.

51. **Non-Local Communication:** In quantum physics, communication between particles happens beyond space and time. Experiments have now shown that this way of communication (directly without the use of any electromagnetic signals) can happen in our everyday world.

52. **Non-Local Consciousness:** Quantum physicists' term for our natural state of being (compared to the local state of consciousness, which is the ego).

53. **Observer effect:** The role of consciousness in shaping our reality.

54. **Original Consciousness:** The source of life, the ground of being from which everything comes, and into which everything goes back. It is our ground state—pure or primary awareness. It exists independent of the brain. See also Awareness.

55. **Pain:** It can be both physical and emotional (or mental) discomfort.

Glossary

56. **Peak Experience:** Transpersonal experiences that take us into an altered state of mind, our natural state of being.

57. **Presence:** Inner awareness or our natural state of being.

58. **Probability Field:** The chances of a particle being at any particular point within the wave formation.

59. **Psychological Time:** This is different from chronological time. Psychological or inward time is a mental concept, an idea, or a thought, an illusion, created by the ego and goes from the past to the future, avoiding the present moment.

60. **Quantum Collapse:** To materialize, to bring about.

61. **Quantum Entanglement:** Connected or linked beyond space and time. When two entities or objects interact and then separate, they are forever intimately connected to each other, and they act as one entity. Change to one entity will affect the other no matter the distance between them. Information between them travels instantaneously.

62. **Quantum Jump:** Abrupt changes or transitions when the electrons of an atom disappear from one orbit and reappear in another orbit jumping over the space between orbits instantaneously. One cannot predict when the electrons will jump or where they will reappear. It also applies to an abrupt transition in thought when we have an insight.

63. **Quantum Physics:** Study of the subatomic world—the world of the very, very small that cannot be seen.

64. **Routine Trap:** The "same old, same old" way of living and responding to life and its perceived stressors.

65. **Spirituality:** The process of going inward and reconnecting with our true self.

66. **Stress:** The present-day term for what the Buddhists call suffering or mental anguish. It is a self-created disturbance of the mind caused by our restless and anxious, chattering mind, the voice in the head.

67. **Subatomic Particles:** Particles smaller than atoms—example electrons, protons and neutrons.

68. **Subatomic World:** The world of the very, very small which exists as a web of interconnections and interrelationships of millions and millions of subatomic particles, as one organic, living, conscious, and sentient being. A non-sensory reality beyond space and time.

69. **Subconscious Mind:** Most of our mind (over 95%) is hidden or subconscious and runs our automatic body processes like breathing, blood circulation, and the pumping of the heart. The subconscious mind also includes our conditioned framework of beliefs, habits, and attitudes that we have accumulated since when we were young. Within the subconscious mind, there are many levels and at the deepest level is our original mind or natural state of being.

70. **Suffering:** Mental anguish—psychological and emotional distress.

71. **Superposition:** Every subatomic particle exists in multiple states at the same time until it is observed (or measured). After observation, it collapses into one of its basic states.

72. **Survival Mode:** Living in stress—our automatic way of living and doing things and sleepwalking through life—just surviving.

73. **Unconscious:** When we are "lost" in thought, we are awake, but lose awareness of our actions, behaviors, and surroundings. Our responses then become automatic and "unconscious."

74. **Voice in the Head:** Mind chatter.

75. **Wave-Particle Duality:** In the subatomic world, the particles have a dual nature (or physical characteristics)—they exist as particles and waves at the same time.

76. **Wisdom:** Knowledge that comes from our natural state of being.

77. **Worry:** Worry starts when we are unable to solve our problems adequately. Then the voice in the head takes over—with a running commentary of what could have been, should have been, didn't happen and on and on.

Endnotes

Epigram

1. Quote from the Book of Exhortation, quoted in José Saramago, *Blindness* (Harcourt, 1997), Epigram

Introduction I: The Art of Ascending the Inner Mountain

2. Jon Kabat-Zinn, *Wherever You Go There You Are: Mindful Meditation in Everyday Life* (New York: Hyperion, 1994), 211.

3. Amit Goswami, *The Visionary Window: A Quantum Physicist's Guide to Enlightenment* (Wheaton, IL: Quest Books, 2000), 59.

4. Ibid., 16, 45–60, 72.

5. Merriam-Webster Online, https://www.merriam-webster.com/dictionary/mystica.

6. Bruce H. Lipton, *The Biology of Belief: Unleashing the Power of Consciousness, Matter & Miracles* (London, New York: Hay House Inc., 2015), 201.

7. Amit Goswami, *The Visionary Window: A Quantum Physicist's Guide to Enlightenment* (Wheaton, IL: Quest Books, 2000), 158.

8. Sogyal Rinpoche, *The Tibetan Book of Living and Dying* (Harper: San Francisco, New York, 1992), 53.

9. Ross Pittman, "If You Want a Better World, Become a Quantum Activist," Conscious Life News, August 5, 2012. http://consciouslifenews.com/become-quantum-activist/115832/August 25, 2016.

10. Robert E. Ornstein, *The Psychology of Consciousness* (San Francisco: W.H. Freeman and Company, 1972), 133.

11. Ibid., 133.

12. "Is God Already Scientifically Proven?" A Discussion with Dr. Amit Goswami, Science and Spirituality website, http://Suprememaster.tv.

13. Paul Lewis, "'Our minds can be hijacked': the tech insiders who fear a smartphone dystopia," *The Guardian*, October 6, 2017. https://www.theguardian.com/technology/2017/oct/05/smartphone-addiction-silicon-valley-dystopia.

14. Brian Luke Seaward, *Managing Stress: Principles and Strategies for Health and Well-Being*, (Sudbury, MA: Jones & Bartlett Publishers, Inc., 2006), 160.

15. Drew Hendricks, The Complete History of Social Media: Then and Now, May 8, 2013,

https://smallbiztrends.com/2013/05/the-complete-history-of-social-media-infographic.html.

16. Annie Leonard, "The Real Meaning of Consumer Demand," video, *The Story of Stuff 2007 Official Version*, April 22, 2009, https://www.youtube.com/watch?v=9GorqroigqM.

17. Paul Lewis, "'Our minds can be hijacked,': the tech insiders who fear a smartphone dystopia," *The Guardian*, October 6, 2017." https://www.theguardian.com/technology/2017/oct/05/smartphone-addiction-silicon-valley-dystopia.

18. C. G. Jung, *Psychology and Religion: West and East* (Princeton University Press, 1969), 556.

Introduction II: Mountain—The Preparation

19. Lynne McTaggart, *Intention Experiment: Using Your Thoughts to Change Your Life and the World* (New York: Atria paperback, 2007), xvi, xxi.

20. Richard Carlson, *You Can Be Happy No Matter What* (New York: MJF Books, 1997), 15.

21. We think the mind chatter is normal. However, if we heard someone talking to himself or herself, we would immediately think that person was insane or crazy. But we do it all the time except we keep our mouths shut!

22. Rumi, quoted in Ram Dass, *Journey of Awakening: A Meditator's Guidebook* (New York: Bantam Books, 1990), 208.

23. Shunryu Suzuki, *Zen Mind, Beginner's Mind* (Boulder, CO: Shambhala Publications, 1970), 1.

Introduction III: The Beginner's Mind

24. Ibid.

25. Bruce H. Lipton, "The Programmable Mind," video, presented at UPLIFT 2014, Dec 17, 2014. https://www.youtube.com/watch?V=GZMJ4sJspZY.

26. I have not been able to find the original source of the quote but the quote has been attributed to the Dalai Lama, Frank Zappa (1940–1993) and Sir Thomas Robert Dewar (1864–1930).

27. Fyodor Dostoevsky quoted in Lea Winerman, "Suppressing the 'white bears,'" *American Psychological Association Monitor on Psychology*, 42, no. 9, (October 2011).

28. Amit Goswami, *The Visionary Window: A Quantum Physicist's Guide to Enlightenment* (Wheaton, IL: Quest Books, 2000), 167.

29. Byron Katie with Stephen Mitchell, *A Thousand Names for Joy: Living in Harmony with the Way Things Are* (New York: Three Rivers Press, 2007), 60.

Endnotes

30. Sogyal Rinpoche, *The Tibetan Book of Living and Dying* (New York, San Francisco: Harper, 1992), 53.

31. Philo of Alexandria quoted in Stephen Mitchell, compiled and adapted, *The Second Book of the Tao,* (New York: Penguin Press, 2009), 150.

Chapter 1: How We Live Today

32. G I. Gurdjieff quoted in P D. Ouspensky, *In Search of the Miraculous*, (New York: Harcourt, 2001), 144.

33. Ann Zimmerman, "Toys for Tight Schedules," *The Wall Street Journal,* July 23, 2013, https://www.wsj.com/articles/SB10001424127887324783204578622472279102826

34. Annie Leonard, "The Real Meaning of Consumer Demand," https://www.youtube.com/watch?v=9GorqroigqM.

35. Paul Lewis, "'Our minds can be hijacked,': the tech insiders who fear a smartphone dystopia," *The Guardian*, October 6, 2017." https://www.theguardian.com/technology/2017/oct/05/smartphone-addiction-silicon-valley-dystopia.

36. Ibid.

37. Virginia Smart, Tyana Grundig, "'We're designing minds': Industry insider reveals secrets of addictive app trade," CBC News Marketplace, Nov 03, 2017, http://www.cbc.ca/news/technology/marketplace-phones-1.4384876.

38. Vito Pilieci, "Canadians now have shorter attention span than goldfish thanks to portable devices," *National Post,* May 12, 2015, http://news.nationalpost.com/news/canada/canadians-now-have-shorter-attention-span-than-goldfish-thanks-to-portable-devices-microsoft-study.

39. Paul Lewis, "'Our minds can be hijacked,': the tech insiders who fear a smartphone dystopia," *The Guardian*, October 6, 2017." https://www.theguardian.com/technology/2017/oct/05/smartphone-addiction-silicon-valley-dystopia.

40. Ibid.

41. Virginia Smart, Tyana Grundig, "'We're designing minds': Industry insider reveals secrets of addictive app trade," CBC News Marketplace, Nov 03, 2017, http://www.cbc.ca/news/technology/marketplace-phones-1.4384876.

42. Paul Lewis, "'Our minds can be hijacked,': the tech insiders who fear a smartphone dystopia," *The Guardian*, October 6, 2017." https://www.theguardian.com/technology/2017/oct/05/smartphone-addiction-silicon-valley-dystopia.

43. Elizabeth Renzetti, "Life of Solitude: A loneliness crisis is looming," *Globe and Mail,* November 23, 2013: "A study from the University of Michigan has

shown that, on the surface, Facebook provides an invaluable resource for fulfilling the basic human need for social connection. Rather than enhancing well-being, however, these findings suggest that Facebook may undermine it."

44. Josh Trapper, "Internet addict face constant temptations, non-believers," Toronto Star, February 1, 2013; Paul Lewis, "'Our minds can be hijacked': the tech insiders who fear a smartphone dystopia," *The Guardian*, October 6, 2017. https://www.theguardian.com/technology/2017/oct/05/smartphone-addiction -silicon-valley-dystopia.

45. Daniel Tencer, "Ex-Facebook Chief Warns Site Was Built To Exploit People's Weaknesses," HuffPost, 11/09/2017, http://www.huffingtonpost.ca/2017/11/09/ex-facebook-chief-warns-site-was- built-to-exploit-people-s-weaknesses_a_23272438/?utm_hp_ref=ca-homepage.

46. Paul Lewis, "'Our minds can be hijacked': the tech insiders who fear a smartphone dystopia," *The Guardian*, October 6, 2017. https://www.theguardian.com/technology/2017/oct/05/smartphone-addiction -silicon-valley-dystopia.

47. Sufi saying, quoted in "Right Attitude And Alignment," Learning Institute for Growth, Healing and Transformation (LIGHT), 1, http://www.lightwinnipeg.org/Spiritual%20Writings/RIGHT%20ATTITUDE% 20AND%20ALIGNMENT.pdf

48. Rumi, quoted in Robert E. Ornstein, *The Psychology of Consciousness* (San Francisco: W. H. Freeman and Company, 1972), 37.

Chapter 2: Consciousness—The Universal Intelligence

49. Einstein, quoted on Musetude Trust website, http://musetude.com/brain-r-d/altruism/.

50. Joe Dispenza, *Evolve your Brain: The Science of Changing Your Mind* (Dearfield, Florida: Health Communication, 2007), 69.

51. Thomas Cleary, trans., *The Secret of the Golden Flower: The Classic Chinese Book of Life* (San Francisco: Harper, 1991), 138–139.

52. Richard Carlson, *You Can Be Happy No Matter What* (New York: MJF Books, 1997), 28.

53. Thomas Cleary, trans., *The Secret of the Golden Flower: The Classic Chinese Book of Life* (San Francisco: Harper, 1991), 138–139.

Chapter 3: Our Individualized Thought System

54. Gandhi, quoted in Bruce H. Lipton, *The Biology of Belief: Unleashing the Power of Consciousness, Matter & Miracles* (London, New York: Hay House Inc., 2015), 138.

Endnotes

55. Alison Gopnik, *The Philosophical Baby: What Children's Minds Tell Us About Truth, Love, and the Meaning of Life* (London: Picador, 2009), 10.

56. Joe Dispenza, *Breaking the Habit of Being Yourself: How to lose your mind and create a new one* (London, New York: Hay House 2012), 175–215; Alison Gopnik, *The Philosophical Baby: What Children's Minds Tell Us About Truth, Love, and the Meaning of Life* (Picador 2009), esp. 5–18, 106–163 [Gopnik's book, especially chapters four and five, provides a fascinating insight into the children's consciousness up to the age of five or six years]; Bruce H. Lipton, *The Biology of Belief: Unleashing the Power of Consciousness, Matter & Miracles* (Hay House Inc.2015), 172–200.

57. Joe Dispenza, *Breaking the Habit of Being Yourself: How to lose your mind and create a new one* (London, New York: Hay House 2012), 203.

58. Joe Dispenza, *Breaking the Habit of Being Yourself: How to lose your mind and create a new one* (London, New York: Hay House 2012), 175–215; Alison Gopnik, *The Philosophical Baby: What Children's Minds Tell Us About Truth, Love, and the Meaning of Life* (Picador 2009), especially 5–18, 106–163; Bruce H. Lipton, *The Biology of Belief: Unleashing the Power of Consciousness, Matter & Miracles* (Hay House Inc.2015), 172–200.

59. Alison Gopnik, "Your baby is smarter than you think," *The New York Times*, August 15, 2009, http://www.nytimes.com/2009/08/16/opinion/16gopnik.html.

60. Peggy Phillips, review of *The Philosophical Baby: what children's minds tell us about truth, love and the meaning of life*, by Alison Gopnik, Birth Psychology, The Association of Prenatal and Perinatal Psychology and Health, June 2009, https://birthpsychology.com/book-review/philosophical-baby-what-childrens-mind-tell-us-about-truth-love-and-meaning-life.

61. Alison Gopnik, *The Philosophical Baby: What Children's Minds Tell Us About Truth, Love, and the Meaning of Life* (Picador 2009), 129.

62. Ibid., 154.

63. Ethan Remmel, "Brainstorming Babies," review of *The Philosophical Baby: what children's minds tell us about truth, love and the meaning of life*, by Alison Gopnik, *American Scientist*, September– October 2009, https://www.americanscientist.org/article/brainstorming-babies

64. Joe Dispenza, *Evolve your Brain: The Science of Changing Your Mind* (Dearfield, Florida: Health Communication, 2007), 219.

65. Michael Green, "What Babies Know and We Don't," review of *The Philosophical Baby: what children's minds tell us about truth, love and the meaning of life*, by Alison Gopnik, *The New York Review of Books*, March 11, 2010, http://www.nybooks.com/articles/2010/03/11/what-babies-know-and-we-dont/.

Green writes, "Gopnik offers the captivating idea that children are more conscious than adults but also less unconscious, because they have fewer automatic behaviors."

66. Bruce H. Lipton, "The Programmable Mind," video, presented at UPLIFT 2014, Dec 17, 2014. https://www.youtube.com/watch?V=GZMJ4sJspZY.

67. Bruce H. Lipton, *The Biology of Belief: Unleashing the Power of Consciousness, Matter & Miracles* (Hay House Inc.2015), 173-174.

Chapter 4: The Monkey Mind

68. This Sanskrit Shloka is quoted in Anand Patkar, *Master the Mind Monkey: Experience Your Excellence* (Mumbai: Jaico Publishing House, 2006), esp. ch. 10.

69. Eckhart Tolle, *The Power of Now: A Guide to Spiritual Enlightenment* (Novato, CA: Namaste Publishing and New World Library 2004), 52.

Chapter 5: The Walking Dead

70. Nancy Routley, "A shadow of my future self," *Globe and Mail*, June 4, 2013.

71. Eli Pariser, "Beware online 'filter bubbles,'" TED2011, March 2011.

72. Kevin Salvin, "How algorithms shape our world," TEDGlobal, July 2011; Eli Pariser, "Beware online 'filter bubbles,'" TED2011, March 2011; Leo Hickman, "How algorithms rule the world," *The Guardian*, July 1, 2013, https://www.theguardian.com/science/2013/jul/01/how-algorithms-rule-world-nsa.

73. Joe Dispenza, *Breaking the Habit of Being Yourself: How to lose your mind and create a new one* (London, New York: Hay House 2012), 61–63.

74. Bruce H. Lipton, *The Honeymoon Effect: the science of creating heaven on earth* (London, New York: Hay House Inc. 2013), 75.

75. Monty Mckeever, "The Brain and Emotional Intelligence," interview with Daniel Goleman, Tricycle, May 18, 2011, http://tricycle.org/trikedaily/brain-and-emotional-intelligence-interview-daniel-goleman/.

76. This is the prefrontal cortex area of the brain, which is at the center of everything that happens in the head. Now we know why we say and do things when we are stressed that we come to regret later! We will look at it in some more detail later in the chapter on the working of the brain. Travis Bradberry, "How Successful People Stay Calm," Forbes, February 6, 2014. http://www.forbes.com/sites/travisbradberry/2014/02/06/how-successful-people-stay-calm/#6603ed629c8c.

77. Joe Dispenza, *Evolve your Brain: The Science of Changing Your Mind* (Dearfield, Florida: Health Communication, 2007), 8.

Endnotes

78. Charles Garfield, quoted in William Arntz, Betsy Chasse and Mark Vicente, *What the Bleep Do We Know? Discovering the Endless Possibilities for Altering Your Everyday Reality* (Health Communications 2005), 195.

Chapter 6: How "Dead" Are We?

79. Nicole Winfield, "Pope issues mission statement for papacy," *Boston Globe*, November 26, 2013, https://www.bostonglobe.com/2013/11/26/pope-issues-mission-statement-for-papacy/T5z1XB1xRcsD5av60zxDBK/story.html

80. Cam Marcus, "Brain Scans Can Reveal Your Decisions 7 Seconds Before You 'Decide," Exploring the Mind! (website), http://exploringthemind.com/the-mind/brain-scans-can-reveal-your-decisions-7-seconds-before-you-decide.

81. As neuroscientist David Eagleman says "Our conscious minds are really just a summary of what our brains get up to all the time—without "us" having any idea... the conscious you, which is the part that flickers to life when you wake up in the morning, is the smallest bit of what's happening in your head... It's like broom closet in the mansion of your brain." As quoted in Chris Baraniuk, "The Enormous Power of the Unconscious Brain," BBC Future, March 16, 2016. http://www.bbc.com/future/story/20160315-the-enormous-power-of-the-unconscious-brain

82. Blaise Pascal, quoted in Dr. Wayne W. Dyer, "Can You Turn Down the Noise? The spirituality of silence," You Can Heal Your Life (website), Oct 23, 2009, http://www.healyourlife.com/can-you-turn-down-the-noise.

83. Maia Szalavitz, "Awkward Silences: 4 Seconds Is All It Takes to Feel Rejected," Time.com, Dec. 30, 2010, http://healthland.time.com/2010/12/30/awkward-silences-4-seconds-is-all-it-takes-to-feel-rejected/.

Chapter 7: Living in Survival

84. Sri Nisargadatta Maharaj, *I AM THAT*, Maurice Frydman, trans., Sudhakor S. Dikshit, edit., (Durham, NC: Acorn Press, 2012), part 8, ch. 57.

85. William Shakespeare, The Tragedy of Hamlet, Prince of Denmark, Act 2, scene 2, http://nfs.sparknotes.com/hamlet/page_106.html.

86. Joe Dispenza, *Evolve your Brain: The Science of Changing Your Mind* (Dearfield, Florida: Health Communication, 2007), 286.

87. "Thought Du Jour," *Globe and Mail*, October 10, 2013.

88. Bruce H. Lipton, *The Biology of Belief: Unleashing the Power of Consciousness, Matter & Miracles* (Hay House Inc.2015), 140.

89. Daniel J. Siegel, *Mindsight: The New Science of Personal Transformation* (New York: Bantam Books, 2010), 18, 55.

Chapter 8: The Anxiety Gap

90. Thomas Merton, quoted in Sogyal Rinpoche, *The Tibetan Book of Living and Dying* (New York, San Francisco: Harper, 1992), 356.

91. Elizabeth Renzetti, "Life of Solitude: A loneliness crisis is looming," *Globe and Mail*, November 23, 2013.

92. Jonathan Webb, "Do people choose pain over boredom?" BBC News, July 4, 2014, http://www.bbc.com/news/science-environment-28130690; Wilson, et al., "Just think: The challenges of the disengaged mind," Science, 04 July 2014/vol. 345, Issue 6192, pp. 75-77; DOI: 10.1126/science.1250830 http://science.sciencemag.org/content/345/6192/75?variant=full-text&sso=1&sso_redirect_count=1&oauth-code=63586e2b-07a9-4ce3-b1a7-8fad95cd0c1b

93. Byron Katie with Stephen Mitchell, *A Thousand Names for Joy: Living in Harmony with the Way Things Are* (New York: Three Rivers Press, 2007), 58.

94. Marilyn Ferguson, quoted in Germain Decelles, *Change Your Future, Now! Questions, Reflections and Answers* (WebTech Managing and Publishing Inc., 2013), 414.

Chapter 9: The Routine Trap

95. Joe Dispenza, *Evolve your Brain: The Science of Changing Your Mind* (Dearfield, Florida: Health Communication, 2007), 251.

96. Bruce H. Lipton, *The Biology of Belief: Unleashing the Power of Consciousness, Matter & Miracles* (Hay House Inc.2015), 150.

97. Joe Dispenza, *Evolve your Brain: The Science of Changing Your Mind* (Dearfield, Florida: Health Communication, 2007), 251–293; Monty Mckeever, "The Brain and Emotional Intelligence," An interview with Daniel Goleman, Tricycle, May 18, 2011. http://tricycle.org/trikedaily/brain-and-emotional-intelligence-interview-daniel-goleman/

98. Jo Marchant, "Can Meditation really slow ageing?" Mosaic, Wellcome Trust, July 1, 2014, http://mosaicscience.com/story/can-meditation-really-slow-ageing.

99. Joe Dispenza, *Evolve your Brain: The Science of Changing Your Mind* (Dearfield, Florida: Health Communication, 2007), 10–12.

Endnotes

Chapter 10: The Four-in-One Brain

100. Marilyn Ferguson, *The Aquarian Conspiracy: Personal and Social Transformation in Our Time* (Jeremy P. Tarcher/Penguin, 2009), 51.

101. Robert E. Ornstein, *The Psychology of Consciousness* (San Francisco: W. H. Freeman and Company, 1972), esp. 50–72, 224–225; Joe Dispenza, *Evolve your Brain: The Science of Changing Your Mind* (Dearfield, Florida: Health Communication, 2007), esp.103–143, 337–380;

Joe Dispenza, *Breaking the Habit of Being*, 123–146; Daniel J. Siegel, *Mindsight: The New Science of Personal Transformation* (New York: Bantam Books, 2010), esp. 15, 21–22, 26–30;

102. Joe Dispenza, *Evolve your Brain: The Science of Changing Your Mind* (Dearfield, Florida: Health Communication, 2007), 108; Paul Maclean, Four Brain Model, Musetude Trust website, http://musetude.com/brain-r-d/four-brain-model/; Lydia Desai, "Tune up with Music!" *Sound Arts, The Menza Magazine* 3, no. 1 (February 2007): http://musetude.com/wp-content/uploads/19.-Article-in-Menza-Magazine-%E2%80%93-Tune-up-with-music1.pdf

103. Robert E. Ornstein, *The Psychology of Consciousness* (San Francisco: W. H. Freeman and Company, 1972), esp. 50–72, 224–225; Joe Dispenza, *Evolve your Brain: The Science of Changing Your Mind* (Dearfield, Florida: Health Communication, 2007), esp. 103–143, 337–380;

Joe Dispenza, Breaking the Habit of Being Yourself: How to lose your mind and create a new one (London, New York: Hay House 2012), 123–146.

Chapter 11: The Survival Brain

104. Albert J. Bernstein, quoted in Germain Deceles, *Change Your Future Now!* (WebTech Management and Publishing Inc., 2013), 68.

105. "The Hierarchy of Human Needs: Maslow's Model of Motivation," Personality and Spirituality (website), http://personalityspirituality.net/articles/the-hierarchy-of-human-needs-maslows-model-of-motivation/.

106. "How dark is your personality?" BBC Future, December 3, 2015. http://www.bbc.com/future/story/20151123-how-dark-is-your-personality?ocid=fbfutcom;

David Robson, "Psychology: the man who studies everyday evil," BBC Future, January 30, 2015
http://www.bbc.com/future/story/20150130-the-man-who-studies-evil.

Chapter 12: The Emotional Brain

107. Robert Sylwester, "How Emotions Affect Learning," *Educational Leadership* 52, no. 2, Oct 1994, 60–65. http://www.ascd.org/publications/educational-leadership/oct94/vol52/num02/How-Emotions-Affect-Learning.aspx

108. Jill Bolte Taylor, *My Stroke of Insight: A Brain Scientist's Personal Journey* (New York: Penguin Group, 2009), 16.

109. Daniel Goleman, *Working with Emotional Intelligence* (New York: Bantam Books, 2000), 74–75.

110. "The Science Behind WSL," Whole System Learning (WSL) website, http://whole-system.com/discovery-learning/discovery-learning-method.shtml

Chapter 13: The Conscious Brain

111. *Collected Works of C.G. Jung*, vol. 6; Psychological Type by C. G. Jung, Edited by Gerhard Adler and R.F.C Hull (Princeton University Press, 1976), 628.

112. Daniel J. Siegel, *Mindsight: The New Science of Personal Transformation* (New York: Bantam Books, 2010), 20.

113. Paul Maclean, Four Brain Model, Musetude Trust website, http://musetude.com/brain-r-d/four-brain-model/; Lydia Desai, "Tune up with Music!": http://musetude.com/wp-content/uploads/19.-Article-in-Menza-Magazine-%E2%80%93-Tune-up-with-music1.pdf.

114. Joe Dispenza, *Evolve your Brain: The Science of Changing Your Mind* (Dearfield, Florida: Health Communication, 2007), 348.

115. Ibid., 141.

116. Daniel J. Siegel, *Mindsight: The New Science of Personal Transformation* (New York: Bantam Books, 2010), esp. 15, 21–22, 26–30; Joe Dispenza, *Evolve your Brain: The Science of Changing Your Mind* (Dearfield, Florida: Health Communication, 2007), esp. 139–143,337–380.

117. Daniel J. Siegel, *Mindsight: The New Science of Personal Transformation* (New York: Bantam Books, 2010), 14-15.

118. "The Hierarchy of Human Needs: Maslow's Model of Motivation," Personality and Spirituality (website), http://personalityspirituality.net/articles/the-hierarchy-of-human-needs-maslows-model-of-motivation/.

119. Roger Highfield, "Scientists discover brain trigger for selfish behaviour," *The Telegraph*, October 6, 2006, http://www.telegraph.co.uk/news/1530715/Scientists-discover-brain-trigger-for-selfish-behaviour.html; Elizabeth Svoboda, "Hardwired for Giving," *The Wall*

Endnotes

Street Journal, August 31, 2013, http://www.wsj.com/articles/SB10001424127887324009304579041231971683854.

120. Elizabeth Svoboda, "Hardwired for Giving," *The Wall Street Journal*, August 31, 2013, http://www.wsj.com/articles/SB10001424127887324009304579041231971683854.

121. Ibid.

122. Roger Highfield, "Scientists discover brain trigger for selfish behaviour," *The Telegraph*, October 6, 2006, http://www.telegraph.co.uk/news/1530715/Scientists-discover-brain-trigger-for-selfish-behaviour.html.

123. Elizabeth Svoboda, "Hardwired for Giving," *The Wall Street Journal*, August 31, 2013, http://www.wsj.com/articles/SB10001424127887324009304579041231971683854.

124. Ibid.

125. William von Hippel, "Do people become more prejudiced as they grow older?" *BBC*, July 17, 2015, http://www.bbc.com/news/magazine-33523313; Roger Highfield, "Scientists discover brain trigger for selfish behaviour," *The Telegraph*, October 6, 2006, http://www.telegraph.co.uk/news/1530715/Scientists-discover-brain-trigger-for-selfish-behaviour.html.

126. Roger Highfield, "Scientists discover brain trigger for selfish behaviour," *The Telegraph*, October 6, 2006, http://www.telegraph.co.uk/news/1530715/Scientists-discover-brain-trigger-for-selfish-behaviour.html.

127. William von Hippel, "Do people become more prejudiced as they grow older?" *BBC*, July 17, 2015, http://www.bbc.com/news/magazine-33523313

The effect of this change is clearly highlighted in the fiction work of author Harper Lee. In *To Kill a Mockingbird*, Atticus Finch as a young man was a "kind, wise, honorable, an avatar of integrity," who defended a black man accused of raping a white woman. In her second novel, "Go Set a Watchman," which was released in 2015, Harper Lee shows Atticus Finch, who is now 72 as a racist "sprouting hate speech." [Michiko Kakutani, "Harper Lee's 'Go Set a Watchman' Gives Atticus Finch a Dark Side, *The New York Times Books of the Times*, July 10, 2015. https://www.nytimes.com/2015/07/11/books/review-harper-lees-go-set-a-watchman-gives-atticus-finch-a-dark-side.html]

Chapter 14: The Famous Left and Right Brains

128. Musetude Trust website, http://musetude.com

129. Robert E. Ornstein, *The Psychology of Consciousness* (San Francisco: W. H. Freeman and Company, 1972), 51, 55.

130. Jill Bolte Taylor, *My Stroke of Insight: A Brain Scientist's Personal Journey* (New York: Penguin Group, 2009), esp. 139.

131. Ibid., 26–35, 51, 138–187.

132. Ibid., 140.

133. Ibid., 71.

134. Ibid., 116.

135. Fritjof Capra, *The Turning Point: Science, Society, and the Rising Culture* (New York: Bantam Books/Simon and Schuster, 1982), 27; Robert E. Ornstein, *The Psychology of Consciousness* (San Francisco: W. H. Freeman and Company, 1972), 65-72.

136. Richard Rohr, *Eager to Love: The Alternative way of Francis of Assisi* (Cincinnati, OH: Franciscan Media, 2014), 123-124.

137. Bruce H. Lipton, *The Biology of Belief: Unleashing the Power of Consciousness, Matter & Miracles* (Hay House Inc.2015), 147.

138. Daniel J. Siegel, *Mindsight: The New Science of Personal Transformation* (New York: Bantam Books, 2010), 108.

139. Jill Bolte Taylor, "My Stroke of Insight," TED Talk (video), Feb. 2008, https://www.ted.com/talks/jill_bolte_taylor_s_powerful_stroke_of_insight.

140. Daniel J. Siegel, *Mindsight: The New Science of Personal Transformation* (New York: Bantam Books, 2010), 108.

141. Ibid., 107.

142. Robert E. Ornstein, *The Psychology of Consciousness* (San Francisco: W. H. Freeman and Company, 1972), 62-63.

143. Joe Dispenza, *Evolve your Brain: The Science of Changing Your Mind* (Dearfield, Florida: Health Communication, 2007), 215–221.

Chapter 15: The Right Brain Missing in Action

144. Rene Descartes, quoted in Fritjof Capra, *Tao of Physics: An Exploration of Parallels between Modern Physics and Eastern Mysticism* (Boulder, CO: Shambhala Publications, 2010), 23.

145. Marilyn Ferguson, *The Aquarian Conspiracy: Personal and Social Transformation in Our Time* (Jeremy P. Tarcher/Penguin, 2009), 65.

146. Gary Zukav, *The Dancing Wu Li Masters: An Overview of the New Physics* (New York: William Morrow & Company, 1979), esp. 37–41.

Endnotes

Tool for the Journey 3—Understanding the Brain Waves

147. Jonathan Star, *Two Suns Rising: A Collection of Sacred Writings* (New Jersey: Castle Books, 1996), 51.

148. Joe Dispenza, *Breaking the Habit of Being Yourself: How to lose your mind and create a new one* (London, New York: Hay House 2012), 207.

149. Robert Ornstein, *The Right Mind: Making Sense of the Hemispheres* (New York: Harcourt Brace & Company, 1997), 71.

150. Musetude Trust website, http://Musetude.com; Rebecca Turner, "Lucid Dreams Found to Take Place at Gamma Brainwave Frequencies," http://www.world-of-lucid-dreaming.com/lucid-dreams-found-to-take-place-at-gamma-brainwave-frequencies.html; Jeffrey L. Fannin, "Understanding Your Brainwaves," http://drjoedispenza.com/files/understanding-brainwaves_white_paper.pdf; "What are Lambda & Epsilon waves? Out of body experiences with theta and lambda waves," updated on January 20, 2014, http://hubpages.com/education/What-are-Lambda-Epsilon-waves-Out-of-body-experiences-with-theta-and-lambda-waves; Joe Dispenza, *Breaking the Habit of Being Yourself: How to lose your mind and create a new one* (London, New York: Hay House 2012), 184, 190.

Chapter 16: The Science of Wholeness

151. Ervin Laszlo, quoted in William Arntz, Betsy Chasse, and Mark Vicente, *What the Bleep Do We Know?*, 256.

152. "Is God Already Scientifically Proven?" A Discussion with Dr. Amit Goswami, Science and Spirituality (website), http://www.suprememaster.tv/ss/Is-God-Already-Scientifically-Proven-A-Discussion-with-Dr-Amit-Goswami.html.

153. The following books provide a fascinating look into the new science of quantum physics and its implication in today's world: Fritjof Capra, *Tao of Physics: An Exploration of Parallels between Modern Physics and Eastern Mysticism* (Shambhala Publications, 2010); Amit Goswami, *The Visionary Window: A Quantum Physicist's Guide to Enlightenment* (Quest Books, 2000), esp. 27–133; Gary Zukav, *The Dancing Wu Li Masters: An Overview of the New Physics* (New York: William Morrow & Company, 1979); William Arntz, Betsy Chasse, and Mark Vicente, *What the Bleep Do We Know? Discovering the endless Possibilities for Altering your |Everyday Reality* (Health Communications 2005).

Chapter 17: We Are Machines

154. *Mindwalk*, directed by Bernt Amadeus Capra, based on Fritjof Capra's book *The Turning Point* (1990; Triton Pictures).

155. Amit Goswami, *The Visionary Window: A Quantum Physicist's Guide to Enlightenment* (Wheaton, IL: Quest Books, 2000), esp. 6.

Chapter 18: A Paradigm Shift—Science Discovers Consciousness

156. *Mindwalk*, directed by Bernt Amadeus Capra, based on Fritjof Capra's book *The Turning Point* (1990; Triton Pictures).

157. Amit Goswami, *The Visionary Window: A Quantum Physicist's Guide to Enlightenment* (Wheaton, IL: Quest Books, 2000), 15.

158. Gary Zukav, *The Dancing Wu Li Masters: An Overview of the New Physics* (New York: William Morrow & Company, 1979), 31–32.

159. William Arntz, Betsy Chasse, and Mark Vicente, *What the Bleep Do We Know? Discovering the endless Possibilities for Altering your |Everyday Reality* (Health Communications 2005), 64-65.

160. Lynne McTaggart, *Intention Experiment: Using Your Thoughts to Change Your Life and the World* (New York: Atria Books, 2007), xxii.

161. Amit Goswami, *Quantum Creativity: Think Quantum, Be Creative* London, New York: Hay House 2014), 18.

162. Gary Zukav, *The Dancing Wu Li Masters: An Overview of the New Physics* (New York: William Morrow & Company, 1979), 193.

163. Avery Thompson, "The Logic-Defying Double-Slit Experiment Is Even Weirder Than You Thought," Aug 11, 2016, http://www.popularmechanics.com/technology/startups/reviews/a22280/double-slit-experiment-even-weirder/; Lynne McTaggart, *Intention Experiment: Using Your Thoughts to Change Your Life and the World* (New York: Atria Books, 2007), xxii-4; Amit Goswami, *The Visionary Window: A Quantum Physicist's Guide to Enlightenment* (Wheaton, IL: Quest Books, 2000), esp. 37–42; Gary Zukav, *The Dancing Wu Li Masters: An Overview of the New Physics* (New York: William Morrow & Company, 1979), 60–90.

164. Lynne McTaggart, *Intention Experiment: Using Your Thoughts to Change Your Life and the World* (New York: Atria Books, 2007), xxiv.

Chapter 19: Quantum Billiards

165. Richard Feynman, quoted in William Arntz, Betsy Chasse, and Mark Vicente, *What the Bleep Do We Know? Discovering the endless Possibilities for Altering your |Everyday Reality* (Health Communications 2005), 61.

166. Bruce H. Lipton, *The Biology of Belief: Unleashing the Power of Consciousness, Matter & Miracles* (Hay House Inc.2015), 83.

167. George Ganov, *Mr. Tompkin in Paperback (includes Mr. Tompkin in wonderland and Mr. Tompkin explores the atom)* (The Press Syndicate of the University of Cambridge, 1965), Chapter 10 Quantum Billiards, esp. 65–69;

Endnotes

"Quantum Physics and Billiards," Physics 24/7 website, http://www.physics247.com/physics-tutorial/quantum-physics-billiards.shtml.

168. Amit Goswami, *The Quantum Activist Workbook*, 1
This workbook, which accompanies the documentary film *The Quantum Activist* (released in 2009), is an exploration of the idea of quantum activism. Dr. Amit Goswami defines quantum activism as "The idea of changing ourselves and our societies in accordance with the transformative and revolutionary message of quantum physics. This change is taking its cue from the emergence of a new paradigm within science; the paradigm of a consciousness based reality as articulated by Quantum Physics." (http://www.quantumactivist.com).

169. George Ganov, *Mr. Tompkin in Paperback (includes Mr. Tompkin in wonderland and Mr. Tompkin explores the atom)* (The Press Syndicate of the University of Cambridge, 1965), Chapter 10 Quantum Billiards, esp. 67; Physics 24/7 website, "Quantum Physics and Billiards," http://www.physics247.com/physics-tutorial/quantum-physics-billiards.shtml.

170. Physics 24/7 website, "Quantum Physics and Billiards," http://www.physics247.com/physics-tutorial/quantum-physics-billiards.shtml.

171. Lynne McTaggart, *Intention Experiment: Using Your Thoughts to Change Your Life and the World* (New York: Atria Books, 2007), 8.

172. Michael Ricciarch, "Quantum Entanglement Experiment Proves 'Non-Locality' For First Time, Will Permit Multi-Party Quantum Communication," (March 28, 2014),

https://planetsave.com/2014/03/28/quantum-entanglement-experiment-proves-non-locality-for-first-time-will-permit-multi-party-quantum-communication/.

173. Amit Goswami, *The Visionary Window: A Quantum Physicist's Guide to Enlightenment* (Wheaton, IL: Quest Books, 2000), 33.

Chapter 20: Our Mechanistic World

174. Amit Goswami, *The Visionary Window: A Quantum Physicist's Guide to Enlightenment* (Wheaton, IL: Quest Books, 2000), xvii.

175. Rupert Sheldrake, "The Science Delusion—the Default Worldview," Tedx Whitechapel—The "Banned" Talk, January 12, 2013, https://www.youtube.com/watch?v=1TerTgDEgUE.

176. Annie Leonard, "The Real Meaning of Consumer Demand," https://www.youtube.com/watch?v=9GorqroigqM.

177. I Ching—The Book of Changes, quoted in William Arntz, Betsy Chasse and Mark Vicente, *What the Bleep Do We Know? Discovering the endless Possibilities for Altering your |Everyday Reality* (Health Communications 2005), 214.

178. Samuel Arbesman, "It's complicated: Human ingenuity has created a world that the mind cannot master. Have we finally reached our limits?" Aeon Essay,

January 6, 2014,
https://aeon.co/essays/is-technology-making-the-world-indecipherable.

Chapter 21: The Holographic World

179. Joe Dispenza, *Breaking the Habit of Being Yourself: How to lose your mind and create a new one* (London, New York: Hay House 2012), xvi.

180. "Dr. Amit Goswami and Non-local Consciousness," Jeff Kober Meditation (website), September 3, 2012, http://jeffkobermeditation.com/2012/09/dr-amit-goswami-and-non-local-consciousness-september-3-2012/.
Amit Goswami, *Quantum Creativity: Think Quantum, Be Creative* London, New York: Hay House 2014), 20-21.

181. Amit Goswami, "Quantum Physics, Consciousness, Creativity, and Healing," audio lecture, Institute of Noetic Sciences (ION), 2006, http://library.noetic.org/library/audio-lectures/quantum-physics-consciousness-creativity-and-healing-amit-goswami-part-1-3.

182. Malcolm Godwin, *The Lucid Dreamer: A Waking Guide for the Traveller between Worlds* (New York: Simon & Schuster, 1994), esp. 191–205; Amit Goswami, *Quantum Creativity: Think Quantum, Be Creative* London, New York: Hay House 2014), 93–94.

183. Jonathan Star, *Two Suns Rising: A Collection of Sacred Writings* (New Jersey: Castle Books, 1996), 142.

184. William Blake, quoted in Ram Dass, *Journey of Awakening: A Meditator's Guidebook* (New York: Bantam Books, 1990), 63.

185. Daniel Goleman, *Working with Emotional Intelligence* (New York: Bantam Books, 2000), 244.

186. Gary Zukav, *The Dancing Wu Li Masters: An Overview of the New Physics* (New York: William Morrow & Company, 1979), 37–41.

187. Daniel Goleman, *Working with Emotional Intelligence* (New York: Bantam Books, 2000), 317-318.

188. Dan Brown, *The Lost Symbol* (Transworld Publishers, 2009), 86 and page that states: FACT "All rituals, science, artwork, and monuments in this novel are real"; Lynne McTaggart, "The Key to the Lost Symbol: The Power of Intention, September 18, 2009, https://lynnemctaggart.com/the-key-to-the-lost-symbol-the-power-of-intention/.

189. Lynne McTaggart, *Intention Experiment: Using Your Thoughts to Change Your Life and the World* (New York: Atria Books, 2007), 33.

190. Bruce H. Lipton, *The Biology of Belief: Unleashing the Power of Consciousness, Matter & Miracles* (Hay House Inc.2015), 187.

Endnotes

191. Amit Goswami, *The Quantum Activist Workbook*, Center for Quantum Activism, http://www.amitgoswami.org.

Chapter 22: Science and Mysticism

192. Fritjof Capra, Tao of Physics: *An Exploration of Parallels between Modern Physics and Eastern Mysticism* (Shambhala Publications, 2010), 306.

193. William Arntz, Betsy Chasse, and Mark Vicente, *What the Bleep Do We Know? Discovering the endless Possibilities for Altering your |Everyday Reality* (Health Communications 2005), 41–214; Fritjof Capra, *Tao of Physics: An Exploration of Parallels between Modern Physics and Eastern Mysticism* (Shambhala Publications, 2010), 130–305, 330–341; Marilyn Ferguson, *The Aquarian Conspiracy: Personal and Social Transformation in Our Time* (Jeremy P. Tarcher/Penguin, 2009), 173–176, 399–440.

194. Masaru Emoto, *The Hidden Messages in Water* (New York: Atria Books, 2005), 40.

195. J. Krishnamurti, *The First and Last Freedom* (New York: Harper & Row, 1975); Eckhart Tolle, *The Power of Now: A Guide to Spiritual Enlightenment* (Namaste Publishing and New World Library, 2004).

Tool for the Journey 4—The Art of Observation

196. Quote from the Book of Exhortation, quoted in José Saramago, *Blindness* (Harcourt, 1997), Epigram.

Chapter 23: Touchpoints of Sanity

197 Rumi, quoted in Ram Dass, *Journey of Awakening: A Meditator's Guidebook* (New York: Bantam Books, 1990), 12.

198. I have not been able to verify the author of this quote, which has been attributed to Viktor Frankl. Stephen Covey writes in the forward to Alex Pattakos's book, *Prisoners of Our Thoughts,* that he came across it while browsing books in the university library while on a sabbatical in Hawaii.
[Alex Pattakos, *Prisoners of Our Thoughts: Viktor Frankl's Principles for Discovering Meaning in Life and Work*, (Berret-Koehler Publishers, 2010), foreword by Stephen R. Covey, vi.]

199. Sogyal Rinpoche, *The Tibetan Book of Living and Dying* (New York, San Francisco: Harper, 1992), 11.

200. Sylvia Maddox, "Where Can I Touch the Edge of Heaven?" http://ExploreFaith.org.

201. Eric Weiner, "Where Heaven and Earth Come Closer" *The New York Times*, March 9, 2012,

http://www.nytimes.com/2012/03/11/travel/thin-places-where-we-are-jolted-out-of-old-ways-of-seeing-the-world.html.

202. Kendra Cherry, "What are Peak Experiences?", February 13, 2016, http://psychology.about.com/od/humanist-personality/f/peak-experiences.htm.

203. C. George Boeree, "Personality Theories: Abraham Maslow," http://webspace.ship.edu/cgboer/maslow.html.

204. Daniel Goleman, *Working with Emotional Intelligence* (New York: Bantam Books, 2000), 107.

205. Mihaly Csikszentmihalyi, *Flow: The Psychology of Optimal Experience: Steps Toward Enhancing the Quality of Life* (New York: Harper & Row, 1990), esp. 1–22, 43–70, 214–215; Mihaly Csikszentmihalyi, "Flow, the secret of happiness," TED October 24, 2008, https://www.ted.com/talks/mihaly_csikszentmihalyi_on_flow.

206. Mihaly Csikszentmihalyi, *Flow: The Psychology of Optimal Experience: Steps Toward Enhancing the Quality of Life* (New York: Harper & Row, 1990), esp. 214.

207. Michael Jackson quoted in Jan Bommerez, comment on Michael Jackson, "Flow, Shiva's dance and Michael Jackson," July 30, 2011, the taoflow blog, http://www.the-tao-of-flow.com/flow-shiva-and-michael-jackson/.

208. Carlos Santana quoted in Leila Reyes, comment on Carlos Santana, "Carlos Santana Lives His Divine Purpose," The Divine Purpose Unleashed blog, http://www.divinepurposeunleased.com/carlos-santana-lives-his-divine-purpose/.

209. Jonathan Star, *Two Suns Rising: A Collection of Sacred Writings* (New Jersey: Castle Books, 1996), 120.

210. Amit Goswami, *Quantum Creativity: Think Quantum, Be Creative* London, New York: Hay House 2014), esp. 7–35, 67–70, 175–195.; Amit Goswami, *The Visionary Window: A Quantum Physicist's Guide to Enlightenment* (Wheaton, IL: Quest Books, 2000), esp. 165–189, 247–259.

211. Amit Goswami, *The Visionary Window: A Quantum Physicist's Guide to Enlightenment* (Wheaton, IL: Quest Books, 2000), 169

Chapter 24: Mountain—The Climb

212. Rumi, quoted in "States of Spiritual Development," Learning Institute for Growth, Healing and Transformation (LIGHT), 1, http://www.lightwinnipeg.org/Spiritual%20Writings/STAGES%20OF%20SPIRITUAL%20DEVELOPMENT.PDF

213. Bhante Henepola Gunaratana, quoted in "Mindfulness," Learning Institute for Growth, Healing and Transformation (LIGHT), 4, http://www.lightwinnipeg.org/Spiritual%20Writings/MINDFULNESS.pdf.

Endnotes

214. Stephen Mitchell, trans., foreword to *tao te ching: A New English Version* (New York: HarperCollins, 2006), vii–viii.

215. Zenrin, quoted in Ram Dass, *Journey of Awakening: A Meditator's Guidebook* (New York: Bantam Books, 1990), 127.

216. Robert Cribb, "ALS sufferer defies odds, celebrates life," *Toronto Star*, October 20, 2012. Steven Wells, who has a passion for online stock trading, suffers from Lou Gehrig's (ALS) disease (a slow and steady neuromuscular breakdown of nerves, brain and spinal cord). He was diagnosed in his second year of university and has lived 33 years with the disease when most of the people with ALS die within the first five years He uses a wheelchair with his head stabilized in a brace at the back of his chair and communicates using a computer.

217. Eckhart Tolle, *Realizing the Power of Now: An In-Depth Retreat* (Sounds True, August 29, 2003), (audiobook).

218. *Life as a House*, directed by Irwin Winkler, New Line Cinema, Nov. 9, 2001.

219. Sadhguru Joggi Vasudev, "Spirit of Eastern Wisdom: The Intelligence Within," (video), November 17, 2015, https://www.youtube.com/watch?v=LQC-A6Aukus.

Chapter 25: The Science and the Power of Meditation

220. Bruce H. Lipton, *The Honeymoon Effect: the science of creating heaven on earth* (London, New York: Hay House Inc. 2013), 11.

221. Krishnamurti Foundation of America, *The Collected Works of J. Krishnamurti: Volume XII1 962-1963: A psychological revolution by Jiddu Krishnamurti*, (Kendall/Hunt, 1992), 215.

222. Joe Dispenza, *Evolve your Brain: The Science of Changing Your Mind* (Dearfield, Florida: Health Communication, 2007), 10.

223. Lynne McTaggart, *The Intention Experiment: Using Your Thoughts to Change Your Life and the World* (New York: Atria Books, 2007), 66.

224. Peter Baksa, Can our Brainwaves affect our physical reality? HuffPost, Nov 26, 2011, https://www.huffingtonpost.com/peter-baksa/-can-thoughts-manipulate-_b_971869.html.

225. Catharine Paddock, "How Meditation Benefits The Brain," Medical News Today, Nov. 23, 2011, https://www.medicalnewstoday.com/articles/238093.php?utm_source=TrendMD&utm_medium=cpc&utm_campaign=Medical_News_Today_TrendMD_1; Alice G. Walton, "7 Ways Meditation Can Actually Change The Brain," Forbes.com, Feb. 9, 2015, https://www.forbes.com/sites/alicegwalton/2015/02/09/7-ways-meditation-can-actually-change-the-brain/#a7a364314658.

226. Jack Forem, *Transcendental Meditation: The Essential Teachings of Maharishi Mahesh Yogi,* (London, New York: Hay House, 2012), 72–91.

227. Alice G. Walton, "7 Ways Meditation Can Actually Change The Brain," Forbes.com, Feb. 9, 2015, https://www.forbes.com/sites/alicegwalton/2015/02/09/7-ways-meditation-can-actually-change-the-brain/#a7a364314658.; Carolyn Gregoire, "5 Ways Modern Science Is Embracing Ancient Indian Wisdom," HuffPost, December 8, 2014, http://www.huffingtonpost.ca/entry/science-embraces-ancient-indian-wisdom_n_6250978.

228. Jeffery L. Fannin and Robert M. William, "Neuroscience Reveals the Whole-Brain State and its Applications for International Business and Sustainable Success," *The International Journal of Management and Business* 3, no. 1 (August 2012), https://psych-k.com/v42012.pdf.

229. Lynne McTaggart, *Intention Experiment: Using Your Thoughts to Change Your Life and the World* (New York: Atria Books, 2007), 74.

230. Tom Ireland, "What Does Mindfulness Meditation Do to Your Brain?" *Scientific American,* June 12, 2014, https://blogs.scientificamerican.com/guest-blog/what-does-mindfulness-meditation-do-to-your-brain/.

231. Lynne McTaggart, *Intention Experiment: Using Your Thoughts to Change Your Life and the World* (New York: Atria Books, 2007), 74-75.

232. Jack Forem, *Transcendental meditation: The Essential Teachings of Maharishi Mahesh Yogi,* (London, New York: Hay House, 2012), 72–87.

233. Alarik Arenander, "Brainwaves, Total Brain Functioning, and the Development of Higher States of Consciousness: A Tutorial," Brain Research Institute, Maharishi University of Management, September, 2005, http://www.biosignalsedu.com/articles/BrainwaveTutorialv8.pdf.

234. Jack Forem, *Transcendental meditation: The Essential Teachings of Maharishi Mahesh Yogi,* (London, New York: Hay House, 2012), 72–86.

235. Carolyn Gregoire, "5 Ways Modern Science Is Embracing Ancient Indian Wisdom," HuffPost, December 8, 2014, http://www.huffingtonpost.ca/entry/science-embraces-ancient-indian-wisdom_n_6250978.

236. Alarik Arenander, "Brainwaves, Total Brain Functioning, and the Development of Higher States of Consciousness: A Tutorial," Brain Research Institute, Maharishi University of Management, September, 2005, http://www.biosignalsedu.com/articles/BrainwaveTutorialv8.pdf.8

237. Stephan A. Schwartz, "Meditate on This: The Practice Can Heal You in Less Than 11 Hours," HuffPost, Nov. 4, 2011, https://www.huffingtonpost.com/stephan-a-schwartz/effect-of-meditation-on-brain-_b_941082.html.

Endnotes

238. Jack Forem, *Transcendental meditation: The Essential Teachings of Maharishi Mahesh Yogi*, (London, New York: Hay House, 2012), 90–91.

239. Tom Ireland, "What Does Mindfulness Meditation Do to Your Brain?" Scientific American Online, June 12, 2014, https://blogs.scientificamerican.com/guest-blog/what-does-mindfulness-meditation-do-to-your-brain/.

240. William J. Cromie, "Meditation found to increase brain size," Harvard News Office, Feb. 2, 2006, http://news.harvard.edu/gazette/story/2006/02/meditation-found-to-increase-brain-size/

241. Bruce H. Lipton, *The Biology of Belief: Unleashing the Power of Consciousness, Matter & Miracles* (Hay House Inc.2015), xxiv, 138.

242. Jo Marchant, "Can Meditation really slow ageing?" July 1, 2014, https://mosaicscience.com/story/can-meditation-really-slow-ageing.

243. James Kingsland, "Could meditation really help slow the ageing process?" *The Guardian*, May 9, 2017, https://www.theguardian.com/science/blog/2016/mar/03/could-meditation-really-help-slow-the-ageing-process.

244. Kelly McGonigal, "The Big Brain Benefits of Meditation," *Yoga Journal*, https://www.yogajournal.com/lifestyle/brain-meditation.

245. Deepak Chopra, "Meditation: Change Your Brain, Change Your Life," beliefnet (website), http://www.beliefnet.com/columnists/intentchopra/2011/02/meditation-change-your-brain-c.html.

246. Johns Hopkins Medicine, "Meditation for anxiety, depression?" Science Daily, Jan 6, 2014, https://www.sciencedaily.com/releases/2014/01/140106190050.htm.

247. Connor Wood, "Gamma waves help meditation change the brain," March 18, 2012, http://www.patheos.com/blogs/scienceonreligion/2012/03/gamma-waves-help-meditation-change-the-brain/

248. Deepak Chopra, Leonard Mlodinow, *War of the Worldviews: Where Science and Spirituality Meet-and Do Not* (Ebury, 2011), 73-79.

249. Harald S. Harung and Frederick Travis, *Excellence through Mind-Brain Development: The Secrets of World-Class Performers* (London: Routledge, 2016), esp. ch. 7 and ch. 8.

250. Claire Bates, "Is this the world's happiest man? Brain scans reveal French Monk has 'abnormally large capacity for joy'—thanks to meditation," Mail Online, October 31, 2012, http://www.dailymail.co.uk/health/article-2225634/Is-worlds-happiest-man-Brain-scans-reveal-French-monk-abnormally-large-capacity-joy-meditation.html.

251. Lynne McTaggart, *Intention Experiment: Using Your Thoughts to Change Your Life and the World* (New York: Atria Books, 2007), 7–71.

Chapter 26: Meditation—At a Distance and Without Entanglement

252. Bruce H. Lipton, *The Honeymoon Effect: the science of creating heaven on earth* (London, New York: Hay House Inc. 2013), 90.

253. Amit Goswami, *The Visionary Window: A Quantum Physicist's Guide to Enlightenment* (Wheaton, IL: Quest Books, 2000), esp. 117, 178–179.

254. Ibid.

255. Jon Kabat-Zinn, *Wherever you go there you are: Mindfulness meditation in everyday life* (New York: Hyperion, 2005), 35; Jon Kabat-Zinn, *Full Catastrophe Living: Using the Wisdom of Your Body and Mind to Face Stress, Pain, and illness* (New York: Bantam Dell, 2005), 20.

256. Swami Brahmananda, quoted in Ram Dass, *Journey of Awakening: A Meditator's Guidebook* (New York: Bantam Books, 1990), 38.

257. Marilyn Ferguson, The *Aquarian Conspiracy: Personal and Social Transformation in Our Time* (Jeremy P. Tarcher/Penguin, 2009), 53.

258. Ven. Henepola Gunaratana, *Mindfulness in Plain English*, http://www.vipassana.com/meditation/mindfulness_in_plain_english.php.

259. Amit Goswami, *The Visionary Window: A Quantum Physicist's Guide to Enlightenment* (Wheaton, IL: Quest Books, 2000), esp. 255–256.

Chapter 27: Meditation—The Undoing of Our Personality

260. "Who Am I? (Nan Yar?) The Teachings of Bhagavan Sri Ramana Maharshi," Dr. T. M. P. Mahadevan, trans., (published by V. S. Ramanan), https://www.sriramanamaharshi.org/teachings/instructions/.

261. "Self-Enquiry, Teachings of Sri Ramana Maharshi," David Godman, edit., http://www.hinduism.co.za/self-enq.htm.

262. Ibid.

263. Ibid.

Chapter 28: Mountain—The Summit

264. Jean Klein, quoted in "States of Spiritual Development," Learning Institute for Growth, Healing and Transformation (LIGHT), 18,

http://www.lightwinnipeg.org/Spiritual%20Writings/STAGES%20OF%20SPIRITUAL%20DEVELOPMENT.PDF

Endnotes

Chapter 29: The Unconscious Person Awakens

265. Byron Katie with Stephen Mitchell, *A Thousand Names For Joy: Living in Harmony with the Way Things Are* (New York: Three Rivers Press, 2007), 75.

266. Sogyal Rinpoche, *The Tibetan Book of Living and Dying* (New York, San Francisco: Harper, 1992), 40.

267. Stephen Mitchell, trans., forward to *tao te ching: A New English Version* (New York: HarperCollins, 2006), 1.

268. Shunryu Suzuki, quoted in Ram Dass, *Journey of Awakening: A Meditator's Guidebook* (New York: Bantam Books, 1990), 138.

269 Osho, *The Book of Secrets: 112 Meditations To Discover The Mystery Within* (New York: St. Martin's Press, 2010), 1050

270. Eckhart Tolle, *A New Earth: Awakening to Your Life's* Purpose (New York: Penguin Group, 2005), 160.

271. Shunryu Suzuki, *Zen Mind, Beginner's Mind* (Boulder, CO: Shambhala Publications, 1970), 20.

272. Eckhart Tolle, *A New Earth: Awakening to Your Life's* Purpose (New York: Penguin Group, 2005), 267.

Chapter 30: Mountain—The Return

273. Rene Daumal, quoted in Ram Dass, *Journey of Awakening: A Meditator's Guidebook* (New York: Bantam Books, 1990), 213.

274. "Two-thirds of the accidents happen on the way down...If you get euphoric and think 'I have reached my goal,' the most dangerous part is still ahead of you." Eric Arnold, the Dutch climber who scaled Mount Everest on his fifth try in May 2016 only to die from altitude sickness descending the mountain. Quoted in Binaj Gurubacharya, "Terrifying weekend on Everest," *Toronto Star*, May 23, 2016.

275. Amit Goswami, *The Visionary Window: A Quantum Physicist's Guide to Enlightenment* (Wheaton, IL: Quest Books, 2000), esp.279.

276. Thomas Cleary, trans., *The Secret of the Golden Flower: The Classic Chinese Book of Life* (San Francisco: Harper, 1991), 2.

277. Robert Sibley, "Why the force is still with us," George Lucas 1999 interview for *Time Magazine, Ottawa Citizen*, May 26, 2007.
https://www.aarweb.org/sites/default/files/pdfs/Programs_Services/Journalism_Award_Winners/2008Sibley.pdf

278. Jean Klein, quoted in "States of Spiritual Development," Learning Institute for Growth, Healing and Transformation (LIGHT), 17,
http://www.lightwinnipeg.org/Spiritual%20Writings/STAGES%20OF%20SPIRITUAL%20DEVELOPMENT.PDF

Index

addiction
  stress, 60
  technology, 8–10
adrenaline, 74, See also stress
aging
  conditioning and, xxxix, 32, 39, 42, 44, 68
  loneliness and, 64, See also loneliness
  meditation and, 212–14
  neuroplasticity and, 78, 206
  stress and, 77, 107
aha insight. See insights
algorithms, 40, See also technology
alpha waves
  coherence of. See meditation
  creative state and, 21
  during meditation. See meditation
  during relaxation, 127
  frequency range of, 27, 127
  in adults, 127–28
  in children, 27
  relaxed and awake state and, 127
  right brain and, 127
  subconscious and conscious state and, 22, 127
altitude
  meaning of, xxxv
  principle of life, xxxi–xxxii
  trust factor, xxxv
amygdala
  early warning system, 73–75, 84
  hijack, 46, 86, 209
  stress center, 79
anxiety
  beginning of, 31
  fear and, 44–45, 74
  gap, 17, 64, 69
  silence and, 53
  voice in the head and, 37, 45–46, 65–71, See also voice in the head
Arbesman, Samuel, 159
atoms. See also matter
  building blocks of universe, 136–40
  electrons and, 140–47
  elementary/subatomic particles and, 136, 139–46
  emptiness/energy of, 140–46, 161, See also energy; void
  neutrons and, 140
  nucleus of, 140–41
  protons and, 140
  subatomic world of, 140
attention
  control of, 8, 220, See also technology
  defination of, xxvi, xxxiv–xxxv
  expansion into awareness, 26, 220, 243
  flow and, 199
  goldfish/short span and, 8, 198
  intention and, xxxiv
  life force, xxvi, xxxv, 8
  mindfulness, 200
  moment by moment awareness or, xxxv, 198, 220, 257, See also mindfulness
  observation and, xxxv, See also observation
  prefrontal cortex and, xxxiv, 99
  social media and, xxvi, 8, See also technology
  thought and, xxxv, 227
  training of, xxvii, 220
attitude
  behavior and, xl
  intention and, xxxiii
  meaning of, xxxiii
  principle of life, xxxi–xxxii

awareness. *See also* being, natural state of
  aware of itself, 227
  deep stillness, 211
  defination of, 25
  heightened or expanded, 26, 117, 179, 215–17, 226, 238, 257, *See also* meditation;peak experiences
  intuitive mind and, 222
  lack of, 24, *See also* unconscious
  passive, 27
  prefrontal cortex seat of, 98, 208
  primary or pure, 14–15, 179, 230–31, 246, *See also* consciousness
  secondary, limited or everyday, 15–16, 26, 177, 231
  self, 99, 117, 166
  shift in, xxviii, 198, 205, 235

bardo, 188, See also gaps
beginner's mind
  child's mind, xlii, 25
  I don't know mind, xxxvii
  loving and compassionate, xxxix
  non-judgemental, xli, 220, 255
  patient, xxxviii
being, natural state of
  awake brain on idle, condition of, 128, 210
  awareness, xxvii, 26–27, 174, 256
  bliss, 162
  Buddha nature. *See* Buddha nature
  creative state, xxiv, 14
  encounter with, 185–95, 199, 230, 243–46
  existence of, 133–34
  higher states of consciousness and, 129
  living in awareness, 36
  maintaining, 175
  nonlocal state of consciousness, 134, 143, 162, 172–73
  operating from, xxvi
  original mind, 14
  presence, 14
  quantum consciousness, 143
  silence, 230
Bernstein, Albert J., 87
beta waves
  active or awake state and, 20, 125
  conscious state and, 22
  during meditation, 207
  during relaxation, 127
  frequency range of, 30, 127, 216
  high, 30, 73, 77, 116
  high alpha waves and low, 31, 127
  in adults, 30, 125–27
  in children, 30
  left brain and, 127, *See also* left brain
  low, 30
  medium, 30
  stress and, 30, 37, 45–46, 73, 77, 116, 127, 198
Blake, William, xxiv, 163
Book of Exhortations, xvii, 177
boredom. *See also* loneliness
  beginning of, 31
  condition of, xli
  mind and, 6
  pain experiment, 65
brain
  corpus callosum in, 109
  development in adults, 30–32, 107
  development in children, 24–31, 95, 107
  evolution of, 83–85, 87–88, 91–92, 95–99, 107
  four sub brains in, xxviii, 84
  integration of, xxvii, 78, 83, 86, 99, 103, 112, 165–66, 196, 266, *See also* meditation
  left and right, 85, 97, *See also* left brain; right brain
  limbic/emotional or mammalian, 84
  lobes in, 85, 98
  mind relationship to, 14
  neocortex/prefrontal or human, 85, 99, See also prefrontal cortex
  neocortex/primate or intellectual, 85, 98
  reptilian or survival, 84
  split-brain, 110, 122

Index

brain waves. *See also* specific brain waves
  coherence of. *See* alpha waves
  electrical activity and, 22, 207
  frequencies, 20
  mental states and, 20
  synchrony of. *See* gamma waves
Brown, Dan, 167
Brown, Ramsay, 8
Buddha nature, xxv
Buddhism, Chan, 15, 16

Campbell, Joseph, 263
Capra, Fritjof, 139, 171–72
cerebral cortex. *See* brain, neocortex
chattering mind. *See* voice in the head
Chopra, Deepak, 155, 214
classical science
  cause and effect in, 137
  consciousness and. *See* consciousness
  observation and. *See* observation
  reality and, 157
  study of large objects, 139
  subatomic particles and, 142
conditioned conscious spirit, 16, *See also* ego
conditioned self. *See* ego
conditioning
  anxiety, result of, 69
  awareness, constricted by, 26, 177
  beginning of, 16, 24–31
  breaking through, xxix, 54, 195, 222
  change and, 158, 168
  ego and, 17, 19, 51, *See also* ego
  filter bubble and. *See* technology
  force of, 261–65
  memories and, 29, 58
  mental concepts as, xxxix, 28, 40, 58, 175, 249
  personality and. *See* ego; personality
  reinforcement of, xxxix, 8, 68
  reptilian or survival brain and, 88
  subconscious mind and, 42–43, 88, 107, *See also* subconscious mind
  thought and, 39

conscious breath
  as anchor, 80, 258
  power of, 80, 258, *See also* meditation
conscious mind
  analytical/rational, 24
  aspect of, 22–24
  development in children, 25–30
  higher cognitive/executive functions and, 85
conscious or creative force, 8, 31, 194, 261–65
consciousness
  aware of, 162
  classical science and, 135–37, 155
  divine self as, 14, *See also* being, natural state of
  everyday ego, xxiv, xxviii, 15, *See also* ego
  ground of all being as, xxv, 14, 143, 173, *See also* being, natural state of
  lantern, of children, 25
  mind and. *See* mind
  nature of, 14
  optical delusion and, 13
  quantum physics and, 134, 147–48, 161–62, 169, 172–75
  spotlight, of adults, 25
  two modes of, 110, 244
  universal intelligence. *See* intelligence, innate/universal
consumerism
  advertising and, 7
  consumption and, xxvii, 7, 156
  defines us, 7
  unhappiness and, 7
Cooper, Robert K., 73
cortisol, 62, 74, *See also* stress
cosmic consciousness, 14, *See also* being, natural state of
cosmic homesickness, 122, *See also* inner yearning
creative state. *See* being, natural state of
Csikszentmihalyi, Mihaly, 191–94

Daumal, Rene, 259
Davidson, Richard, 216
Dawkins, Richard, 156
decision lag time. *See* subconscious mind
deficiency needs. *See* hierarchy of needs
delta waves
    deep sleep state and, 21
    during meditation, 128
    frequency range of, 25, 128
    in adults, 128
    in children, 24
    subconscious state and, 22, 128
dependence
    codependence, 251
    freedom and, 251
    independence, 251
Descartes, Rene, 121–25, 136–37, 136, 157, 166, 252
designing brains. *See* technology
detachment
    apathy and, 191, 248
    indifference and, 248
    meaning of, 248
    withdrawal from life and, 47, 248
discontentment, 7, 66
discontinuous. *See* quantum jump/leap
Dispenza, Joe, 46, 60, 99, 127, 161
dopamine, xxvi, 9
Dostoevsky, Fyodor, xxxviii
double-slit experiment, 146, *See also* observer effect
Du Sautoy, Marcus, 50
duality. *See also* left brain; perception
    "either or" thinking, xxiii, 110, 115, 136
    stress and, 178
    subject-object split or, 15

EEG (electroencephalogram), 22, 162, 207
effortless effort, 191, 200, *See also* flow; meditation
ego. *See also personality*
    "I" thought as, 26, 28
    anxiety gap and, 17
    conditioned programs and. *See* subconscious mind
    conditioning and, 40, *See also* conditioning
    death of, 54, 236, 243–46, 250
    development of, 14–16, 25–30, 234
    everyday consciousness as, 28, 111
    false or conditioned self, xxviii, 32
    free will and. *See* free will
    function of, 68
    home of, 24, 26, 98
    left brain and, 111
    materialist mindset and, 157
    mental concepts and, 29, 120, 234, 255
    silence and, 53
    strengthening of, 194
    stress and, xxiv
    vigilance and, 257–58
    voice of, 59, *See also* voice in the head
Einstein, Albert, xxiii, xxiv, xxix, 13, 153
elementary/subatomic particles. *See* atoms
emotional center. *See* amygdala
emotional intelligence
    defination of, 166
    difficulty of teaching, 165
    lack of, 73, *See also* stress
emotions and feelings, 91, 93
emptiness/energy. *See* atoms; void
energy
    attention and, xxxv
    brain waves and, 207
    desire and, xxxiii
    during flow, 191
    intention and, xxxi, xxxiii–xxxv
    life sustaining, 75, 197
    quantum field and, 164, 167
    stress and, 60, 76, 125
    subatomic universe and, 133, 139, 141–44, 145, 161, 173
    thought and, xxxi, xxxiii

Index

transformation and, 244, 250
enlightenment. See also liberation; transcendence
   expansion of consciousness, 112, 186
   gaps of, 186–89, See also present moment awareness
   non-dualistic or unitive perspective, 186
   profound common sense, as, xxiii
   self-transcendence and, 104, 175
epsilon waves
   frequency range of, 129, 216
   higher states of consciousness and, 129, 215
exoteric/esoteric, xxii

Facebook, 8–10, 40, See also technology
false self. See ego
Faraday chambers, 162
feelings, 199, 253–55, See also emotions and feelings
feminine/masculine principles, 112, 117, 119, 260
Ferguson, Marilyn, 70, 83, 122, 227
Feynman, Richard, 149
fight or flight response, 73, 76, 92, See also stress
filter bubble. See technology
Fischer, Bobby, 192
flow, 117, 191–94, 216, 260, See also being, natural state of
fMRI (Functional Magnetic Resonance Imaging), 49, 106
Ford, Henry, xxxvii
fourth brain. See prefrontal cortex
free will
   limited by ego, 50, 158
   prefrontal cortex and, xxxiv, 99
   unlimited beyond ego, 51
freedom, 247, 250–51, See also liberation; enlightenment; transcendence
future, 33–36, See also time

gamma waves
   during meditation, 129, 207, 216
   frequency range of, 129, 215
   higher states of consciousness and, 129, 215
   synchrony, 216, See also happiness
Gandhi, Mahatma, 19, 30, 168
gaps, 186–89, 229–31, See also meditation
Garfield, Charles, 47
genes
   epigenetics and, 213
   meditation affecting. See meditation
   stress and, 214
Goleman, Daniel, 92, 165–66, 191
Gopnik, Alison, 20, 24–26, 119, 267
Goswami, Amit, xxiii, xxxix, 144–45, 170, 231
Goyal, Madhav, 215
guest, 16, 18, See also ego
Gunaratana, Bhante Henepola, 198
Gurdjieff, G I., 3
gut feeling, 112, 118, 209, See also intuition

Hanyashingyo, Buddhist Wisdom and Heart Sutra, 174
happiness
   effect of stress on, 46–47
   external world and, 9, 157
   gamma synchrony and, 216
   insights and, 195
   natural creative state of mind and, xliii
   pleasure and, 77
   right brain and, 119
   source of, 69, 119
   touchpoints of, 187
   transcendence and, xliii
Harbaugh, Bill, 106
Haynes, John-Dylan, 49
hierarchy of needs, 88, 92, 103
hologram, 162–64
host, 15, 18, See also being, natural state of
human beings
   lumbering robots, 156

machines, 135, 155
  stressed-out computing machines, 159
hypnosis, xxvi, See also theta waves

illusion (maya), 165, 174
individualized thought system, 16, 20, 58
inner creativity/inner journey
  aha moments/insights and, 195, 266
  doing phase and being phase in, 202
  letting go in, 201–3
  meaning of, xxxix
  process of, xx, xxxii–xxxv, 195, 197–204, 224, 243–46, 260–67
  progress in, 203–4
  role of guides in, 201, 266
inner yearning, 104, 262–65
insights, 117–18, 170, 194–96, 255, See also inner creativity/inner journey
instincts
  force of, 261–65
  gut. See gut feeling
  reptilian or survival brain and, 84, 87
  stress and, 76
  survival mode, 50, 104, 256
intellect
  development of, 27–28
  function of, xxxiv, 45, 97, 114, 252
  intelligence and, 253–55, See also intelligence, innate/universal
  stress and, 78, 107
intelligence, innate/universal, 13, 28, 50, 79, 117, 143, 175, 253, See also being, natural state of; wisdom
intention
  attention and, xxxiv, See also attention
  attitude and, xxxiii, See also attitude
  chaotic mind and, 169
  meaning of, xxxi
  meditation and, 257
  prefrontal cortex and, xxxiv, 99
  process of, xxxiii
internal reference point

  ego as, xxiv, 177, 248, 249, See also ego
  true self as, xxiv, 104, 178, 248, See also being, natural state of
intuition
  beyond mind, 252, See also being, natural state of
  common sense, xxvii, 115
  feminine principle, 113, See also feminine/masculine principles
  gut feeling. See gut feeling
  insights, 170, See also insights
  meditation and, 209
  right brain and, 118, 122
  theta waves and, 128

Jackson, Michael, 193
Jung, Carl, xxvi–xxvii, 97, 263

Kabat-Zinn, Jon, xix
Katie, Byron, xl, 66, 247
Klein, Jean, 243
knowledge
  intellectual/rational, xxii, xxxiv, xli, 28, 114, 115, 118, 121, 179, 195, See also left brain
  intuitive/creative, xxii, xxviii, xxxiv, 117–18, 175, 194–95, 235, See also right brain; wisdom
Krishnamurti, J., 175, 206

lambda waves
  frequency range of, 129, 216
  higher states of consciousness and, 129, 215
language
  limitation of, 174, 237, 251–52
  of logic, xli
  of love, xli
Lao-Tzu, 125, 200, 251
Laszlo, Ervin, 133
laughter, xlii, xliii, 252
learning
  accelerated, 27–28
  children and, 25–31

Index

dual-brain processing, 27, 119
lopsided. *See* left brain
Lebow, Victor, 156
left brain
    analytical/rational/intellectual, 78
    ego and, 114
    focus on survival of physical body, 115
    in adults, 113–16
    in children, 25
    intellect and, 114
    lopsided development of, 28, 31, 115, 121, 123, 157
    mental concepts and, 114
    noisy/ voice in the head and, 114–16
    rational/logical mind and, 110
    yang/masculine characteristics of, 112, *See also* feminine and masculine principles
Leonard, Annie, 7
liberation, 112, 175, 188, *See also* enlightenment; freedom; transcendence
Lipton, Bruce, 30, 75, 114, 169, 213, 219
living in creativity. See also being, natural state of
    contentment and, xlii
    natural state of being and, xxix, 263
living in survival/stress. See also ego
    ego consciousness and, xxix
    less divine, 46
    misery/suffering and, xlii, 263
loneliness. *See also* boredom
    aging and, 64
    beginning of, 31
    definition of, 63
love
    experience of, xxxiv
    peak experiences as, 190
    self, xl, 250
    source of, 119
    transformative power of, xl, xli, xliii, 247
    unconditional, 250
Lucas, George, 263

Maharaj, Sri Nisargadatta, 57, 175
Maharshi, Sri Ramana, 233, 235, 239
mammalian brain. *See* brain
Maslow, Abraham, 88, 92, 103, 117, 189–92
materialism. *See also* materialistic/physical
    dangers of, xxvii
    stress and, xxvi
materialistic/physical
    aspect of world, 136, 155
    mindset. *See* ego
    science. *See* classical science
matter
    atoms and, 136
    defination of, 136
    elementary/subatomic particles and. *See* atoms
maya. *See* illusion (maya)
McTaggart, Lynne, xxxi
mechanistic science. *See* classical science
meditation
    aging and, 212–14
    alpha coherence during, 210, 211, 216
    alpha waves during, 207, 210, 223
    amygdala and, 208
    anxiety, depression, pain and, 215
    attention and, 220
    brain integration and, 198, 206–12, *See also* brain
    breath and, 80, 221, 225–26, *See also* conscious breath
    complete psychological revolution, 206
    concentration, 220–26
    creativity and, 208
    default mode network and, 208
    detachment and, 248
    doing-not-doing in, 200
    dose dependent, 209, 225
    effortless effort. *See* effortless effort
    expansion of consciousness and, 26, 172, 205

gamma synchrony and. *See* gamma waves
gene activity and, 213, 214
gut feeling and. See gut feeling
higher states of consciousness and, 80, 215–17, See also gamma waves; lambda waves; epsilon waves
mind-body connection and, 210, 214
observing thoughts in, 200, 220–22, 226–31, *See also* meditation, witness
practice, 222–25, 236–39
prefrontal cortex and, 208–12, 212, 216
quantum leaping in, 231, *See also* quantum jump/leap
self-inquiry, 234–39
sitting, 220, 257
stress and, 206, 209
subconscious programming and, 206
theta waves during, 223
training the brain, 221
voice in the head and, 198
witnessing, 220, 226–31
memories
amygdala and, 94–95
creating, 15, 27
mental concepts as, xxviii, 187
thought forms, 15
wall of, 15, 29, 31, See also mind
mental concepts. *See* conditioning; ego; left brain; memories; thoughts
mental distress, 10, 61, *See also* mind; stress
Merton, Thomas, 63
mind
altered state of. See being, natural state of
chatter. See voice in the head
conscious. See conscious mind
consciousness and, 14
creative, 58
disturbance, 44
intuitive/irrational, xxii, xxxv, 110
levels of, 14, 22, 172

meaning of, xxxii, 14, 233
monkey, 33, 98
natural state of, 58, 69, See also being, natural state of
noisy. See voice in the head
ordinary/superficial, 15, *See also* ego
original, 14, *See also* being, natural state of
rational/logical, xxii, xxxiii, 110, *See also* conscious mind
subconscious. See subconscious mind
thought-making machine, xxxii
working brain and, 14
mindfulness. *See also* attention; meditation
definition of, 198, 220
habit of, 220
practice, 198–201
stress and, 198, 318
Mindfulness Based Stress Reduction (MSRB), 208, *See also* mindfulness
Monroe, George (movie character), 204
mountain climbing. *See also* inner creativity/inner journey
four-stage journey, xx
metaphor for inner journey, xix
mystical/mysticism
Albert Einstein's view of, xxiii
defination of, xxiii
experience, 171
transformative system, as, xxiii
mystics
quantum physics and, 148, 170, *See also* mystical/mysticism
transcending mind, 83

natural state of being. See being, natural state of
neuroplasticity, 78, 206
Nirvana. See right brain
no mind, 14, *See also* being, natural state of
non-duality. *See also* right brain
"and" stance, 118
unitive/holistic perspective, xxiii, 110, 178, *See also* perception

Index

observation. See also meditation; observer effect
   classical science and, 137, 146
   mind and, 83
   observer/observed and, 145
   of thoughts, 76
   pure, 15, 179
   quantum physics and. See observer effect
   right brain, 179
observer effect, 144, 146–47, 167, 169, 173–74, 225, 229
original mind, 14, See also being, natural state of
original spirit, 15, See also being, natural state of
Ornstein, Robert, 110

Parker, Sean, 10
particles. See atoms; quantum
Pascal, Blaise, 53
passive awareness. See awareness
past, 33–37, See also time
Patton, George S., 60
peak experiences, 117, 189–91
pendulum of thought. See also thoughts
   conditioning, reinforcing of, 36
   voice in the head, 36–37, See also voice in the head
perception
   dualistic, 246
   look, 178, 180
   non-dualistic, xxiv, 178, 246
   observe, 179, 180
   see, 177, 180
personal world. See individualized thought system
personality. See also ego
   dark triad of, 88
   differences in left and right brain, 110
   formation of, 29, 42, 64, 234
Philo of Alexandria, xlii
Picasso, 192

pole, pole, or slowly, slowly, 197, See also mindfulness
Pope Francis, 49
prefrontal cortex. See also brain
   altruistic behavior and, 105
   amygdala connection, 208, See also meditation
   deterioration of, 46, 107
   development of, 107
   middle, 99, 104
   seat of awareness, 98
   self-awareness and. See awareness
   stress and, 46
presence. See being, natural state of
present moment. See also awareness
   absence of thoughts, 112
   awareness, xxvi, 112, 186, 188, 208, 236
   children and, 25–26
   meaning of, 35
   natural state of being and. See being, natural state of
   now, 35
   subatomic world and, 154
primary awareness. See awareness
primordial brain. See brain, reptilian/survival
programming. See conditioning

quanta, 140
quantum
   cause and effect relationship, 154
   collapse, 144, 215
   consciousness. See being, natural state of
   discontinuity. See quantum jump/leap
   energy field, 207
   entanglement, 153, 162, 164, 167, 207
   jump/leap, 140, 154, 167, 170, 196, 231, 255, 256, 266
   nature of thoughts, 222
   nonlocality/nonlocal state of consciousness. See being, natural state of

311

observer effect. *See* observation
particle/wave duality, 143, 207
physics and classical science,
    differences, 149–54
probabilities/possibilities, 142–45,
    151–53, 167–69, 172–73
signal-less communication, 161–62
subatomic world. *See* atoms
superposition, 142, 152–53, 207, 215
tunneling, 154
uncertainty, 221
quantum physics, xxii, xxv, 122, 139,
    196, 221, 225, 266

rational mind. *See* intellect; left brain
reality, nature of, 66–67
relaxation
    brain waves during. *See* individual
        brain waves
    escape into, 6
    skill of, 125
Renzetti, Elizabeth, 64
Ricard, Matthieu, 216
right brain
    compassion, 111
    cultivating, 197
    heart as, 118
    in adults, 116–19
    in children, 24–32
    intuitive/irrational mind and, 110
    Nirvana and, 110
    present moment and, 116
    silent, 117
    wisdom and, 117
    yin/feminine characteristics of, 112,
        117, *See also* feminine and
        masculine principles
Rinpoche, Sogyal, 188, 248
Rohr, Richard, 112
Routley, Nancy, 39
Rumi, 11, 185, 194, 197, 205
runner's high, 193

same old, same old, 47, 75, 94
Sanskrit shloka, 33

Santana, Carlos, 193
Saramago, José, 177
sat chit ananda, 162, See also being,
    natural state of
secondary awareness. *See* awareness
self-actualization, 191, 263
self-help books
    for survival of egos, xliii, 4
    why they don't work, 42–44, 158
self-talk. *See* voice in the head
servant, 16, *See also* ego
Shabistari, Mahmud, 163
Shakespeare, 58
silence, xxx, 54, 230, 252, *See also*
    meditation; relaxation
Sledge, Sharlande, 189
social media. *See* technology
Sperry, Roger, 110
spirituality
    meaning of, xxiii, 263
    stress and, xxiii, *See also* stress
split-brain. *See* brain
Star Wars movie, 263
Story of Stuff, 7
stress. *See also* fight-or-flight response
    addiction to, 60
    aging and, 77, *See also* aging;
        meditation
    aliveness and, 46–47
    beta waves and. *See* beta waves
    brain freeze and, 75, 88
    breathing and, 79
    cause of, 11, 63–71
    chemicals of. *See* adrenaline; cortisol
    children and, 6
    ego and, xxiv, *See also* ego
    foundation of, 64
    freedom from, 78
    genes and. *See* genes
    instincts and, 76
    intellect and, 78
    key ingredients of, 61
    physical/mental health and, 62
    routine trap and, 75
    spirituality and, xxiii, *See also*
        spirituality

Index

stopgap fixes and, 62
suffering and, 57
survival or protective mode and, 73
thoughts and, 58
uncertainty and, xxviii
voice in the head and, 58, 68, See also voice in the head
way of life and, 61
worry and, 59, 70–73, 202
stroke of insight, 110
subatomic world. See atoms
subconscious mind
   aspects of, 22–24
   conditioned/automatic programs in, 22, 30, 219
   decision lag time and, 49
   ego and, 59, See also ego
   emotional, 84
   forces of, 262
   in children, 25, 27
   instinctive, 84
   power of, 43
Sufi, xxiv, 10, 163
survival
   anxiety and, 45–46
   fittest, of the, 61, 76, 88
   reaction, 46
Suzuki Shunryu, xxxv–xxxvii, 252, 256
Swami Brahmananda, 223
Sylwester, Robert, 91

Taylor, Jill, 110, 116
technology
   addiction, 8–10
   attention control and, xxvii
   attention economy and, 7
   dangers of, xxvii, 8, 10, 61, 159, See also conditioning
   designing brains and, 8
   filter bubble, 40–42
   inner self and, xxvii, See also being, natural state of
   social media, xxvi, 6, 9–10, 42, 61, 65
   stress and, xxvi, 4, See also stress
telepathy, 162
telomeres. See genes

theta waves
   frequency range of, 25, 128
   in adults, 128
   in children, 25
   insight and, 128
   semi-awake state, 21, 128
   subconscious state and, 22
Thin places, 189, See also gaps
thought-making machine. See mind
thoughts
   "I" as a network of, xxviii, 28–29, 234
   attacked by, 74
   attention and, 34
   awareness and, 227
   babies and, 25
   beliefs and, 19
   beyond, 51, 164, See also being, natural state of; meditation
   conscious breath and, 79–80
   content of, 39, See also conditioning
   controller of, 229
   energy of, xxxi, 169
   gaps between, 170, See also gaps; meditation
   identification with, xxiv
   interference of, xl
   mental concepts or, 29, 45, 67, 114, 118, 175, 229, 234, 244, 253
   nature of, xxxi, 37, 71, 79, 233
   noisy, 58, See also voice in the head
   observing. See observation
   pendulum of, 34–37
   power to transform, xxxi, 167
   quantum nature of, 221
   reality and, 35–36, 70
   recycled, 37, 228
   stress and. See stress
   targeted or focused, xxxiii, 167, 169, See also intention
   thinker and, xxxii, 67
   thinking and, 227
   wall of, 15, See also memories
   worry. See stress
time. See also future; past; present moment

313

chronological or clock, 36
psychological or inward, 36
Tolle, Eckhart, 35, 175, 203, 256–58
transcendence, 100, 103, 162, 175, 210–12, 231, 247–58, *See also* enlightenment; freedom; liberation
transformation
   beginning of, xl, 230, 244
   change and, 158
   classical science and, 158
   complete psychological revolution, 206
   quantum physics and, 167, 266
   stages of. *See* inner creativity
true nature/self. *See* being, natural state of
trust factor. *See* altitude

uncertainty principle. *See* quantum uncertainty
unconscious
   definition of, 24
   lost in thought, 16, 31
   state, 16, 22–24, 43, 256

virtual world/reality, 29, 40, 59, 114, 164, 175, 234, *See also* ego
voice in the head
   effect of, xxxii, 74
   ego as, xxiii, *See also* ego
   fantasy world, 203

intellectual brain, home of, 98, *See also* brain
silence and, 54, 243, *See also* meditation
stress and. *See* stress
what does it sound like, 60
void, 173, *See also* atom

waves. *See* quantum
Weiner, Eric, 189
Wells, Steven, 202
whole-brain functioning, 166, 170, 195, *See also* brain, integration of
Williams, James, xxvii, 8
Wilson, Timothy, 65
wired ego, 7, *See also* ego
wired world, 8, 220, *See also* technology
wisdom, xlii, 15, 122, 195, See also intelligence, innate/universal; knowledge
worry. *See* stress

yin/yang, 112, *See also* feminine/masculine principles

Zenrin, 201
Zimmerman, Ann, 6
zone, being in. *See* flow
Zukav, Gary, 141, 145

Acknowledgments

There have been many people who have come into my life over the years and helped me on my journey of self-exploration. Whether brief or long each encounter has left an ever-lasting impression and I am eternally grateful to all of them.

I want to acknowledge and thank some of the people who have given generously of their time, expertise, energy, and wisdom to make **Calm Brain, Powerful Mind** a reality.

My sincere gratitude to my remarkable editor, Cristina Joyce Fuller, whose knowledge and astute querying helped clarify many of the key concepts in the book. The book you are holding in your hands is very different from the draft I first discussed with Cristina many months ago in Portland, Oregon. Her insightful suggestions regarding the rearrangement of some of the sections have made the content flow smoothly, conveying the depth and richness of the experiential content.

I want to express my appreciation to all the members of "Searching for Meaning Reading Group" which include Beth Langhorst, Gwyneth Mast, Adam Alfsen, Isabelle Bruce, Branden Rennie, Helga Brown, Mike, and Richard Targett, and the late Larry Tod. Larry was the driving force of the group for many years. We miss you, Larry. The wonderful discussions we have at these meetings have helped me grow immensely. A special thank you to Katherine Selby, who continues to be a source of inspiration to the group.

I am greatly indebted to John Mclachlan, Jim Pappas, and Preetum Anauth. What started off as a discussion on the artwork for the book cover with John, ended up with John playing a significant role in the design of the book. He created the artwork, the illustrations, and the layout of the book. Working with Jim, he even designed the **Calm Brain, Powerful Mind** website.

John became part of a unique group of individuals that included Jim and Preetum, who all played a crucial role in getting the book ready for publication. I don't know where to begin to thank these three extraordinary creative friends and natural problem solvers. Nothing was too difficult for them. We connected at a different level of consciousness, and they brought incredible energy, fun, and laughter to the project. They critiqued the many draft versions of the manuscript, developed marketing strategies and databases, and took it upon themselves to spread the message I am trying to convey. They also got their friends and families together to help launch the "Conversations with Friends Series of Seminars." These seminars are based on the teachings of **Calm Brain, Powerful Mind**. Preetum even took care of the logistics providing space and refreshments for these seminars.

We certainly didn't set out to create a Mastermind Group, but we morphed into one over countless breakfasts and hours of enlightening conversations over the last couple of years. They are a joy to be with, and words cannot adequately express my gratitude to them.

I would also like to especially thank Jim Pappas for writing the foreword for the book and coming up with the title. With just a few words, he captured the essence of the book.

Thanks to my friend Ed Shields, for his love, advice, and support for this project.

Acknowledgements

I also want to thank Sifu Tommy Cheng, a gifted, wise, and patient Tai Chi Master, who showed me another way to ground myself in the present moment. Tai Chi, with its rich heritage of centuries of moving meditation and internal energy practices, brings together the opposing forces of yin (feminine) and yang (masculine) within us. It is a way of being that I write about in this book. The world needs more people like Tommy, and I hope one day, he decides to write about his teachings.

Special thanks to my travel buddies and dear friends Shafiq and Farzana Khimji. Shafiq, thank you for your invaluable comments on the earlier versions of the draft manuscript and the many delightful early morning conversations we had in those far away (and not so far away) lands. I am looking forward to our next adventure.

I also want to express my deepest appreciation to my brothers Anvarali Velji, Iqubal Velji, my sister-in-law Yasmin Jiwani, and my brother-in-law Alnashir Alibhai for critiquing the different versions of the draft manuscript, and for the many illuminating conversations over the years. They were not only my sounding boards, but their experience and in-depth knowledge of some of the material I have discussed helped me articulate many of the concepts in the book. I look forward to many more of these conversations, as we go through this life together.

Special thanks to my daughter Faheema Velji-Shears, for reading the earlier versions of the draft and giving me a young person's perspective on the concepts discussed in the book. Her insightful comments helped me simplify some of the content. I am also grateful to my son-in-law Scott for the many conversations we had on his common-sense approach to engineering or for that matter, everything he does in life. This approach resonates with the many ideas I talk about in the book.

Profound thanks to my late parents, Shirin and Madat Meghji. They are not around to see the publication of the book, but we did get a chance to spend many hours discussing some of the ideas and concepts I talk about.

I am filled with gratitude for the many past and present-day spiritual teachers, some of who I have quoted in the book, who have guided me on this journey. I have never met any of them, but I feel I know them intimately through their work. Without their wisdom, I wouldn't even have known there was a journey. I am truly indebted and grateful to all of them.

A special thank you to our Mount Kilimanjaro team headed by our guides Loisolo Lobulu and Nile Msaro, for safely guiding us to the summit and back. In climbing Kilimanjaro, I was reminded again and again that when we are mindful, it is difficult to be stressed on the journey. We are so completely focused on the path that we are not worrying and being overwhelmed by what lies ahead.

I wish to express my deep gratitude and respect to Meena, my life partner, and soulmate on this incredible journey of life. I owe so much to her. Without her unconditional love, encouragement, patience, and wisdom, **Calm Brain, Powerful Mind** would not have had the opportunity to manifest.

About the Author

Aziz Velji is a student, teacher, and author. His background encompasses specialized areas of study and expertise in philosophy, psychology, meditation practices, quantum physics, brain enhancement, neuroscience, and lucid dreaming (or what is called Dream Yoga). His formal education includes postgraduate degrees in engineering and business management. He has applied these areas of study and training to better understand the nature of reality, the relationship between the brain and the mind, and to further advance society, humanity, and, most importantly, our potential as human beings.

This is the way he describes his career change... "In my previous career, I was in the construction field— maintaining, renovating, and building physical structures. Now I am into demolition-dismantling and tearing down all the mental structures I have ever built that were imprisoning me..."

Manufactured by Amazon.ca
Bolton, ON